CLASSIC TEXTS IN
MUSIC EDUCATION 13

MUSIC EXPLAINED TO THE WORLD

CLASSIC TEXTS
IN MUSIC EDUCATION

1 J. J. Rousseau *Project Concerning New Symbols for Music (Projet Concernant de Nouveau Signes pour la Musique* 1742)

2 Bernarr Rainbow and various authors *English Psalmody Prefaces* (1562–1835)

3 Wm Bathe *A Briefe Introduction to the Skill of Song* (c.1587–90)

4 Loys Bourgeois *The Direct Road to Music* (*Le Droict Chemin de Musique* 1550)

5 Sarah Glover *Scheme for Rendering Psalmody Congregational* (1835)

6 John Turner *A Manual of Instruction in Vocal Music* (1833)

7 John Hullah *Wilhem's Method of teaching Singing* (1842)

8 Pierre Galin *Rationale for a New Way of Teaching Music* (from *Exposition d'une nouvelle méthode* 1818)

9 Joseph Mainzer *Singing for the Million* (1841)

10 W. E. Hickson: *The Singing Master* (1836)

11 M. A. Langdale and S. Macpherson: *Early Essays on Musical Appreciation* (1908–1915)

12 J. Mainzer: *Music and Education* (1848)

13 F. J. Fétis: *Music Explained to the World* (1844)

14 J. S. Curwen: *Singing for Schools and Congregations* (1843: edn of 1852)

15 J. S. Curwen and J. Hullah: *School Music Abroad* (1897–1901)

GENERAL EDITOR of the Series
BERNARR RAINBOW MEd PhD

F. J. Fétis

MUSIC EXPLAINED TO THE WORLD

(1844)

(With the text enlarged by ten per cent)

Introduced by
BERNARR RAINBOW

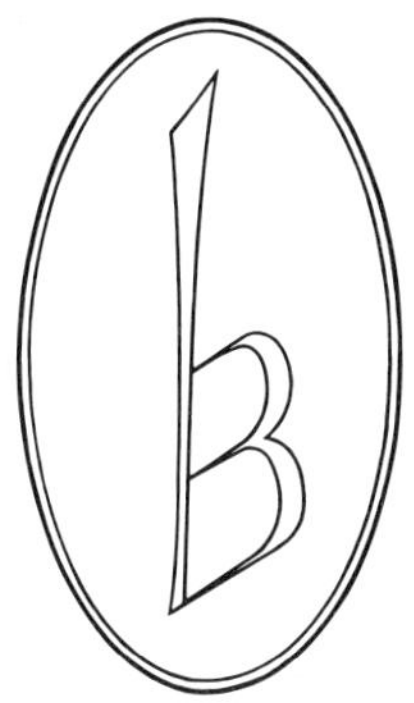

Reproduced under the direction
of Leslie Hewitt for
BOETHIUS PRESS

British Library Cataloguing in Publication Data

Fétis, F. J.
Music explained to the world (1844) : how to understand music and enjoy its performance.—(Classic texts in music education; 13)
1. Music appreciation
I. Title II. La musique mise à la portée de tout le monde. *English* III. Series
780'.1'5 MT6

ISBN 0-86314-044-0

The publishers would like to thank
Dr Bernarr Rainbow for lending his copy
for reprinting.

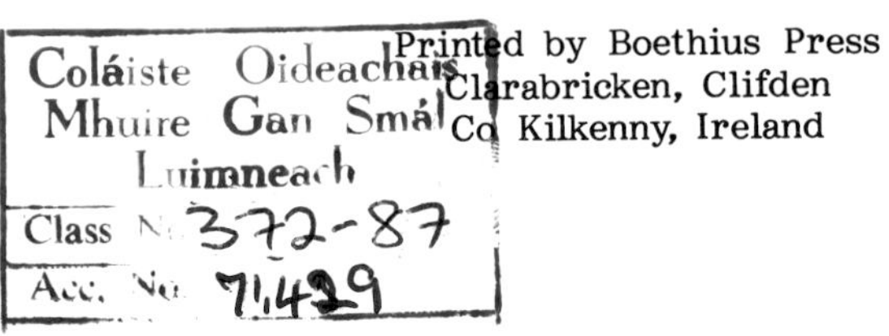

Printed by Boethius Press
Clarabricken, Clifden
Co Kilkenny, Ireland

INTRODUCTION

One indirect consequence of the French Revolution had been to bring to the people at large musical performances on a scale hitherto available only to the monarch and his court. The earliest demonstration of the new trend was to be found in the vast military-cum-musical *spectacles* staged on the Champs de Mars in Paris to thronged citizen audiences. Another appeared later in the vogue for 'heroic' operas designed to whip up patriotic feeling during the Napoleonic Wars, and again in the morale-building 'rescue' operas that celebrated human courage withstanding villainy, misfortune or natural catastrophe. Much of the appeal of these performances lay in the elaborate staging of the earthquakes, volcanic eruptions, avalanches or shipwrecks against which the heroes were pitted, while the musical scores relied heavily upon melodramatic devices for their effectiveness.

At first the new popular audience's response to the musical component in such spectacular performances was limited to an exuberant tremor when some bold orchestral or vocal stroke echoed a violent incident in the plot, a head-wagging sensuality when a particular tune caught the fancy. Textural, structural and harmonic features made little or no impression upon this musically inexperienced audience. Indeed, experiments conducted in Paris early in the nineteenth century revealed that at least some part of such an audience believed that the orchestra played in unison with the singers.[1] It was in an effort to educate audiences in France to higher standards of muscial awareness that François-Joseph Fétis (1784–1871) wrote his *La musique mise à la portée de tout le monde* at the request of the publisher, Alexandre Mesnier, in 1830.

Fétis was at that time well known for the erudite musical articles which he contributed to daily newspapers and to the *Revue Musicale*, a weekly journal which he founded and edited. But beneath his popular image as a journalist lay one of the century's most influential musical scholars, a leading teacher at the Conservatoire and a musical historian who was not content to record the past but sought to revive early works in performance. In assuming the role of populariser for his art such a man inevitably held strong reservations about the propriety of attempting over-simplification. In his *Introduction* Fétis speaks of his attempt to provide information with as little use of technical language as possible, and the risk this entails of supplying only superficial knowledge. Since this is enough to meet most people's needs he does not propose to apologise on that account. Yet the reader who expects to find orthodoxy replaced in his book by some new-fangled method is warned that he will be disappointed.

* * *

1. The reference is taken from p. 46 of the present book; but in the original French the passage reads: 'Il y a environ vingt ans qu'on s'est assuré, par diverses expériences, qu'une partie du public de nos spectacles croyait que l'orchestre jouait à l'unisson des chanteurs'. (Edn of 1830, p. 57)

Fétis was writing as the movement to teach singing to children in French schools gathered strength. Already Wilhem, Galin and their disciples had demonstrated new ways of teaching sight-singing. But to a teacher of Fétis's stature, accustomed to working only with talented pupils, musical training was essentially a lengthy and demanding process. The idea that its elements might advantageously be brought within the reach of ordinary children at school was outside his comprehension, and he warns his readers against simplistic methods:

> Let no one trust in the promise of certain charlatans. In vain do they declare that they will make musicians impromptu. Knowledge is not gained in a moment . . . (p. ix)

In particular, the introduction of substitute forms of notation designed to simplify the task of reading music calls for his scornful condemnation:

> Discouraged by the multitude of the signs of musical notation, men of talent, but who were scarcely more than indifferent musicians, have attempted to introduce other systems, seemingly more simple, and composed of ciphers or arbitrary signs . . . (p. 41)

With Rousseau's proposals particularly in mind Fétis explains, and with justification, that such alternative forms of notation cannot be expected to replace the accepted system. Only because the likelihood of such a step never enters his mind he fails to comment upon their introduction as temporary ancillary devices to help young beginners.

On another page Fétis warns that children's voices may be ruined if they are taught sight-singing by teachers unversed in vocal techniques. To avoid this risk he recommends that sight-reading should be taught without the pupil's singing at all:

> The reading of music is independent of the art of singing; and it is therefore useless to unite in study two things which are naturally separated. The instructions of the professor of solfeggio, if limited to teaching the pupil to read music, by merely naming the notes, without singing them, and to dividing with exactness all the times of the combinations of the notes, would surely be sufficient to attain the end proposed in this preliminary study. (pp. 198–99)

With these various objections in mind we turn to the section of Fetis's book dealing with musical notation with raised expectation. But instead of encountering explanations which enable the reader to bring his aural senses into play when scrutinising the symbols of notation, we find the topic treated purely as an intellectual exercise in which the visual symbol is introduced to the eye accompanied only by a verbal definition. This was the standard approach adopted by teachers of instrumental music both then and subsequently; and its re-appearance in Fétis's book should perhaps not cause surprise when we recall his warning that no new methods would appear in it. Yet the discovery draws renewed attention to his fallible suggestion that young pupils should learn to read music by naming the notes, instead of singing them. Such a process could only perpetuate the state of affairs criticised by Pierre Galin in his *Exposition d'une Nouvelle Méthode* (1818):

> One thing that constantly puzzles observers is that among the vast number of those who have learned music, so few can sing at sight. Most of them have to consult their violin, their pianoforte, or their flute, in order to learn a new tune; and it is actually the instrument which does the reading for them . . . Here you have a strange process; the sight of the written symbols causes the fingers to move, and the instrument produces the sound. But why does the sight of the symbols themselves convey nothing to the reader's mind?[2]

If pressed to answer that rhetorical question Fétis would doubtless have replied with other eminent musicians of his day that 'knowledge is not gained in a moment' while the acquisition of skill 'can only be the result of long labour'. And to that extent Fétis and Galin respectively may be seen as personifying that conflict of ideas existing between professional musician on one hand, and philanthropic universal music educator on the other, which first appeared in France when Rousseau sought to simplify musical instruction. It was to continue both there and elsewhere as successive generations of amateurs took up a task largely ignored by the professional musician until our own day.

Yet in the present book we encounter Fétis in the unfamiliar role of populariser. Just how far

2. *op. cit.*, pp. 10–11; and in the translated version in 'Classic Texts in Music Education' No. 8. *Rationale for a New Way of Teaching Music*, pp. 41–42

that strange errand was undertaken at his publisher's instigation against his own inclination is open to question. Certainly it is not surprising in the circumstances that this scholarly musician failed to appreciate and sympathise with all the beginner's problems. Perhaps the greater marvel is that he should have succeeded so well in the larger part of his book.

* * *

It is perhaps desirable to remind ourselves that *Music Explained to the World* was not an elementary treatise intended for use in schools, but a book designed for adult readers among the growing class of cultured bourgeoisie. When it first appeared it was a book difficult to categorise; Fétis himself claimed a place for it among 'that department of the literature of art called aesthetics'. To classify it in that way invited comparison with much more substantial texts by German writers from Kant to Schumann and Hegel—a comparison to which *Music Explained* is not equal. The fact is that, however modest, this was a book of a new type, bordering both aesthetics and criticism and having perhaps a single precedent in Hans Georg Naegeli's *Vorlesungen über Musik*, a collection of the Swiss educationist's most celebrated lectures on music to popular audiences, published in Stuttgart in 1826.

But where Naegeli's book attracted a wide readership in Switzerland and Germany the fame of Fétis's equally unassuming publication addressed to general readers led to its appearance in translation in Germany, Belgium, Italy, Spain, Russia, England and the United States, all within a dozen years of its first publication in Paris in 1830. Introducing the second edition (the version from which the present English translation of 1844 was made) Fétis acknowledged that the favourable reception accorded to his book had exceeded his expectation and led him to amplify certain sections, notably by the addition of Chapter V (on ethnic scales) and Chapter XI (on acoustics). Otherwise the book remained essentially as it had first appeared, divided into four parts respectively treating Notation, Texture and Structure, Performance, and Listening.

Even today it remains obvious that some part of the book's success depends on its cumulative effect upon the reader. Passing from the mundane details rehearsed in the section on Notation (upon which observations have already been made) the narrative gathers pace as mere description of the raw materials of sound leads to discussion of their metamorphosis into the substance of an art depending for its full effect upon the listener's awareness of the very processes so described. All this information Fétis was well-placed to provide for the edification of adult readers. Both his descriptions and the illuminating incidents which he introduced to give point to them were calculated to hold the attention of those intent upon self-betterment. Much that he records also provides the modern reader with an unexpected insight into the musical world of his day. With the knowledge that hindsight gives us of the development of the so-called Musical Appreciation movement in the present century it is well worth recalling the aims which Fétis set himself in writing this book, as recorded in the original subtitle not preserved in the English version:

A concise summary of all that is necessary
to form a judgement of this art,
and to discuss it without having studied it.

MUSIC EXPLAINED.

MUSIC

EXPLAINED TO THE WORLD:

OR,

HOW TO UNDERSTAND MUSIC AND ENJOY ITS PERFORMANCE.

FROM THE FRENCH OF

FRANCIS JAMES FETIS,

DIRECTOR OF THE MUSICAL REVIEW OF PARIS.

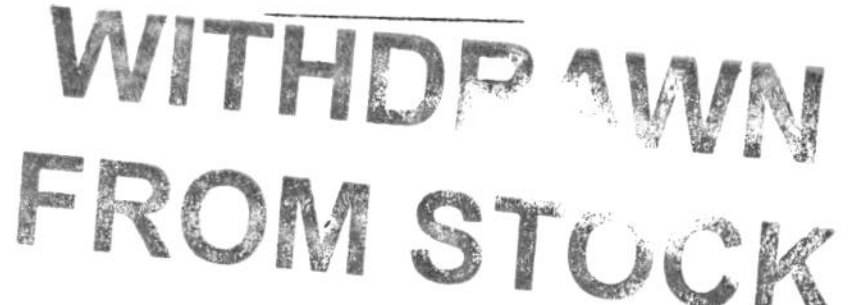

LONDON:
H. G. CLARKE & CO. 66, OLD BAILEY.

1844.

LONDON:
PRINTED BY MANNING AND MASON, IVY LANE,
PATERNOSTER ROW.

ADVERTISEMENT.

The Publishers have been induced to offer a translation of the work of Mr. Fetis to the musical public, in consequence of perceiving, as they thought, its remarkable adaptation to the state of musical knowledge among us, and the probability that its perspicuous and lively style, its scientific accuracy, and its just criticisms, founded on the surest principles of the art, would attract numerous readers, both in and out of the profession. The qualifications of the author will not be doubted by any one who possesses a thorough knowledge of the principles of music and of musical taste; and he has been singularly happy in explaining the difficulties of the art, in pointing out its true objects, and the best means of attaining them. He conveys all this with a freedom and force, which, while they shew his own intimate acquaintance with the whole subject, are at the same time agreeable to the student, satisfactory to the professor, and useful to all who give any attention to music. The amateur will find in it all that is necessary; and the student and professor will derive great advantage from the clear, comprehensive views it contains, and the sort of chart it presents of the whole field of their labours.

The work was translated, several years ago, from the first Paris edition; and has recently been carefully revised, and made to correspond with the second edition, in which many improvements were introduced by the author, several paragraphs having been omitted, and others inserted, and two entire chapters having been written for it, and the opinions having been here and there corrected throughout the book. These alterations have all been carefully adopted in this translation; and no voluntary changes have been made, except the following: In the vocal scale, the syllable *do* has been used instead of *ut*, which is still retained by the French; and in speaking of keys, the letters have been substituted, in the English fashion, for the syllables of the scale. Thus what we understand by the key of G is the key of *sol*, in the French mode of speaking; the key of D is their key of *re*, etc. Three paragraphs have been omitted, which had reference merely to the use of certain musical terms in the French language, where the English is better provided with proper expressions. These paragraphs occur on the 20th, 28th, and 30th pages of the second Paris edition, and relate to the use of the words *ton, doubles croches, triples croches*, etc., and *mesure*.

The dictionary of terms, and the catalogue of works on music, added by the author to the second edition, have also been omitted. The first is not now needed in this country, and the second would not be interesting to the general reader.

INTRODUCTION.

Science is not born with us. No knowledge is so simple that we are not forced to acquire it either by experience or by education. This proposition, so true in every thing, is indisputable in all that relates to art. The unpractised eye cannot distinguish the qualities or defects of a painting, nor the untutored ear the combinations of harmony. Undoubtedly, the habitual use of the eye and the ear is sufficient in many cases to enable us to perceive the beauties of painting or music; but this is in itself an education.

There is, however, a great difference between this vague feeling, which has no other origin than mere sensations, and that certainty of judgment which is the result of positive knowledge. Every art has its principles, which we must study, in order to increase our enjoyment, while we are forming our taste. Those of music are more complex than those of painting; and besides, music is at once a science and an art. This complexity renders the study of it long and difficult for those who wish to acquire a certain degree of skill. Unfortunately, it is scarcely possible to shorten the time which must be devoted to it. With whatever readiness we may be gifted, to whatever process we resort, whatever method we adopt, still it will be necessary to accustom our organs to read with ease the great number of characters of which musical writing is composed, to produce the prescribed tones with precision, to feel the divisions of the measures, and, finally, to combine all these elements of the art. Time alone can enable us to accomplish this.

But time is precisely that which we have the least at command in the course of life, especially in the present high state of civilization. Obliged to learn a multitude of things, we can give but very slight attention to each, and we are compelled to select those which will be most useful in the business of life. The arts, considered as recreations, or sources of pleasure, are among those objects with which in general we become acquainted only as we pass along through life, and of which every one thinks himself a competent judge by nature, and without study; not that one would not like to have correct ideas concerning them, provided it cost us no more labour to obtain them than it does to keep up with the politics of the day by reading the newspapers. But where is the book which meets this want? The attempt to give general and sufficient information on all that contributes to the effect of the art of music, with as little use of technical language as possible, is a task which no writer has undertaken; and this task I now propose to myself. Perhaps it may be said that there is nothing in my book but the knowledge of the superficial. Be it so.

This is enough for most people, and I shall not think it derogatory to my character of professor to have taught it. To extend the taste for the art I cultivate is my object. Every thing which conduces to this end seems to me good in itself. I trust that this will be my apology with my learned colleagues.

Whoever expects to find in this book a new method, a system, or anything of that sort, will be mistaken. Its title sufficiently explains the object which I have in view. To give sufficiently clear ideas of what is necessary to increase the pleasure which music affords, and to speak of the art without having studied it profoundly, is my design. But, to those who wish really to acquire the principles of music, my work will still be useful, as it will prepare the mind for studies which are usually very disagreeable, because the connexion between their first rudiments is not perceived; though, besides this, particular methods, masters, and, especially, devoted attention and patience, will be necessary. In this case, it will no longer be enough to feel and to reason about sensations; but the object will be to produce these sensations ourselves. This is more difficult, and requires more time. Let no one trust in the promise of certain charlatans. In vain do they declare that they will make musicians impromptu. Knowledge is not gained in a moment; or, rather, we know well only that which it has cost us trouble to learn. It is easy to understand the mechanical structure of the science and of the language of music, as any one may be convinced by reading the treatise which I here present to the public; but to become skilful is another thing, which can only be the result of long labour.

Some critics, in speaking of the first edition of this book, have said that it did not deserve its title, and that it did not make music simple; that is to say, that it did not render the study of it either shorter or easier. I suspect these critics have not read the Introduction; for they would then have seen that I have answered their objections in anticipation, and that my object was not what they have supposed.

This work belongs to that department of the literature of art called æsthetics. No book of this kind has been published in France, though there are many such in Germany. But they are only imperfect treatises, which, without doubt, will ere long be superseded; they have the merit of having opened the road, and this will always belong to them. I trust it will be so with my own work; better ones may be made, but its usefulness will be felt and acknowledged.

The favourable reception it has met with from the public has surpassed my expectation. In less than two years, besides the Paris edition, there were two others; one at Liege, in 12mo., the other at Brussels, in 18mo. Mr. Charles Blanc has made a translation of it into German, Berlin, 12mo., 1830, and has added some notes; and lastly, the journals of Italy have announced a translatien of it into Italian.

This general success of my book is a better defence of it than I could make in a preface; though it does not blind me to its defects, nor diminish my desire to improve it, and increase its usefulness. This wish has induced me to alter several passages, and to add a second volume, though I am perfectly aware that the merit of a work is not measured by its size. I have thought this new volume would be convenient to the general reader, and even to those artists who have not time to study every branch of their art. It contains, first, a dictionary of terms in most common use; and secondly, a systematic catalogue of the principle French works on the different departments of music.

TABLE OF CONTENTS.

PART I.

OF THE MUSICAL SYSTEM, CONSIDERED IN THE THREE QUALITIES OF SOUNDS; NAMELY—TONE, LENGTH, AND STRENGTH.

PART II.

OF SOUNDS, CONSIDERED IN THEIR RELATIONS OF SUCCESION AND OF SIMULTANEOUSNESS; AND OF THE CONSEQUENCES OF THESE RELATIONS.

PART III.

OF EXECUTION.

PART IV.

HOW TO ANALYSE THE SENSATIONS PRODUCED BY MUSIC, IN ORDER TO JUDGE OF IT.

MUSIC EXPLAINED.

PART I.

OF THE MUSICAL SYSTEM, CONSIDERED IN THE THREE QUALITIES OF SOUNDS; NAMELY, TONE, LENGTH, AND STRENGTH.

CHAPTER I.

OBJECT OF MUSIC—ITS ORIGIN—ITS MEANS.

Music may be defined the art of producing emotions by the combinations of sound. It is not on the human species alone, that the power of this art is felt. The greater part of organized beings are more or less under its influence. The sense of hearing, on which it acts immediately, seems to be only its agent: its power is most developed on the nervous system; and hence the variety of its effects. The dog, the horse, the stag, the elephant, reptiles, and even insects, are sensible of the effects of music, but in different ways. In some, the sensation resembles a nervous agitation, so violent as to become painful; in others, pleasure is exhibited under different forms. The attention of all is fixed, as soon as the sounds are heard.

The phenomena, produced by music in the human frame, are especially worthy of observation. In a given number of persons equally sensible to its tones, some remain unmoved by combinations of sounds which excite pleasure in others. A combination which does not move us at one moment, transports us with pleasure at another. Sometimes this pleasure is only a delicious sensation, to which we seem to yield ourselves passively; under other circumstances, the action of the art becomes violent, and the whole vital system is agitated. The delicate constitution of females adapts them to experience more vivid sensations than men from the hearing of music; and it is in them that the action of this art carries the delirium of the senses to its greatest height.

But, if the taste for music is given to us by nature, education adds much to it, and may even create it. Hence it is, without doubt, that we see in the world men otherwise distinguished by the qualities of their minds, and by talents of another kind, who shew not only indifference, but even aversion, to this art. Some philosophers have thought that such persons were imperfectly or badly organised; but it may be that their insensibility is merely a result of the long inertness of nerves unaccustomed to musical sounds.

The action of music upon the physical organs, and upon the moral faculties, has given rise to the idea of employing it as a means of cure, not only in mental affections, but even in certain diseases in which the physical organization alone seems to be attacked. Many physicians have made interesting researches on this subject; which, however, are defective in philosophical spirit. The number of the works in which they have recorded them is very considerable, and the facts stated have something in them so improbable, that they have need of the authority of the names of their authors in order to be believed.

Notwithstanding its capacity, the human mind is so limited, that the idea of infinity cannot be attained without effort. We wish to find the origin of every thing; and, to common minds, music seems to require a beginning, like other branches of knowledge. Neither the book of Genesis nor the poets of antiquity mention the inventors of this art, but only the names of those who made the first instruments—Tubal, Mercury, Apollo, and others. It will readily be supposed that I believe the book of Genesis on this point, as well as on others of more importance; but this is not now the question. As to the origin of music, every one has his own ideas; but the opinion which traces it to the singing of birds is the most common. It must be confessed that this is an odd idea, and it implies a strange opinion of man, to suppose that he finds one of his most delightful pleasures in the imitation of the language of animals. No, no, it is not so. Man sings, as he speaks, moves, and sleeps; in consequence of his organization, and the constitution of his mind. This is so true, that nations the most savage, and most completely insulated in their situation, have been found to possess some kind of music, even where the severity of the climate would scarcely permit birds to live or to sing. Music, in its origin, is composed only of cries of joy or expressions of pain: as men become civilised, their singing improves; and that which at first was only the accent of passion, becomes at last the result of study and of art. There is a wide interval, no doubt, between the indistinct sounds which come from the throat of a woman of Nova Zembla, and the warblings of a Malibran or Sontag; but it is not the less true that the delightful singing of the latter has its foundation in something as rude as the croaking of the former. Still it is of little consequence to know what was the origin of music: all that interests us is to know what it has become, since it deserved the name of an art; to prepare ourselves to receive all the agreeable impressions it can make; and to increase its effect as much as possible. This it is which we should examine and study.

By what means does music act upon organised beings? This is a question often repeated under different forms, and the solution of which includes the whole mechanism of the art. In general, without entering into details, every one gives an answer according to his own taste, and says that it is melody, or harmony, or the union of the two, but without explaining, and, perhaps, without knowing exactly, what melody or harmony is. I shall attempt to remove all doubts on this subject; but first, it is to be observed, that music possesses a third means of producing effect, which has not been regarded; that is, accent, the presence or absence of which is the reason that the same melody or harmony does or does not produce an effect. This also will be explained.

CHAPTER II.

OF THE DIFFERENCE OF SOUNDS, AND OF THE MANNER OF EXPRESSING THEM BY NAMES.

Every one has remarked, that the voices of women and children differ entirely in character from those of men; the one being more or less elevated, and the other more or less depressed. The number of possible sounds between the highest of the one and the lowest of the other is infinite; and each of them, to a practised ear, is readily distinguishable. It is easy to see that if a different name had been given to each, the multitude would have been so great, that, far from being any aid, it would have been a useless burden to the memory; but those learned philosophers, who first undertook to arrange sounds in a regular manner, having remarked that, beyond a certain number of sounds, arranged in a particular order, either ascending or descending, the rest are successively reproduced in the same order, and do not differ from the former, except as a high and low voice in accordance differ from each other,—they came to the conclusion, that the last were only a repetition of the first, at a certain distance, which they called an *octave*. For instance, having designated the first sound by the letter C, the second by D, the third by E, etc., in this order, C D E F G A B, they commenced a second series by *c d e f g a b;* the third, by *cc dd ee,* etc. The invention of the syllables *ut, re, mi, fa, sol, la,* now commonly used, is attributed to an Italian monk, whose name was Guido d'Arezzo, who took them from a hymn to Saint John—

> *Ut* queant laxis, *re*sonare fibris,
> *Mi*ra gestorum, *fa*muli tuorum,
> *Sol*ve polluti, *la*bii reatum
> Sancte Joannes.

But, in a letter to another monk, Guido merely advises him to recollect the air of this hymn, which rises one note on each syllable, —*ut, re, mi,* etc.—in order to find the tone of each degree of the scale. Five hundred years afterwards, a Fleming added the syllable *si* to the first six, and completed the series; after which, *ut, re, mi, fa, sol, la, si,* were repeated for the second octave, and so on for the third, fourth, and succeeding octaves. About 1640, Doni, a learned musician, substituted *do* for *ut,* as being more agreeable in solmization. The Italians, the French, the Spanish, and the Portuguese, have adopted these syllables to designate sounds; the Germans and the English have preserved the letters for the same purpose. This series of names, or letters, is called the *gamut.** Sounds having been thus distinguished, it was perceived that there were also intermediate tones, which the ear perfectly appreciated. For example, we recognise that between the sounds designated by *do* and

* The word *gamut (gamme)* is derived from the name of the lowest note in the scale of sounds, represented by the third letter of the Greek alphabet, called *gamma,* which letter corresponds to the syllable *sol.*

re, there is a third, equally distant from both. To avoid multiplying names, we suppose that this sound is sometimes *do* raised, and sometimes *re* lowered. We call the raised *do*, *do sharp;* and the *re* lowered, *re flat;*—and we do the same thing with regard to the intermediate sounds between *re* and *mi*, and *fa* and *sol*. This makes the word *sharp* synonymous with *raised*, and the word *flat* synonymous with *lowered*. It is plain that this is only a fiction, introduced for the sake of greater simplicity; for a sound cannot be modified in its tone, or be changed into another, without ceasing to exist. *Do* sharp is no longer *do*. But those musicians who are merely practical,—and these are the most numerous,—having attached an idea of reality to the signs which represent sounds, and seeing that the signs of *do* and *re* are not changed, but that the signs of raising and lowering are simply added to them,—that is to say, the sharp (♯), or the flat (♭),—these musicians, I say, have imagined that *do* is always *do*, whether there be a sharp added to it or not. Similar errors are frequent in music, and have thrown much obscurity over its theory.

Do sharp and *re* flat being between *do* and *re*, it would seem that these two notes should be exactly in unison; but, according to the theory, founded on the calculation of the length of strings, and the phenomena of their vibration, it appears that *do* sharp is not exactly the same sound as *re* flat, and that their difference is as 80 to 81 in certain cases, and as 125 to 128 in others. The name of *comma* is given to these differences. But the difficulty of constructing keyed instruments, such as the piano or the organ, to express these proportions, and the embarrassment which such instruments would cause in the performance, have given rise to the plan of tuning them by distributing these differences over the whole extent of the key-board, so that the differences may be less sensible to the ear. The name of *temperament* is given to this operation. All tuners practise it from habit, without understanding the theory. It will be perceived that, by the temperament, we obtain only a proximate accuracy. But this is enough for the ear, in ordinary cases.

If every one were at liberty to name the first sound he happened to hit upon *do*, the next one *re*, and so on, ascending, there would be produced an extreme confusion in music, and harmony would be destroyed. To prevent this inconvenience, little instruments of steel, in the form of forks, have been constructed, so as to produce a standard tone, called *diapason*, which name has also been given to the instrument itself. By the sound thus established, all instruments are tuned, and all voices guided. In France, this sound is called *la;* in Italy, it is called *do*. Hence have come the expressions used in orchestras, when tuning instruments. In France, they say, *donner le la;* in Italy, *suonar il do*. The *diapason* is not identically the same in all countries; it has even undergone different modifications in the same place. Each of the theatres at Paris had formerly its own; that of the Opera was the lowest, and that of the Italian theatre the highest. There is now very little difference between them. A diapason which is too low injures the brilliancy of the effect, because the strings of the instruments are not sufficiently strained; a diapason which is too high fatigues the voice.

The use of the diapason is not sufficiently common. Most pianos, in the provinces of France, are tuned too low. Singers who acccompany themselves on these pianos acquire a sort of lazy habit of voice, which they cannot overcome when obliged to sing at concert pitch.

CHAPTER III.

METHOD OF REPRESENTING SOUNDS BY SIGNS.

The operation of mind, by which man first thought of representing the sounds of speech by signs, will for ever be a mystery; but, having once attained to this discovery, he could not meet with much difficulty, we conceive, in finding the means of expressing the sounds produced in singing. The Greeks and Romans, for that purpose, made use of the letters, and parts of the letters, of their alphabet, variously combined. The Mahometans have no signs for musical sounds. The Chinese have signs for music, which are as complicated and as odd as their language.

After several ages of unceasing struggle with the barbarians of the North, the Western empire was subdued, and fell; the arts perished with it; and there scarcely remained any thing more than an indistinct recollection of them, which was gradually weakened, down to the eighth century, when even that was entirely lost. Music, especially,—that is to say, the music of the Greeks, which had delighted Rome and Italy,—was absolutely forgotten; and all that remained of it was what those two fathers of the church, Saint Ambrose and Saint Gregory, had preserved for divine service. The melodies were so simple, or rather so limited, that few signs were necessary to write them; and these signs were formed of certain letters of the alphabet.

But, while the Latin nations made use of these signs, the Lombards and Goths, whose power was established in Italy, introduced others, on a different plan; for the latter represented not only individual sounds, but combinations of sounds, and even whole phrases. The large libraries contain manuscripts, in which we find these signs applied to the vocal music of the church; and thus we are enabled to decipher them, by comparing them with the same music written in the Latin signs.

It is remarkable, moreover, that those nations of the East, who have thought of representing sounds by signs, have understood the use of these only as means of expressing collections of sounds by a single sign, instead of separating them into their most simple elements. This peculiarity must be ascribed to their taste for excessive ornament in their melodies, which would have rendered the reading of music extremely difficult, if they had not found means to represent several sounds by a single sign. The signs which are still in use in the Greek churches of the East are of this kind; they were invented by a monk—John of Damascus.

It would be difficult, at this day, to fix the precise epoch when the notes of the *plain-chant*, from which the modern notation is derived, were devised: there are examples of it in the manuscripts of the first half of the eleventh century; but there is no proof that they were not invented at a more distant period. It is well, also, to remark, that at that time there was no uniform system of signs for the writing of music. Every master had his own; he communicated it to his pupils; and one could scarce go from one little district to another, without being obliged to study a new one.

However it may be, the system of notes of the plain-chant, as it is found in the books of the church, finally prevailed, and became the foundation of the notation which is now adopted by all the European nations. Successive improvements have insensibly made of it a very different thing from what it originally was. I shall attempt to give precise ideas of it, with as much conciseness as possible.

The signs of music, collectively, are called *notation*. They are divided into two kinds: the first includes the signs of *intonation;* the second, the signs of *duration*. Both are indispensably necessary; for it is not enough to know, by looking at a sign, the sound which it represents; but we must also know its duration, and be able to measure it. These signs are arranged upon paper, specially prepared for the purpose, which is called *music paper*. This preparation consists in ruling the paper horizontally, with groups of five parallel lines each, which are called the *staff.* They are represented in this manner:*—

Upon these lines, or in the spaces between them, the signs of notation are placed. I have said that musical signs are divided into two kinds—the signs of intonation and those of duration. The signs of intonation are of two sorts; namely, *clefs* and *notes.*

The difference between voices has given rise to clefs, which, being placed at the commencement of the staff, indicate that the music written upon it belongs to such or such a voice. The sign of high voices and instruments is called the G or treble clef, and is made thus . It is commonly placed upon the second line from the bottom of the staff, which indicates that the sign of the sound called G is placed upon that line. The sign of low voices or instruments is called the F or bass clef, and has this form: Its ordinary position is upon the fourth line from the bottom of the staff. It indicates that F is upon this line. The sign of intermediate voices and instruments is called the C or tenor clef; but, as there are several degrees of high and low in these voices, these degrees are expressed by placing the same sign upon different lines. The C clef is made in this manner;

* Some music paper contains ten staves on a page; some twelve, some fourteen, sixteen, and even twenty-four. That which is higher than it is wide is called *French,* and that which is wider than it is high, *Italian paper.*

and gives its name to the note found upon the line upon which it is placed.

The different qualities of voices may be reduced to four: 1, the high voice of women; 2, the low voice of women; 3, the high voice of men; and 4, the low voice of men. The high voice of women is called the *soprano*, or *dessus*, (treble); the intermediate voice of the same sex, *mezzo soprano*, or *second dessus*, (second treble); the low voice of women is called *contralto*, or counter: the high voice of men is called *tenore*, or tenor; the low voice, *basso*, or bass. The *bariton* is the intermediate voice between the tenor and bass. The high voices of men being naturally, and from the effect of their conformation, lower by an octave than the high voices of women, the same clef—that is to say, the G clef—might be used for them both, leaving it to nature to effect the difference of the octave. In regard to the *contralto*, or low voice of women, which is an octave above the bass, its part might, for the same reason, be written in the F clef. We might also reduce those instruments, which, in the orchestra, perform the functions of intermediate voices, to the same simplicity, by marking the differences of octaves by a simple sign, such as ——, drawn across the G or F clefs.

But, if it is possible to suppress the C clefs in ordinary use, these same clefs are of great assistance in certain cases, of which I shall speak hereafter; and, from the necessity of using them on these occasions, we are obliged to become familiar with them, and therefore make habitual use of them. Thence it is, that the complexity resulting from a multitude of clefs is preserved to this day, though the advantages which would result from its removal are perceived and acknowledged.

The clefs are only general signs, which shew, once for all, the kind of voice or instrument which should perform the music. The notes are the particular signs of the several sounds. It must not be supposed, however, that it is necessary to have a sign of a particular form for each of these sounds. Such a multiplicity of signs would produce confusion in the mind, and fatigue the memory without advantage. It is not the form of the note which determines its tone, but the place which it occupies upon the staff. To effect this object, a point, placed upon the line or in the space, would be sufficient.

The note placed upon the lower line of the staff represents a sound comparatively lower than those which occupy other positions upon the same staff: thus the note which is in the space between the first and the second line expresses a higher sound than that which is upon the first; the note placed upon the second line represents one still higher: it is the same with all the other positions, in proportion as we rise on the staff. If, therefore, we call the note on the first line *do*, we give the name of *re* to that which occupies the space between the first and the second line, that of *mi* to the note which is placed upon the second line, and so on, as may be seen in the following example:

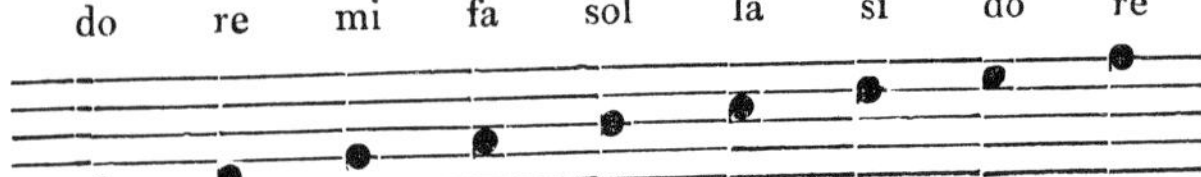

A voice or an instrument, which should be limited to so small a number of sounds, it will readily be conceived, would offer but feeble resources to the singer or player; and, in fact, there are none confined within such narrow limits. Instruments, especially, go very much beyond the extent of the staff of five lines. But if we were obliged to compose the staff of as many permanent lines as would be necessary to embrace the extent of certain instruments, a sort of inextricable labyrinth would ensue from this great number of lines, and the quickest eye would not be able to distinguish a single note without a painful effort.* The method made use of to avoid this inconvenience, is ingenious. It consists in adding short lines to the staff, either above or below, as they may be needed, and in leaving them off when they are no longer of use. These short lines are not confounded with the staff, but are sensibly detached from it to the eye. The following is an example of their use:

Every note placed upon the same line with the clef, at the commencement of the staff, takes the name of that clef, and serves as a point of comparison, from

* This inconvenience formerly existed in instrumental music, especially in the organ music of the sixteenth and seventeenth centuries. From this cause, the works of the great organists of that period are illegible to most musicians.

which to name all the other notes. Thus, when the G clef is found at the beginning of the staff upon the second line, the note placed upon that line is called G, and all the others are named accordingly. If the staff has the F clef upon the fourth line, F is on that line. It is the same with the others. From this, we see that the name of the notes is derived from the position of the clef, and cannot be unchangeably fixed. The difference between voices giving rise to the multiplicity of clefs, is the first cause of these variations.

But, if the position of the notes be variable, it is not so with their tone, which is governed by the model sound, called the *diapason* in French, and *corista* in Italian. Thus a given note, which we call C, for example, can have only one sound, whatever may be its position upon the staff. The only difference which there will be in the different positions of this C, and in its sound, is, that it may belong to the high limits of one voice: such for instance as the upper bass; to the middle or *medium* of another, as the tenor; and to the low limits of a third, which will be the *soprano*.

Example of the same Sound in different Parts.

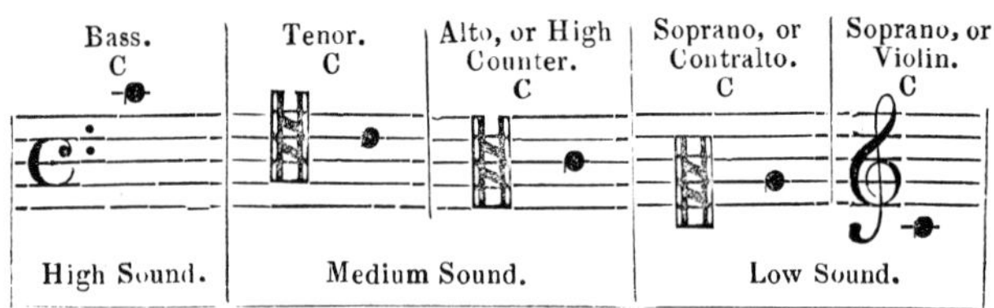

Thus far, we have seen the manner of representing the succession of sounds, which we call *do, re, mi, fa, sol, la, si;* but we have not yet taken notice of the signs of the intermediate sounds, to which we give the name of *sharp* and of *flat*. The sharp is made thus ♯; the flat has this form ♭.

All the lines and all the spaces being occupied by the notes which represent *do*, *re*, *mi*, etc., there is no place left on the staff for the intermediate sounds; but as we suppose, in ordinary language, that the words *do sharp*, or *re flat*, are sufficient to express the idea of the intermediate sound between *do* and *re*, so it has been agreed, that the ♯ put before the note *do*, or the ♭ placed before *re*, is sufficient to represent this intermediate sound to the eye.

Examples.

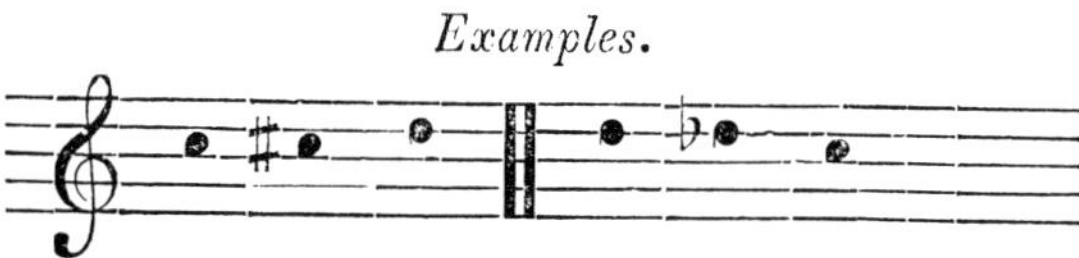

When it is desired to destroy the effect of a sharp or flat, another sign is made use of, called a *natural*, which is formed thus ♮. The natural is put at the side of the note which was preceded by a sharp or flat, and is equivalent to saying, *the sharp is taken off;* or *make this no longer flat*. The natural is a sort of short-hand mark.

We give the name of *tone* to the difference between two sounds, as *do* and *re;* the difference between one of these sounds and the intermediate sound, represented by a sharp or flat, is called a *semitone*. The semitone is the smallest interval that a European ear can appreciate with exactness.

It is remarkable that the difference which is found between the sounds *do* and *re* does not exist equally between all the sounds of the gamut; for the intermediate sound is not found between *mi* and *fa*, nor between *si* and *do*.* The difference between these notes is only a semitone. A succession of sounds, made upon the model of this,—*do, re, mi, fa, sol, la, si, do*,—is called *diatonic;* and if the intermediate sounds are introduced into it, it is then called *chromatic*. It was formerly said of music that it was of the *diatonic* kind when it contained but few of the intermediate sounds, and that it belonged to the *chromatic* kind when sounds of that description were most frequent; but these expressions have been laid aside, since the art has been enriched by a great multitude of combinations resulting from a continual mixture of the two kinds. Some ancient airs and simple melodies may give an idea of the diatonic kind of music. The chromatic kind is frequently employed in modern music, and constitutes, indeed, its distinctive character. In modern music, we sometimes find, also, another kind, which we call the *enharmonic;* but the use of this is more rare. I shall, in another place, explain in what it consists.

The words *diatonic* and *chromatic*, which have passed from the Greek into the modern languages, have only an improper signification in the latter; for *diatonic* comes from *dia*, by, and *tonos*, tone; and it is not true that the music proceeds only by tones in the modern music, since there are two semitones in all the gamuts,

* I do not speak here of the difference between the major tone *do re*, and the minor tone *re mi*, because that is only a difference of interval of tone, which can be estimated better by calculation than by the ear.

as from E to F, and from B to C. This will be clearly seen in the following chapter. The expression is more correct, perhaps, in the word *chromatic;* but it is wanting in clearness. *Chromatic* comes from the Greek word *chroma*, which signifies colour; and in fact, this succession of semitones colours the music, but only in a figurative sense.

CHAPTER IV.

OF THE DIFFERENCE OF SCALES; OF THE NAMES WHICH THEY BEAR; AND OF THE OPERATION CALLED TRANSPOSITION.

THE scale *do, re, mi, fa, sol, la, si, do,* is arranged in such a manner that there is a tone between *do* and *re*, another between *re* and *mi*, a semitone from *mi* to *fa*, a tone between *fa* and *sol*, a tone between *sol* and *la*, a tone between *la* and *si*, a semitone from *si* to *do;* or, in other words, it presents a succession of two tones, a semitone, three tones, and a semitone.

If we should arrange the scale in this manner, *re, mi, fa, sol, la, si, do, re,* the order of tones and semitones would be changed; for there would be a tone between *re* and *mi*, a semitone from *re* to *fa*, a tone between *fa* and *sol*, a tone between *sol* and *la*, a tone between *la* and *si*, a semitone from *si* to *do*, and a tone from *do* to *re;* or we should have a succession of a tone, a semitone, three tones, a semitone, and a tone. This irregularity is removed by substituting *fa* sharp for *fa*, and *do* sharp for *do*. Thus we get a tone from *re* to *mi*, a tone from *mi* to *fa* ♯, a semitone from *fa* ♯ to *sol*, a tone from *sol* to *la*, a tone from *la* to *si*, a tone from *si* to *do* ♯, and a semitone from *do* ♯ to *re*, and the scale is composed in the following manner:

Re, *mi*, *fa* ♯, *sol*, *la*, *si*, *do* ♯, *re*;

which presents a series of two tones, a semitone, three tones, and a semitone, as in the scale which begins with *do*.

In this manner, and preserving the order of the tones and semitones, we may commence the scale by all the notes, and even by the intermediate sounds, and have as many regular scales as there are sounds within the compass of the octave. We give to each scale the name of the note with which it begins; but, instead of saying the scale of *re*, of *mi* ♭, or of *fa*, we say the scale of the *key of re* (D), of the *key of mi flat* (E ♭), of the *key of fa* (F); and we call by the name of a *symphony in re*, a *sonota in mi* ♭, or an *overture in fa*, those pieces which are written with the sounds which belong to the scale of *re*, of *mi flat*, or of *fa*.

All voices not having the same compass, it frequently happens that a piece of music, which is suitable for certain persons, contains sounds which are too high or too low for others;—but the piece pleases; people wish to sing it; and there are no means of doing so, but by setting it lower, if it is too high; or higher, if it is too low; that is to say, by substituting, in the first case, the scale of *do* (C) for the scale of *re* (D), or the scale of *re* (D) for that of *mi flat* (E ♭); and, in the other, by doing the contrary, that is to say, by substituting a higher scale for that of the key in which the piece is written. This operation is called *transposition*.

Persons who are unacquainted with music transpose naturally, and without observing it, by placing the air which they sing in the position which is most favourable to their voice; but the process of the performer, who accompanies a piece *transposed*, is much more complicated; for it consists in playing notes different from those which are written, which requires a sustained attention, and much presence of mind, especially if the instrument be a piano, in which case he must perform a double operation, for the music of the right and that of the left hand.

If it were necessary to make a calculation for each note, and for each sharp, flat, or natural, in order to discover what should be substituted in their place, in the transposition, we can readily conceive that the quickest mind would meet with great embarrassment, on account of the rapidity of execution. But there is a mode of simplifying this operation, which consists in supposing another clef than that which is placed at the commencement of the staff, and in choosing one which corresponds to the key into which the performer is desirous to transpose. For example, if the piece is in the key of *re* (D), written with the G clef, and the performer wishes to transpose into the key of *si* (B flat), he substitutes, in his mind, the C clef upon the lower line of the G clef, supposes two flats at the side of the clef, and the transposition is effected, as may be seen by the following example:

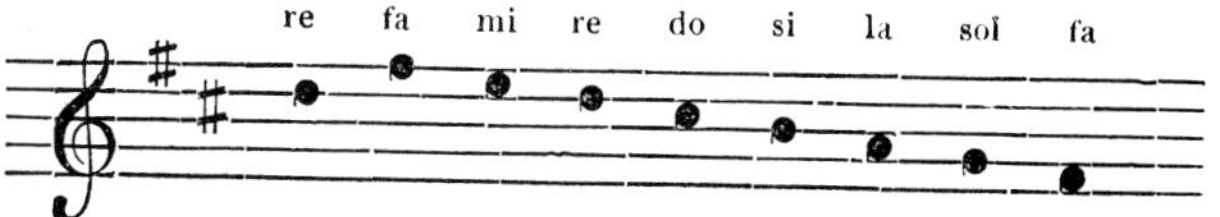

Transposition.

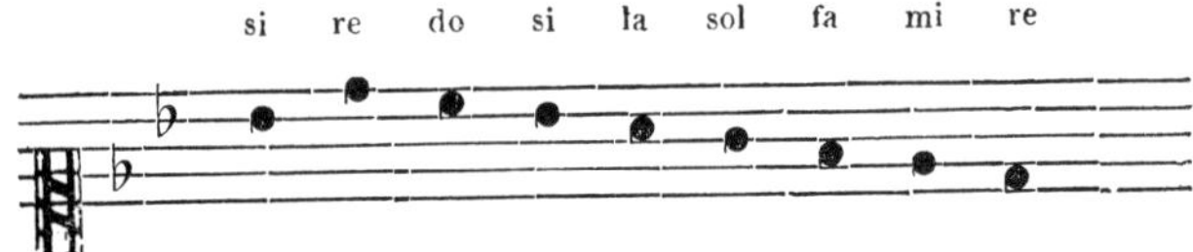

The multiplicity of clefs is particularly useful for this purpose.

Transposition is one of the greatest practical difficulties in music, and requires a peculiar facility, of which even the skilful are not always possessed. In order to remove these difficulties, it has been attempted to make pianos of such a construction as to effect transposition mechanically. They are called *transposing pianos* (*pianos-transpositeurs*).* This invention, though convenient, has met with but little success.

The editors of music, with a view to facilitate the practice of this art to amateurs, frequently transpose the most popular pieces, so as to bring them within the compass of different voices, and to relieve the performer from the operation of transposition; but, as all music cannot be transposed in this manner, it is useful to know how to do it for oneself.

* Several plans have been adopted, to effect a mechanical transposition; but the first transposing pianos introduced into use were those of Messieurs Roller and Blanchet, manufacturers at Paris, Boulevard Poissonnière. Mr. Pfeiffer has improved the invention, by reducing the operation to the pressure of a pedal.

CHAPTER V.

THE SAME SCALE NOT IN USE AMONG ALL NATIONS. THE EUROPEAN SCALE THE BEST, THOUGH NOT PERFECT.

THE gamut, or scale of sounds, which has just been explained, is that which is made use of by the nations of Europe, and in the colonies established by them. The result of a series of modifications, produced partly by accident and partly by design, from ancient times to the seventeenth century, it has become to us, both by education and by habit, the only rule of the metaphysical relations of sounds which the ear will admit, and which renders us, to a certain extent, unable to conceive of any other.

But it is not so with all nations; some of them have had, or still have, very different divisions of the general scale of sounds. These divisions are of two kinds—one founded upon intervals of sounds of the same nature with those of European music, but differently arranged; the other upon smaller intervals, not appreciable by our ears. We will first examine the former.

There is in China and India a major scale, arranged in this manner:

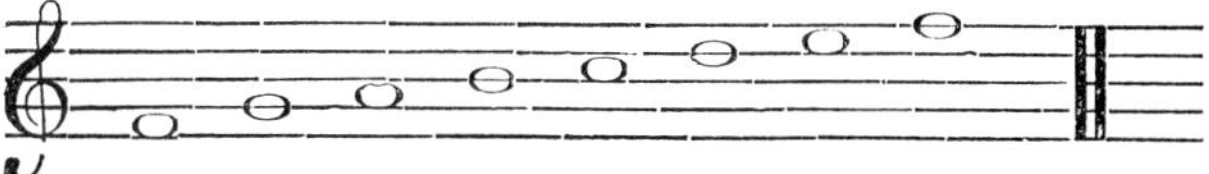

It is manifest that this scale differs from ours in this particular,—that the first semitone, instead of being placed between the third and fourth degree, as it is in ours, occurs between the fourth and fifth, thus creating a total difference in the order of tones, which is shocking to our ears, while the scale of Europeans seems intolerable to the Chinese.*

The Scotch and the Irish have a scale somewhat like that of the Chinese, but still more singular, because there is a whole tone, instead of a semitone, between the seventh and eighth sounds. The following is an example of this scale:—

The defects of this scale are still more shocking to the ear of a musician than those of the Chinese, on account of the double false relation which exists between the major and minor fourth of the key and

* The Abbé Roussier has tried to demonstrate, in his *Memoir on the Music of the Ancients*, and in his *Letters to the Author of the Journal of Fine Arts and Sciences*, etc., that this scale is a natural one, because it is the result of a regular succession of ascending fourths and descending fifths, such as,

This sort of regular movement has something in it pleasing to the imagination, but proves nothing as to the metaphysical connexion of sounds. This scale will always shock the ear of a European musician, because the fourth, first, and eighth, are in a false position relatively to each other.

the seventh. Hence it happens that all the Scotch and Irish airs in this scale must be rearranged for publication.

The Irish have also a minor scale, which is very singular; there are only six notes, and the arrangement of it is thus:—

The logical defect of this scale is the same as that of the preceding; for it consists in a false relation between the third and the sixth sound, which has no place in the scale of other European nations.

The scales of which we have just spoken are divided, like that of the French, Italian, or German music, by tones and semitones: they differ from the latter only in the arrangement of these tones and semitones; but there are some Oriental nations, such as the Arabs, the Turks, and the Persians, whose instruments are constructed on a scale of intervals of thirds. Such intervals, and such a division of the scale, can be appreciated only by organs accustomed by education to their effect: the sensation which they produce on a European ear is that of false sounds and disagreeable successions, while the Arabs find pleasure in them, and are painfully affected by hearing our scale.

Upon considering the effects of such different scales, this question arises:—Is there any scale conforming exactly to principles which are founded in nature? If not, which of them combines the greatest number of desirable conditions? To answer the first of these questions, we must consider it in two ways; that is, we must first inquire if the phenomena of sonorous bodies, and the proportions deduced from them, between the different sounds of the scale, result in precise, invariable tones, and if the physical laws of their order are equally certain.

It must be confessed, the science is yet very imperfect in this respect, as I shall shew in speaking of acoustics. The phenomena have been ill observed, the experiments negligently made; and, as almost always happens, there has been haste in forming conclusions on uncertain data.

The second consideration is entirely metaphysical. The point is, to ascertain if the relations of the sounds of our scale have a sufficient foundation in their agreement with our sensations, and with the laws of the harmony and melody of which our music consists. Now, whatever may be the view we take of the scale, it cannot be denied that its propriety, in the arrangement of the sounds, is perfect, and that another order could not be substituted for it, without greatly affecting melody as well as harmony, nor, consequently, without changing the nature of our sensations.

CHAPTER VI.

OF THE LENGTH OF SOUNDS AND OF RESTS IN MUSIC, AND OF THE MANNER OF REPRESENTING AND MEASURING THEM BY SIGNS.

THE alphabets of all languages have only one object —that of representing sounds. The musical alphabet is more complicated, for it is necessary that its signs of intonation should be combined with those of duration, and even that the notes should indicate both these things at once. This complexity is the principal cause of the difficulty experienced in learning to read music.

It is clear that the sounds which enter into the composition of music have not all the same length, but that they differ greatly in this respect. The notes being intended to represent the sounds, it is necessary to modify their form, in order that they may also express the differences of their length.* With this view, a unit of duration has been supposed, which is called a *semibreve;* the half of this has received the name of a *minim;* the fourth, that of a *crotchet;* the eighth has been called a *quaver;* the sixteenth, *semi-*

* If it were my purpose to explain, philosophically, the principles of the measurement of time in music, I should proceed in a different manner; but I must not forget that the object of this book is not to point out the defects of the technical part of the art. It will be more useful to shew what it actually is.

quaver; the thirty-second, *demisemiquaver;* and the sixty-fourth, *double demisemiquaver.*

Forms of these Signs of Length.

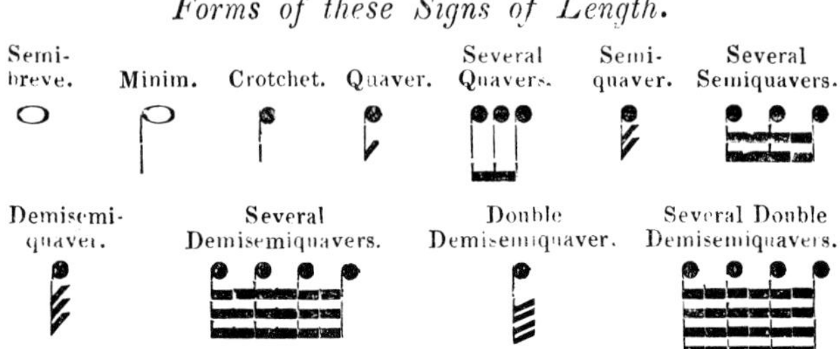

Whatever may be the form of the note, and the duration which it represents, the intonation is not changed, and the name of the note remains the same, as may be seen by the following examples:—

All the forms of the notes in these examples are designed to represent durations of sounds, which are in the proportion of 1 to 2, 1 to 4, 1 to 8, etc.; or $\frac{1}{2}$ to 1, $\frac{1}{4}$ to 1, $\frac{1}{8}$ to 1, etc.; that is to say, which are twice, four times, eight times, longer than others, or which are only the half, fourth, or eighth part of them. But there are certain durations of sounds, which are three times, six times, or twelve times, longer than others, or which are only the third, the sixth, the twelfth, etc. The first are represented by the figure of any note whatever, followed by a point; so that a point increases the duration of such notes by one half. Thus a semibreve pointed has the same duration as three minims, six crotchets, or twelve quavers, etc.; a minim pointed is in the same proportion with respect to crochets, quavers, or semiquavers; and so of others. It follows from this, that a minim has only one third the value of the pointed semibreve, that a crochet represents only the sixth part of it, and a quaver the twelfth, etc. Lastly, there are sounds, which, in regard to others, are in the proportion of 2 to 3. We give the name of *triplets* to those which are in the proportion of 3 to 2, and we denote their value by placing a figure 3 above or below the notes which represent them.

Sounds and their length are not the only elements of music. The cessation of sound, for a greater or less period, is also important. The necessity of subjecting this cessation to rules of proportion, has caused it to be divided, like the forms of notes, and to be represented by analogous signs. The semibreve is taken as the unit of the duration of sound. The cessation of sound of a corresponding length is represented by a *semibreve rest;* the half of this time is called a *minim rest;* the fourth, a *crotchet rest;* the eighth, a *quaver rest;* the sixteenth, a *semiquaver rest.* All these signs of silence have a value equal to that of the different forms of the notes. The following is a table of them:—

Semibreve. Minim. Crochet. Quaver. Semi-quaver. Demisemi-quaver. Double Demi-semiquaver.

Corresponding Rests.

It will be readily perceived, that a semibreve with a point is represented by a semibreve rest followed by a minim rest, a pointed minim by a minim rest followed by a crotchet rest, and so on.

These different proportions of the relative durations of sounds and of cessations of sound, are susceptible of a prodigious number of combinations. The most practised eye would experience some difficulty in distinguishing them, if it were not for the plan which has been devised of separating them, from space to space, by bars crossing the staff perpendicularly. The name of *measure* denotes the space thus comprised between two bars of separation. By means of bars, the eye easily separates each measure of this multitude of signs, in order to consider its contents. The sum total of what is contained in each measure must be of a uniform duration in all the measures; but this duration may, at pleasure, be made equal in value to a semibreve, a minim, or a pointed minim, etc.

The reading of what is contained in each measure is also facilitated by dividing the measures into equal parts, which we call *beats*, and which we mark by movements of the hand. This division may be made into two, three, or four parts; in respect to which, the composer denotes his intention, by a sign which he places at the beginning of each piece. If the division is to be made into two parts, the sign is a 𝄵 ; if into three, the sign is 3 or $\frac{3}{4}$, etc., and, lastly, if the measure is to be divided into four parts, the sign of it is a 𝄴 Upon an inspection of the sign, musicians say that the measure is in common, triple, or quadruple time.

I have said that the semibreve is considered as the unit of duration: we see the proof of this particularly in certain marks of time, which are sometimes found at the commencement of a piece of music, such as $\frac{2}{4}$, $\frac{3}{4}$, $\frac{6}{4}$, $\frac{9}{4}$, $\frac{12}{4}$, $\frac{2}{8}$, $\frac{3}{8}$, $\frac{6}{8}$, $\frac{9}{8}$, $\frac{12}{8}$; for these marks shew that the space between two bars includes *two-fourths, three-fourths, six-fourths, nine-fourths, twelve-fourths*, of the semibreve, or *two-eighths, three-eighths, six-eighths, twelve-eighths*, of the same unit. Amongst these quantities, those which are susceptible of being divided by 2, as $\frac{2}{4}$, $\frac{6}{4}$, $\frac{2}{8}$ and $\frac{6}{8}$, belong to the measures *in common time*, which is marked by a downward and upward motion of the hand, alternately; those which can be divided only by three, as $\frac{3}{4}$, $\frac{9}{4}$, $\frac{3}{8}$ and $\frac{9}{8}$, are of the kind of measures *in triple time*, in which the hand makes three motions—downward, to the right, and upward; and lastly, the quantities $\frac{12}{4}$ and $\frac{12}{8}$, which may be divided by 4, belong to the measures *in quadruple time*, and are marked by four motions of the hand—downward, to the left, to the right, and upward.

All that we have seen thus far of the measure of sounds and of silence presents none but quantities of relative duration; and there is nothing to denote the absolute time which belongs to each of these signs. Indeed, it would have been very difficult, or rather impossible, to express by any signs that mathematical duration, which can only be represented by the vibrations of the astronomical clock, or by divisions of those vibrations. Still, if there did not exist any means of indicating this duration in music, the intention of the composer would be frequently frustrated in the execution; for, inasmuch as every performer would be at liberty to give to the semibreve, considered as a unit, such duration as he pleased, the same piece would run the risk of being executed, sometimes with the slowness of a lament, and sometimes with the liveliness of a *contre danse.* In order to obviate this inconvenience, nothing better was thought of, at first, than to write at the beginning of pieces certain Italian or French words, which indicated, with more or less exactness, the degree of slowness or of quickness to be given to the measure, that is to say, to the length of the semibreve or its parts. Thus the words *largo*, *maestoso*, *larghetto*, *adagio*, *grave*, *lento*, indicate different gradations of slowness; *andantino*, *andante*, *moderato*, *a piacere*, *allegretto*, *comodo*, are the signs of the varieties of a moderate motion; and, lastly, *allegro*, *con moto*, *presto*, *vivace*, *prestissimo*, are signs of a constantly-increasing quickness. It is easy to see, that in these varieties of slowness and of quickness, the semibreve and its rest, and their subdivisions, vary also in duration, to such a degree, that there is no more relation between one semibreve and another, than there is between the relative duration of a semibreve and that of a semiquaver. In fact, there are movements so slow, that five semibreves occupy a minute; and others so quick, that forty semibreves occupy the same space of time. This variety of absolute length does not affect the relative value of the signs.

Formerly, all the pieces of instrumental music, composed by the most celebrated musicians, bore the names of certain dances, such as those of *allemandes*, *sarabandes*, *courantes*, *gigues*, etc.; not that they had the character, but merely the movement, of those sorts of dances; and these movements being known, it was useless to distinguish them in any other manner. Since these pieces have gone out of fashion, it has become necessary to recur to other characteristics; and the Italian words already spoken of, and many others also, have been adopted.

But how vague are these expressions! How many gradations are there not between one *allegro*, or lively movement, and another — between one *adagio* and another! Indications of this kind can never be any thing more than approximations, subject to be modified by the understanding or the particular organization of every performer. The consequence of this is, that music is rarely performed according to the idea of the author, and that the same piece receives different characters in the hands of different musicians. In addition to this, the use of these words is sometimes contradictory; for there are some pieces, the passionate character of which seems to express anger or grief, and yet the movement is marked by the word *allegro*. There is in this a real evil, which has been felt for a long time, and for which no remedy has been discovered until within a few years. From the end of the seventeenth century, it had been acknowledged, that a regular machine would be the best means of regulating the slowness or the rapidity of the movements of music. Many persons, of musical and mechanical talent, have been engaged in studying the principles of the construction of such a machine. In 1698, a professor of music, named Loulie, proposed one which he called a *chronometer* (measurer of time). About the same time, Lafillard, a musician belonging to the chapel of the king, invented another. At a later period, Harrison, a famous English mechanician, and celebrated for his marine time-pieces, invented a machine, which appeared to be perfect, but which was prevented, by its costliness, from being brought into common use. In 1782, Duclos, a watchmaker at Paris, made another machine, which he called a *rhythmometer* (measurer of rhythm), and which at the time received the approbation of some distinguished musicians. To this machine succeeded the chronometer of a mechanician named Pelletier; the form and mechanism of whose invention are not now known. In 1784, Reneaudin, a watchmaker at Paris, constructed a pendulum with the same design. The celebrated watchmaker Breguet also busied himself with the solution of the same problem, without, however, making known the result of his labours. Finally, Despreaux, a professor in the Conservatory of Music, proposed, in 1812, the adoption of a chronometer, having a face to indicate its movements, and a pendulum, or balance, suspended by a silken thread, the different lengths of which would produce, according to well-known physical laws, the different degrees of quickness. Several German musicians had already produced chronometers of this kind, which have the double advantage of being simple in their construction and of trifling expense, but which have the inconvenience of not making sensible to the ear the tick or stroke of the time.

An invention, which is claimed by two skilful mechanicians, — Messrs. Winkel of Amsterdam and Maelzel,—has at length satisfied all wants; I mean the *metronome*, which received the approbation of the Institute in 1816, and the use of which is now generally known. In this machine, each vibration of the balance gives an audible click. The inventor has taken for his unit a *minute*, to the divisions of which correspond the measures of the music. Every gradation of movement, from the slowest to the most rapid, is there expressed and represented by vibrations of the balance, which are divisible, at pleasure, into measures of two, three, or four parts, and which represent according to the fancy of the composer, semibreves, minims, crotchets, or quavers. The simplicity of the principle of this machine is its great merit. This principle consists in displacing the centre of gravity, in such a manner, that we are able to substitute a short rod for a very long one, and to produce great varieties of movement, by very slight changes in the position of the central point. By means of the metronome, the whole system of the division of time in music is represented, both as a whole and in its details.

CHAPTER VII.

OF WHAT IS CALLED EXPRESSION IN THE EXECUTION OF MUSIC; THE MEANS OF EFFECTING IT, AND OF THE SIGNS BY WHICH IT IS INDICATED.

HITHERTO we have considered only two of the attributes of sounds, namely, tone and length: it remains to consider them in the relation of their *intensity*, that is to say, in their different degrees of softness or of strength, which will complete the description of the qualities by which they act upon us.

The softness of sounds generally produces impressions of calmness, repose, tranquil pleasure, and of every gradation of these different states of the mind. Loud, boisterous, and piercing sounds, on the contrary, excite strong emotions, and are proper for the expression of courage, anger, jealousy, and other violent passions; but if sounds were constantly soft, they would soon become wearisome by their uniformity, and if they were always loud, they would fatigue both the mind and the ear. Besides, music is not designed merely to describe the states of the soul: its object is frequently vague and indeterminate, and its result rather to please the senses, than to address the mind. This is particularly to be remarked in instrumental music.

But, whether we consider the excitability of the faculties of the soul, and the numerous changes of which they are susceptible, or have regard to impressions upon the senses only, it will be readily admitted that the intermixtures of soft and loud sounds, and their various successive degrees, are powerful means of expressing the one, and of giving birth to the other. We generally give the name of *expression* to this mixture of softness and strength, to this increase or diminution of force, and, indeed, to all the accidental characteristics of sounds; not because their object is always to *express* either ideas or sentiments,—for they are frequently nothing more than the result of mere fancy, or of a vague, undefinable impression,—but it cannot be denied that their well-ordered intermixture has the effect to excite us so much the more vividly, as the object is less definite. If we should ask skilful singers, or great instrumental performers, what induces them to give strength to particular sounds,—to make others scarcely audible, and gradually to increase or diminish their force,—to produce certain sounds in an animated and very distinct manner, or to connect them together with a graceful negligence and softness,—we should wait long for the answer; or, rather, they would simply reply: "We do not know, but that is the way we feel;" and certainly they will be right, if they transfer their sensations to the souls of their auditors. Further, if they are themselves capable of observing, they will acknowledge that the same passages have not always affected them in the same manner, but that it has happened to them to express them with very different feelings, though the result might be equally satisfactory.

This faculty of expressing the same musical thoughts

in several ways might be very inconvenient, if each one of several performers should follow the impression of the moment; for it might happen that one would be executing his part with force, whilst another would be performing his with softness, and a third would distinctly articulate the sounds of a passage, which his neighbour would think proper to connect together. Hence arises the necessity that the composer should point out his own ideas, in regard to expression, as he does in regard to the time, by unequivocal signs; which, in fact, is always done.

The signs of expression are of several kinds. Some relate to the strength or to the softness of sounds; others are intended to shew whether they are to be separated or connected; and others to shew slight variations of the movement, which contribute to increase the effect of the music.

Some Italian words are used to shew to the performers the different degrees of the force or softness of sounds: *piano*, or simply *p*, signifies that the piece must be sung or played soft; *pianissimo*, or *pp*, indicates an extreme degree of softness; *forte*, or *f*, loud; *fortissimo*, or *ff*, very loud. The transition from soft to loud is expressed by *crescendo*, *cresc.*, or *cr.;* that from loud to soft, by *decrescendo*, *diminuendo*, *smorzando*, or by the abbreviations of these words. A soft followed by a loud sound is indicated by *pf*, and the contrary by *fp*. A small nnmber of sounds, louder than others, is expressed by *rinforzando*, or simply *rf;* *sforzando*, or *sf; forzando*, or *fz*. Lastly, a sudden increase or diminution of strength is indicated by these signs $<$ $>$ Fancy may multiply these marks, and imagine new ones; but those which we have mentioned are enough for singers and players in general. As to the expression which a great artist gives to his playing or singing, it is the voice of the soul, which is scarcely ever heard in the same tone, even under similar circumstances, and which cannot be expressed to the eye by volumes of signs. Such a multitude of delicate shades of expression, prepared beforehand, would be both ambitious and cold, and would injure, instead of increasing, the effect of the music.

The signs of detached sounds are of two sorts. The first consists of lengthened points placed over the notes, which indicate the greatest possible degree of lightness, as well as distinctness, in the sounds.

When the sounds are to be given with a certain degree of emphasis, the notes are surmounted by round points, which are sometimes placed under a curved line, as in this example:—

A curve, without the points placed over the notes, is the sign of connected sounds:—

The alterations of the movement, which are a means of expression sometimes abused, are indicated by the words *calando*, *con fuoco*, *con moto*, when we desire to increase, and by the word *ritardando*, when we desire to diminish, the rapidity of the movement. The composer most frequently leaves slight changes of this description to the understanding of the performers.

There are some accessory signs, the utility of which is felt in execution, but which have no reference to the three principal qualities of sounds, and which, for that as on, I do not think it worth while to explain.

The preceding observations contain a sketch of what is called *notation;* and, if the mechanism of it is understood by the reader, he will be able to follow, with ease, the rest of this work; for it would be a mistake to suppose it necessary to burden the memory with all the terms of art, and with the form of all the signs. The efforts requisite to be made in a study of that sort would be an absolute loss, in reference to the object both of the author and the readers of this book. It is of very little importance, whether people in general, when called upon to form and express an opinion of a musical composition, know how to distinguish a *do* from a *sol*, or a *crotchet* from a *quaver;* but it is necessary that they should understand the use of all these things, were it only to save themselves from the consequential pedantry of those who have made them a profound study. That it is as useful as it is agreeable to possess a knowledge of music, cannot be doubted; but, compared with the entire population of a country, those who possess this advantage are almost always a small number. It is for the others—

that is to say, for those who are prevented, by a thousand obstacles, from studying this difficult art—that this book is written; and the author would consequently fail in his object, if, in order to make himself understood, he should require his readers to obtain a knowledge, the want of which he means to supply.

It would be an error to suppose that the system of notation, above described, has been at all times in use amongst the people of Europe. It was not until towards the close of the tenth century that the notes and staff began to be employed; and the number of lines on the latter underwent many changes. This system of notation, the inventor of which is not known, was not, at first, generally adopted; it suffered divers transformations: many signs, which are now abandoned, were introduced into it, in the fifteenth and sixteenth centuries, and their complication was such, that it was then very difficult to learn to read and to write music. There are not now ten musicians in existence who possess a knowledge of these signs. Notation did not begin to be simplified, and to take its present form, until the reign of Louis XIII.

Discouraged by the multitude of the signs of musical notation, men of talent, but who were scarcely more than indifferent musicians, have attempted to introduce other systems, seemingly more simple, and composed of ciphers or arbitrary signs. But, besides that such changes are no more admissible than it would be to change the alphabet of a language,—since they would produce the great inconvenience of throwing back all those who understand music to a state of entire ignorance, and of destroying every existing monument of the art,—there is another reason, which will always cause the rejection of plans for the reformation of the notation, however simple they may be; that is, that the signs of these systems will not be so sensible to the eye as those which have just been explained, and consequently, that they will offer no facility for the rapid reading of music, equal to that of the system of notation now in use. A reproach is often brought against this system, that there is a want of analogy in its parts. This is a mistake. All the elements seem to me connected in such a manner that no one of them can be removed without destroying the system. The multiplicity of clefs, even, against which some, who are little skilled in the art, have declaimed, far from being an embarrassment, has indisputable advantages in certain cases.

In the origin of modern music, that is to say, about the tenth and eleventh centuries, different systems of notation might be tried, and the advantages and disadvantages of each might be examined; at a later period (the seventeenth century), we were able to give up the ridiculous scaffolding of certain relations which bristled over the reading of music with almost insurmountable difficulties, without the least real use in the art; but, in its actual condition, musical notation is a complete and logical system, which can no longer be changed in the least without injury.

PART II.

OF SOUNDS, CONSIDERED IN THEIR RELATIONS OF SUCCESSION AND OF SIMULTANEOUSNESS; AND OF THE CONSEQUENCES OF THESE RELATIONS.

CHAPTER VIII.

OF THE RELATIONS OF SOUNDS.

THERE is much analogy between the impressions made by music on those who are ignorant of its details, and the sensations of a composer at the first gush of his inspiration. In general, the public is struck only by a combined whole, of which it does not perceive the parts, and the musician is too much excited to analyze his thoughts; but when the latter wishes to write what he has invented, a great difference arises between them: as soon as he takes his pen, his mind becomes gradually calm, and his ideas clear; his musical periods divide themselves into phrases more or less regular under his eye; the voices, the instruments which accompany them, and the dramatic expression of the words, cease to make one homogeneous whole.

Then is developed a musical thought which we call

melody; then is shewn the difference between sounds which succeed one another, and those which are heard together; and then errors of number in the phrases become as perceptible to the musician as faults of quantity to the poet; the arrangement of the voices, the combinations of sounds, the selection of the instruments, rhythm, every thing, indeed, becomes the object of a particular examination; every thing is susceptible of improvements, the necessity of which was not at first perceived, and art lends its aid to genius.

Of all the operations of mind, that by which a composer of music conceives the effect of his composition, without hearing it, seems to be both the most difficult and the most wonderful. What complication! what variety of relations! what talent, perspicacity, experience, observation, even in an inferior composition! for it is not enough to be moved by the situation which he wishes to delineate, or the sentiment which he undertakes to express; it is also necessary to find melodies analogous to these divers objects; that these melodies should be confined and divided among several voices of different characters, of which it is indispensable to anticipate the effect; and, lastly, it is necessary that all this should be accompanied by a greater or less number of instruments, differing in character, power, and quality of tone, and employed in such a manner as will be the most satisfactory and the most conducive to the general effect. Each of these things implies a multitude of details, by the combination of which the elements of this singular art become complicated. The musician has only to throw his eye upon the paper which records his inspirations, to have as just an idea of his composition as if he heard it actually performed!

If we carry our investigations into music with some attention, we remark that it contains four principal things, which concur in its effect, namely, the succession of sounds, which, as we have already seen, is called *melody;* their simultaneousness, from which results *harmony; sonorousness,* (or quality of tone), which is more or less satisfactory, according to the selection and arrangement of the voices and instruments; and, lastly, *accent,* which gives life to all the rest, but which itself escapes analysis. The sensible relations of sounds present themselves, therefore, under three aspects:—I. SUCCESSION. II. SIMULTANEOUSNESS; and III. SONOROUSNESS (QUALITY). Each of these divisions is subdivided, as we shall see hereafter.

CHAPTER IX.

OF MELODY.

THE human voice is the basis and model of music. This first of instruments, at once the most touching and the most fruitful in the variety of its effects, by itself gives only the idea of successive sounds, without even suggesting the possibility of their simultaneous utterance. Hence it is, without doubt, that the melody is first observed, when early education has not modified the natural tendencies; and not only so, it is melody alone which draws the attention of those who are entire strangers to musical studies, and the harmony of the accompaniments strikes their ear in vain; it is not heard. About twenty years ago, it was ascertained by various experiments, that a part of the audience at our theatres believed that the orchestra played in unison with the singers. The people are now better informed, thanks to the improvements in the methods of teaching, and to the influence of the press. It is remarkable that the people of Europe are the only ones who have made use of the union of harmony and melody since the Middle Ages: antiquity seems not to have possessed any knowledge of it, and the Orientals do not understand it when they hear it. It would be easy to shew that the arrangement of the musical scale of some nations does not admit of harmony; and, on the other hand, that it is almost the necessary result of our gamut. Melody is of all countries and of all times; but its forms are variable, like the elements which enter into its composition.

We must not imagine that melody, such as is heard in popular songs and at the theatre, has no other rules than those of fancy. The freest and the most original genius, when it invents airs, obeys, unconsciously, certain laws of proportion, the effect of which is no more conventional than that of the drum upon the masses of soldiers who move at its beat. Let it not be supposed that this regularity of form affects those only who have studied the principles of music: whoever has an ear not absolutely insensible or rebellious, perceives its effect, without analyzing his sensations.

The difference of quickness and of slowness, ranged in any regular order whatever, constitutes what is called *rhythm*, in music. It is by rhythm that this art excites the most lively emotions, and the effect of rhythm increases by repetition. For instance, a crotchet, followed by two quavers, is a succession continually met with in music, without being observed; but let it be prolonged a certain time, it will become a rhythm capable of producing the greatest effects.

Rhythm is susceptible of much variety.

In slow movements, such as the *adagio* and the *largo*, it is almost imperceptible; but in moderate or rapid movements, it is very remarkable. Sometimes it is perceptible only in the leading air; sometimes it is found in the accompaniment; and there are cases in which two different rhythms—the one placed in the air, the other in the accompaniment—combine to produce a mixed effect.

Music deprived of rhythm is vague, and cannot be long continued without becoming wearisome. Still, melodies of this kind are sometimes employed with success, to express a certain melancholy reverie, a repose of the passions, a state of uncertainty, and other things of a similar character. Such cases, however, are rare.

From what has been said, it will be perceived that rhythm is one of the laws of proportion, to which melody is subject. It is the first and the most imperative; it admits the fewest exceptions, and offers the strongest inducements to obedience.

The perception of rhythm in music is either simple or compound. It is simple when only one kind of combination of time is heard; it is compound when different kinds of combinations are heard together.

The fewer the elements of the symmetrical order, the more simple is the sensation. The elements of rhythm are the parts of the measure, and their divisions, whether double or triple.

Examples of some Elements of Simple Rhythm.

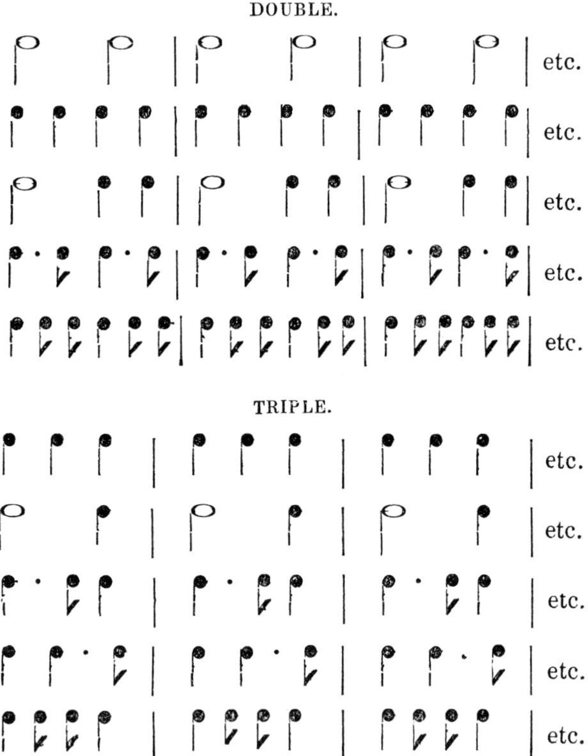

The simplicity of the sensation of rhythm diminishes as the number of elements entering into its composition increases.

Examples of Rhythm composed of several Elements.

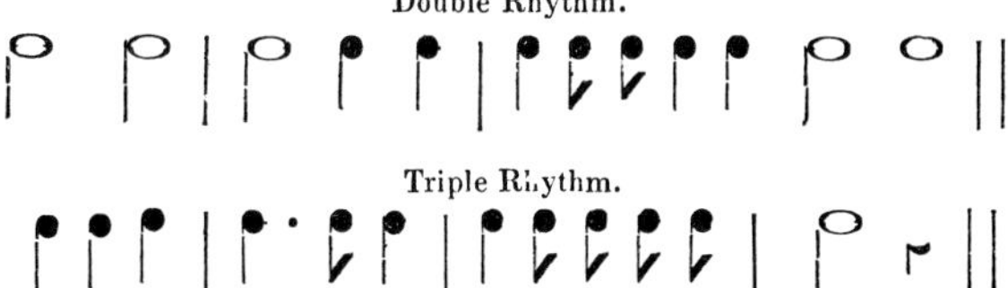

The effect of a very simple rhythm being to affect the organ of hearing in a uniform manner, the perception of it is easy; it is not the same when the rhythm is produced by numerous elements, variously combined. In the two last examples, each measure contains different elements, and each of them, consequently, produces a distinct sensation; from which it follows that the symmetry of arrangement is lost, and therefore the rhythmical relation is weakened.

But a new relation of numbers may result from such combinations. In fact, the ear, without counting the number of measures, is sensibly affected by that number; hence arises the necessity of repetition; and if the ear is satisfied in this respect, a new kind of rhythm is created by the symmetry of the phrases; this rhythm constitutes the *phraseology*, which is called in music, *carrure des phrases*, that is to say, the *quadrature* or *balancing* of the phrases. The necessity of symmetry, in the number of corresponding measures, creates, therefore, a new kind of rhythm, when this symmetry no longer exists in the elements of the rhythm of the time; and this new rhythm is the more satisfactory to the ear, according to the exactness of the resemblance in the arrangement of the rhythmical elements of each measure. Thus the rhythms which have been last given as examples will become regular and perceptible, if phrases similar in the number of measures, and the arrangement of the parts of the measure, should be made to correspond with each of those examples, composed of four measures.

Examples.

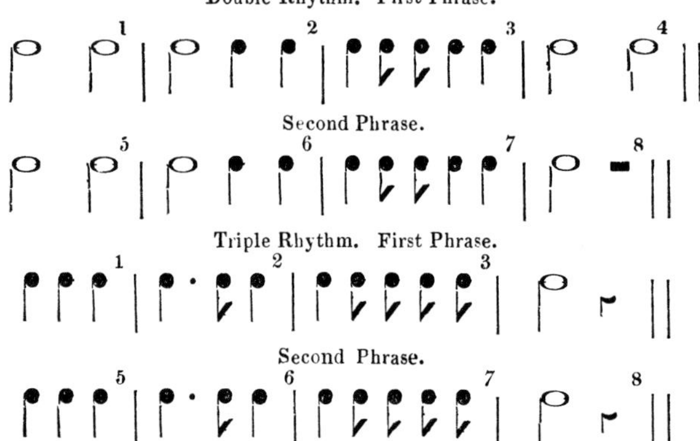

In these examples there is a correspondence, not only in respect to the number of measures in each phrase, but also in respect to the arrangement of the elements of the rhythm in the measures; the fifth agreeing exactly with the first, the sixth with the second, the seventh with the third, and the eighth with the fourth. A difference, however, is observable between the two phrases of the first example; for, instead of two minims in the fourth measure, there is only one in the eighth, followed by a rest. The reason of this difference is, that the rhythmical sense is closed at the end of the two phrases, and that the first half of the last measure is just the point of the termination.

The arrangement of the phraseological rhythm is not always so regular as in these examples; but it may be asserted that the less regularity there is in the arrangement, the more feeble is the perception of this kind of rhythm.

The expression *quadrature of phrases*, which is ordinarily made use of to designate the phraseological rhythm, might make one think it absolutely necessary to compose all phrases in four measures; but there is no such necessity; for, as there is a triple rhythm in the divisions of a measure, there is also a triple rhythm in phrases. A phrase of three measures, if it has another phrase of three measures to correspond with it, will be in perfect rhythm; and the rhythm will be especially agreeable, if the arrangement of the elements of the rhythm of each measure correspond perfectly in the two phrases.

There are also corresponding phrases of five measures each; but, in respect to them, the same observation may be made, as of the rhythm of five divisions of the measure, which some authors have attempted to introduce into music; and that is, that the ear is absolutely unable to apprehend the relation of this quintuple combination, and that if such combinations have been attempted with some success, it is because the ear has separated them into alternate double and triple rhythms, and the symmetry which results from repetition has produced relations of order, which ultimately satisfy the ear. A sequence of measures in five parts presents itself to the ear as an alternate series of measures of two and three parts; a sequence of phrases of five measures is an alternate combination of phrases of two and three measures; whence it follows that the phraseological rhythm of phrases of five measures is the least simple, and, therefore, the weakest in its effect on the ear.

Sometimes the first phrase of four measures is divided by a rest occurring in the middle of it, that is to say, at the end of two measures; and, in this case, the ear requires that the same musical pause should be felt in the supplementary or corresponding phrase. I shall cite, as an example of this, from the romance of *The Prisoner*.

In this example, A is the commencement of a proposition, of which B is the completion. 1, 2, 3, 4, are corresponding and symmetrical members of phrases.

Sometimes the musical sense remains suspended after the second phrase of four measures; and in this case, a third phrase of four must be added, to satisfy the ear. We find an example of this in the celebrated canzonet from *The Marriage of Figaro*, which begins with these words—*Mon cœur soupire*, etc.

It would be a mistake to draw the inference, from what has been said, that a piece of music must always contain an equal number of measures; for it frequently happens, in the *finale* of an opera, or in any other piece written for several voices, that the final measure of one phrase serves also as the first for another phrase, which makes the number of measures at the end unequal, without offending the ear: this kind of overlapping is even an ornament, when judiciously done.

It sometimes happens that a single phrase of five or of three measures occurs in the middle of other phrases which are regular and balanced; but such a defect always offends a delicate ear, and one may affirm beforehand, that the phrase is ill made, and that, by considering it carefully, the author might have balanced it. Cases of this kind are very rare; for the musician conforms himself to the *carrure* of phrases, as a poet does to the measure of his verses, naturally, and without thinking of it.

However, certain popular melodies of mountainous countries, as Switzerland, Auvergne, Scotland, are characterized by numerous irregularities of this kind, and are still not disagreeable. The irregularity is even that which pleases the most in these sorts of melodies, because it contributes to give them a peculiar, strange, and, if you will, wild physiognomy, which excites our curiosity by drawing us out of our accustomed habits. But we must not be deceived; that which attracts us for an instant, in these melodies, soon becomes fatiguing, if we are not relieved by other music; and the irregularity, which we observe in them, and which pleased us at first, ends by becoming monotonous and affected. A musician may make an advantageous use of such melodies; but he must know how to employ them judiciously, and must not be too prodigal of them.

Melody, the fruit of imagination and of fancy, and apparently free from all trammels, is, therefore, subject to three conditions, upon which its existence depends; namely, fitness of tone, rhythm, and number. We shall see presently that there is another, not less important, not less imperative, and more burdensome: I refer to *modulation*, by which we mean the change from one key to another,—that is to say, from the scale of one note into the scale of another. It is necessary to explain the mechanism and the object of these changes of key.

If a piece of music were wholly in the same key, the consequence would be a fatiguing uniformity, which is exactly expressed by the word *monotony* (a single tone). Little airs, in a simple style, alone admit unity of tone, without giving rise to a disagreeable monotony. But, in a piece of some extent, modulation becomes necessary, and is subjected to the demands of the ear, like rhythm and the form of phrases. When a composer desires to make use of modulation, or rather when he is led to it by the nature of the airs which he invents, a difficulty occurs in the selection of keys. In fact, it is not every succession of keys that will please the ear. For this purpose, there must be some analogy between the key which is dropped and that which is taken up; and yet there are a great many cases, in which the modulation must be unexpected in order to be agreeable.

In reflecting upon the contradiction which seems to arise from this double necessity, we perceive that in every piece there are two sorts of modulations—the one, principal, which settles the style of the piece; the other, accessory, and only episodical. The principal modulation, having for its object not only to contribute to the variety of the piece, but to present with clearness the thought of the composer, admits only the analogous keys of which we have spoken; whilst incidental modulations, being designed to arouse the attention of the hearer by their striking effects, are not subject to any such law. The more natural and simple the former, the more satisfactory they are; the more unexpected the latter, the more they enhance the effect.

But here a new difficulty arises, which is this: Whatever may be the principal key chosen by the author of a piece of music, several others are grouped about it, in such a manner as to have much analogy with it; for if it is a major key, we find first the relative minor key,—that is to say, that which has the same number of sharps or of flats,—then that which has a sharp or a flat more, and, lastly, that which has a sharp or flat less; if, on the contrary, it is a minor key, we find first the relative major key—that is to say, that which has the same number of sharps or of flats,—and then those which have a sharp or a flat more or less. But which of all these keys must be adopted? Here, fortunately, there is room for choice; for it is obvious that, if there were only one way in which we could leave the principal key, the modulation would be always foreseen, and from that moment the pleasure derived from the music would be much lessened, or even entirely lost. It is enough to make a modulation agreeable and regular, that it should proceed from the principal key to one of the analogous keys,—that is to say, that it should add a sharp or flat to the melody, or cut off one from it. Let us suppose a major key,*—D, for example,—in which there are two sharps, namely, at F and C: the idea of the composer may be equally simple and natural, whether he conducts his modulation into B minor, in which there is the same number of sharps, whether the modulation passes into A, in which there is one sharp more, into F sharp minor, in which also there is a sharp more, or into G, in which there is a sharp less; fancy alone determines the choice.

* That is, a key in the *major mode*. In the music of the ancients, there was a large number of modes; in modern music, there are but two, and the word has not the same meaning. These two modes are the *major* and the *minor*. The mode is major when the third note of the scale, in any key, is at the distance of two tones, and the sixth at the distance of four tones and a half, from the first. The mode is minor when these two intervals are half a tone less.

Every principal modulation, therefore, may be made into four different keys. And let it not be thought that the pedantry of the schools has reduced us to this limited number of means: the boldest composers —those whose genius is the most independent—have been reluctantly compelled to confine themselves within these limits, because they have ascertained that every thing which goes beyond them offends, instead of pleases, the ear. They do not allow themselves to ramble, nor give themselves up to their imagination, in changes of key, until they have first regularly established the principal modulation; but having done this, other and unexpected changes, far from displeasing the ear, give it the most lively pleasure.

I have said that all composers conform to the regular system of principal modulation; I ought to add, that among the four keys which may be used for this purpose, it is common to adopt one, in preference to all the others, for the most frequent repetition. Thus, though the most simple, natural, and universally-adopted modulation is that in which the melody passes from a major key into another major key, which has a flat less, or a sharp more, as from D to A,—or from a minor key to its relative major key, as from B minor to D major,—yet some musicians have preferred modulations less common, and have made use of them habitually. Rossini, for instance, has adopted the modulation which passes from a major to a minor key, with one sharp more, as from the key of D major to the key of F sharp minor; but he has employed this form so frequently, that he has worn it out, and even rendered it trite.

Such are the principal laws of melody:—1. *Fitness of tone.* 2. *Symmetry of rhythm.* 3. *Symmetry of number.* 4. *Regularity of modulation.* It would be an error to suppose that these laws are so many obstacles to the development of ideas; for rhythm, number, and modulation, are so essential to a musician, that he obeys their laws without observing it, and almost by instinct; his mind being wholly occupied by the graceful, energetic, gay, or impassioned character of his melody. How many other difficulties, much more formidable, is he obliged to overcome, in the development and arrangement of his ideas! If he is composing for words, in the dramatic style, the arrangement of the verses, the prosody, the rapidity of action, and many other circumstances, fetter him much more, as we shall see hereafter; and yet the man of genius triumphs over them all. This faculty of inventing, of preserving the impetus, the excitement, and the delirium of a piece of music, and of becoming impassioned in the midst of so many difficulties,—of remaining independent in the choice of a subject, and of managing it with dexterity, as if nothing stood in the way,—is a mystery which none but composers themselves can comprehend. When we reflect on all these things, we cannot but admit that there may be some merit even in music which is barely tolerable.

There are some melodies which are attractive of themselves, and without extraneous ornament, even that of accompaniment; but they are very few. There are others, which, though purely melodious, require the assistance of harmony of some sort, in order to produce their effect. There are others, again, the origin of which is in the harmony that accompanies them. A person who is not insensible to the effect of sounds, easily seizes the character of melodies of the first kind; hence they quickly become popular. Melodies which do not produce their effect without the aid of an accompaniment of some sort, do not require great musical attainments in order to be felt; but still they can only please ears which are accustomed to hear music. As to melodies of the third kind, which we may call *harmonious melodies*, musicians alone are competent to appreciate them; because, instead of being the result of a simple idea, they are complicated of divers elements, and consequently require a sort of analysis, in order to be comprehended —an analysis which a musician makes with the rapidity of lightning, but which people in general can only make slowly and with difficulty. They are not the less real melodies, and it is wrong to cry out, as is frequently done, that there is no air whatever in a piece which contains a melody of this kind; we ought, in such case, to say only that the air is not readily perceived. To attempt to catch the spirit of it would add to our enjoyment, and would not require a very long study; but our natural indolence exercises its influence even over our pleasures.

Though melody seems to be a thing which everybody can appreciate with ease, it is nevertheless one of the parts of music upon which we pass the most erroneous judgments. There are few frequenters of the opera, who do not think themselves competent to pronounce upon the originality of a melody; and yet, besides that their musical learning is insufficient for that purpose, how often are they not deceived by the ornaments of the singer, which give a seeming novelty to airs that have long gone by? How many old things are there dressed up anew by means of accompaniments of different sorts, and of new instruments, and by changes of movement, of mode, and of key!

And whilst we do not perceive the real analogies which exist between one old melody, and another which we believe to be new, how often it happens that we discover imaginary resemblances, because we observe some similitude of rhythm between two melodies whose character, forms and inspiration have nothing in common! Blunders of this kind are innumerable; but they never make us doubt the infallibility of our judgment; and we are always ready, nevertheless, to fall into the same errors again, with the same assurance.

But, it is said, there is no need of all this examination, to know whether a particular melody is agreeable or otherwise. This is a matter of feeling rather than of analysis, and everybody is capable of judging of his sensations. All this is undeniable; but what must we conclude from it? That every one has the right to say that such a melody pleases him, or that it seems insignificant or disagreeable to him; but not to decide upon its merits, if he is not capable of analyzing it. Thank heaven, we are not obliged to analyze the measures of phrases, in order to ascertain whether they are properly balanced; such a labour, unworthy of any one who has the sentiment of music, is never necessary, when the ear has been properly cultivated, in respect to rhythm and number. We must labour to give perfection to this organ; and to do this, attention alone is required, without resorting to the aid of science. Let any one, instead of giving himself up, without reserve, to the vague pleasure which he receives from an air or a duet, set himself to examine its construction, to consider the arrangement and the repetition of its phrases, the principal rhythms, the cadences, etc. At first, the labour will be painful, and will break in upon his enjoyment; but, by degrees, a habit of attention will be formed, which will soon become spontaneous. Then that which, at first, seemed to be merely a matter of dry calculation will become the foundation of a ready judgment, and the source of the most lively gratification.

There is another objection, which is very freely made, and which must not be left without an answer, as it is specious, and may give rise to doubts even in well-constituted minds. "Beware of all this science," say those who are under the dominion of an unconquerable indolence; "it only weakens your pleasures. The arts procure us enjoyment only so far as their effects are unforeseen. Do not seek, therefore, to acquire a knowledge, the result of which will enable you to judge rather than to feel." All this reasoning is founded upon the following axiom of philosophy: "Feeling is the result of perception; judgment, of comparison." But the improvement of the organ of hearing, which results from an observation of the effect of sounds, is nothing more than the means of perceiving better, and of thereby increasing the amount of its enjoyments. For this reason, attention is necessary for all, while none can derive much advantage from imperfect knowledge. Everybody passes judgment upon music: some under the influence of a blind instinct, and very hastily; others by means of a cultivated taste, and with reflection. Who will venture to say that the first is better than the last?

When I come to treat of dramatic expression, I shall explain what portion of the melody it is that the least practised ear can instinctively appreciate.

CHAPTER X.

OF HARMONY.

When several sounds are heard simultaneously, and, united together, strike the ear more or less agreeably, they receive the collective name of *chords*. The general system of chords, and the laws of their succession, belong to a branch of the musical art which is designated by the name of *harmony*.

Harmony is a generic word, when it signifies the science of chords; but we say also the *harmony* of a chord, when used to point out the effect which it produces upon the ear. This is an example of the poverty of musical language.

In consequence of the education of modern civilized nations, it might be supposed that the sentiment of harmony is so natural to man, that it must have existed in him from all time. This is a mistake, for there is much probability that the ancients had no idea of it; and the Orientals, even at the present day, are wholly unacquainted with its mysteries. The effect of our music in chords is unpleasant to them. The question whether the Greeks or the Romans had any knowledge of harmony has been warmly controverted, but to no purpose; since it is impossible to allege any proofs on either side.* The equivalent of the word *harmony* is nowhere found used in the Greek or Latin treatises of music which have reached our times: † the air of an ode of Pindar, and that of a hymn to Nemesis, with some other fragments, are all that has been preserved of the ancient Grecian music; and in them we find no traces of chords; in fact, the form of the lyre and of the harp, the small number of their strings,—which could not be modified like those of our guitars, those instruments being destitute of necks,—all these reasons, I say, give much probability to the opinion of those who do not believe in the existence of harmony in the music of the ancients. Their adversaries object that harmony exists in nature. True, but how many things exist in nature, which are not observed for a long time! Harmony is in nature, and yet the ear of the Turk, the Arab, and the Chinese, has not become accustomed to it.

* I think, however, it might be shewn, from the nature of the musical scale of the Greeks, that they could not make use of harmony, in the sense we attach to the word; but this is a delicate question, which need not be discussed here.

† These treatises were written between the time of Alexander and the end of the Greek empire. The most important are those of Aristoxenus, Aristides, Quintilian, Alypius, Ptolemy, and Boece.

The first traces of harmony make their appearance in the writers of the Middle Ages, towards the ninth century; but it remained in a state of barbarism until towards the middle of the fourteenth, at which time some of the Italian musicians began to give it more agreeable forms. Among these musicians, the most distinguished were Francis Landino, surnamed *Francesco Cieco*, because he was blind, or *Francesco d'egli organi*, on account of his skill upon the organ, and James of Bologna. Harmony was afterwards improved in the hands of two French musicians, William Dufay and Giles Binchois, and an Englishman, John Dunstable, all of whom lived in the first half of the fifteenth century. Their scholars added to their discoveries; and, since that time, harmony has been continually enriched by the production of new effects.

The habit of hearing harmony from our infancy makes us feel the need of it in music. It seems, besides, that nothing is more natural, and in the state of musical civilization to which we have arrived, it is rare that two voices sing together without endeavouring to harmonize, that is to say, to make concords. As each voice is able to produce only a single sound at a time, two voices, when united, can only make chords of two sounds; and these are the simplest possible chords. They are designated by the name of *intervals*, because there is necessarily some distance from one sound to another; and the names of these intervals express the distances which exist between the two sounds. Thus the interval between two adjoining sounds is called a *second;* that between two sounds separated by another, a *third;* that which includes four sounds, a *fourth;* and so on, according as the distance from one sound to the other is increased,— a *fifth*, *sixth*, *seventh*, *eighth* (or *octave*), and *ninth*. The intervals greater than a ninth preserve the names of *third*, *fourth*, *fifth*, etc., because they are nothing more than double or triple thirds, fourths, fifths, etc. and because their effect is analogous to that of the simple intervals.

If we have not forgotten that different sounds, such as D♭, D♮, and D♯, preserve the common denomination of D, by means of the idea of positive existence attached to the names of the notes, we shall have no difficulty in conceiving that each interval may be presented under different aspects; for, if D is always the second of C, the D or C may be in the state of *flat*, *natural*, or *sharp*, and then the second will be more or lest extended or contracted. An interval reduced to its smallest extent, and in which we find only the signs of a single key and mode, is called a *minor*. The same interval, in its greatest extension, relative to the key, is *major*. For example, the interval from C♮ to D♭ is a *minor second;* that from C♮ to D♮ is a *major second*. But if, by a momentary alteration, which does not conform to any key, we construct intervals smaller than minors or greater than majors, we designate the first by the name of *diminished*, and the others by that of *augmented*. For example, the interval from C♯ to F♮ is a *diminished fourth*, which can be considered only as a momentary alteration; for there is no key in which C is *sharp*, whilst F is not so likewise; and for the same reason, the interval from C♮ to G♯ is an *augmented fifth*. The different degrees of extension of the intervals are, therefore, of four kinds—*diminished*, *minor*, *major*, *augmented.*

Formerly, the terms *true* and *false* were used for the varieties of extension of the *fourth* and *fifth;* but, as there is no place in music for what is false, these improper expressions have been abandoned.

The same effect is not produced by all the intervals or chords of two sounds: some of them please by their harmony, whilst others affect the ear less agreeably, and can satisfy it only when united with the others. We give the name of *consonance* (or *accord*) to the agreeable intervals, and that of *dissonance* (or *discord*) to the others.

The consonant intervals are the *third*, *fourth*, *fifth*, *sixth*, and the *octave.* The dissonant are the *second*, *seventh*, and *ninth.*

The intervals, both consonant and dissonant, have the property of *inversion;* that is to say, any two notes whatever may be, in regard to each other, in an inferior or superior position. For example, C being an inferior note, and E the superior, the interval between them is a *third;* but if E is the inferior note, and C the superior, they form a *sixth.*

The inversion of consonances produces consonances; that of dissonances begets dissonances: thus the third inverted produces the sixth, and the fourth the fifth; the latter produces the fourth, the sixth produces the third, the second the seventh, and the seventh the second.

It was a long time in dispute whether the fourth is a consonance or a dissonance; and two large books have been written on the question: the disputants might have been spared much bad reasoning, if they had thought of the law of inversion. The fourth is a consonance inferior in quality to the others; but still it is a consonance; for it is derived from another, the fifth, of which it is the inversion.

Inversion is a source of variety to the harmony; for it is merely necessary to change the position of the notes, in order to obtain different effects.

I have said that the consonant intervals are agreeable of themselves, and that the others become so only by their combination with the first. The result of this difference is, that the succession of consonances is free, and that we may make as great a number of them to succeed each other as we please. Two dissonances, on the contrary, cannot succeed each other; and in the resolution of a dissonance upon a consonance, the dissonant note must be made to descend one degree. This rule, which cannot be violated without offence to a delicate ear, is not, however, always respected by Rossini and the composers of his school; but, if the master of Pésaro may be pardoned for his negligence on account of his genius, it is not the less certain that the rule is founded upon undeniable relations of sounds, which cannot be violated with impunity.

If we unite two or three intervals, as the third, fifth, and eighth, in one chord, this will be a *consonance;* but if to several consonances we add a dissonance, the chord will become dissonant. In the greater number of dissonant chords, there is only one dissonant; there are some, however, which contain two.

If we were obliged to enumerate all the intervals

which enter into the composition of a chord of four or five sounds, the nomenclature of these chords would be embarrassing in the language of the science, and fatiguing to the memory; but it is not so. The chord which is formed by a union of the third, fifth, and octave, is called, *par excellence*, the *perfect* (or *common*) *chord*, because it is the most satisfactory to the ear,—the only one which can be used for the conclusion of every kind of harmonic period, and which gives the idea of repose. All the others are designated by the interval which is the most characteristic of their composition. Thus a chord formed of the third, sixth, and octave, is called the *chord of the sixth*, because that interval establishes the difference which exists between this and the perfect chord; we give the name of the *chord of the second* to that which is composed of the second, fourth, and sixth, because the second is the dissonance, which requires to be resolved by descending: and we call the chord of the seventh that which is composed of the third, fifth, and seventh, etc.

It is particularly in chords composed of three or of four notes, that the variety resulting from inversion is manifested; for the harmony of these chords may strike the ear under as many different relations as there are notes in their composition. For example, the perfect chord is composed of three notes, either of which may be placed in the inferior position. In the first arrangement, the chord is composed of the third and fifth: this is the perfect chord. In the second, the chord includes the third and sixth: this is the chord of the sixth. Lastly, in the third, the intervals are the fourth and sixth; and this is the chord of the fourth and sixth. The same operation may be performed, in regard to all the chords, and gives rise to groups of different forms and denominations, which it is not necessary to enumerate here, since this book is not a treatise on harmony. It is enough to get a clear idea of the operation.

There are some dissonant chords which do not offend the ear, even when heard directly, and without any preparation; and these are called *natural dissonant chords*. There are some others, which would have a disagreeable effect, if the dissonant note were not at first heard in a state of consonance. The necessity for this gives rise to the term *preparation of the dissonance;* and this kind of chords is designated by the name of *chords by prolongation*. In other chords, one note is substituted for another which enters more naturally into their composition. In this condition, these chords are called *chords by substitution. Chords by alteration* are those in which there is a momentary alteration of one or several notes, by the introduction of an accidental sharp, flat, or natural. Lastly, there are some harmonies in which prolongation, substitution, and alteration, are combined, two by two, or all together. If it be considered, also, that all these modifications are reproduced in all the inversions, we may have some idea of the prodigious variety of forms of which harmony is susceptible. This variety is still further increased by the caprice of certain composers, who, in their chords, sometimes anticipate the harmony of the following chords: this kind of modification, though incorrect in many cases, is not without effect.

In all the chords of which we have spoken, the

sounds have a relation to each other, more or less direct, more or less *logical;* but there are some cases in which this relation almost entirely disappears. In these sorts of harmonic anomalies, a low, middle, or high voice, or instrument, is made to sustain a single sound during a certain number of measures. This prolonged sound is called the *pedal*, because, in the origin of its invention, it was employed only in the music of the church by the organist, who, for that purpose, made use of the *pedals* of his instrument. Upon the pedal or sustained note a varied harmony is executed, and frequently produces a very good effect, though—which is a singular thing—the pedal sound and the harmony bear only a remote relation to each other: it is sufficient if the relation is re-established in a proper manner at the conclusion.

When instrumentation had not as yet acquired importance in the music of the church, the organ was almost the only instrument made use of for that kind of music. Its use was even limited, for a long time, to supporting the voices in the order in which their part was written, without mingling any thing foreign with them. When the vocal bass was silent, the bass of the organ was also silent, and the left hand of the artist was then occupied in executing the part of the tenor or contralto. We commonly ascribe to Louis Viadana, chapel-master of the cathedral of Mantua, the invention of a bass independent of the voice, to be executed upon the organ, or any other keyed instrument, and which, from its not being interrupted, like the ancient bass, received the name of *continued bass*. Several musicians seem to have had the idea of this bass at the same time; but Viadana first gave the precise rules for it, in a treatise published in 1606, at the end of a collection of his compositions. By means of figures placed above the notes of this bass, he expressed the chords of the different voices, and thus dispensed with writing, upon the part designed for the organist, all that belonged to the voices. This part, surmounted by figures, received in Italy the name of *partimento*, and in France that of *figured bass.*

If a figure were written for each interval which enters into the composition of a chord, the eye of the organist would frequently be more confused by it than by the reading of all the parts written in the ordinary notation, and the end proposed would fail. Instead of this, the charactéristic interval only is indicated. For the common chord, for example, a 3 only is written, which indicates the third. If this third accidentally becomes major or minor, by the introduction of a ♯ or a ♮, these signs are placed at the side and before the figure; if it becomes minor by the introduction of a ♭ or ♮, the same means are used. When two intervals are characteristic of a chord they are joined together: for example, the *chord of the fifth and sixth* is expressed by $\frac{5}{6}$. Diminished intervals are marked by a diagonal line drawn across the figure, in this manner, $\not{7}$; and augmented intervals are expressed by placing the ♯, ♭, or ♮, which modifies them, at the side of the figures. When the written note is characteristic of an interval, it is expressed by the sign +

Every epoch and every school have had different systems for the figuring of basses. These differences are of little importance. It is enough that we know of their existence, and that an organist, or other accompanier, is instructed in the different methods.

In the existing state of music, the organ no longer holds the first rank among the mass of instruments with which it is surrounded, so that the figured or continued bass has lost some of its interest; but it is not the less necessary to study it, in order to develope the sentiment of harmony in young artists, and to preserve a knowledge of the fine compositions of the ancient school. Formerly, we did not say in France, *it is necessary to study harmony;* but, *it is necessary to learn continued bass.* The Germans have preserved the equivalent of this expression in their *general bass,* and the English in their *thorough bass.*

The history of harmony is one of the most interesting parts of the general history of music. Not only is it composed of an uninterrupted succession of discoveries in the collective properties of sounds,—discoveries which owe their origin to the desire of novelty, to the boldness of some musicians, to the improvement of instrumental music, and, without doubt, also, to chance,—but there is a portion of this history which is not unworthy of interest; it is that of the efforts which have been made to combine together, in a complete and rational system, all the scattered facts presented by practice to the greedy curiosity of theorists. And it is to be remarked that the history of the theory is necessarily dependent upon that of the practice; for, as fast as the genius of composers hazarded new combinations, it became more difficult to combine them in a general system, and to discover their origin. The numerous modifications which the chords underwent so much changed the character of their primitive forms, that we ought not to be astonished if many errors have been committed in their classification.

Until about the end of the sixteenth century, none but consonant chords and some prolongations, which produced prepared dissonances, were in use: with such elements, the harmonic forms were so limited that no one thought of uniting them into an organized science, or even imagined that there could be any systematic connexion between the chords then in vogue. The intervals were considered two by two, and the art of employing them according to certain rules constituted the whole learning of the schools. Towards the year 1590, a Venetian, named Claude Monteverde, for the first time, made use of natural dissonant chords and of substitutions; from that time, the dominion of harmony was greatly extended, and the science which resulted from it became an object of attention to masters in the art. It was about fifteen years after the happy attempts of Monteverde, that Viadana and some Germans, who contest the invention with him, thought of representing harmony by figures, and for that purpose were obliged to consider each of the chords by itself. The name of *chord* was then introduced into the vocabulary of music, and harmony, or *continued bass*, as it was called, became a branch of the science of music. For nearly a century things remained in this state, though numerous elementary works were published during that interval, with a view to clear away the difficulties of this new science.

An experiment in physics, pointed out by a monk, named Father Mersenne, in 1636, in a large book, filled with trifles more curious than useful, under the title of *Universal Harmony*,—an experiment repeated by the celebrated mathematician Wallis, and analyzed by Sauveur, of the Academy of Sciences,—afterwards suggested to Rameau, a skilful French musician, the origin of a system of harmony, in which all the chords were reduced to a single principle. In this experiment, it had been remarked that, when a string was made to vibrate, there were heard, beside the principal sound, produced by the entire length of the string, two other feebler sounds, one of which was the twelfth, and the other the seventeenth, of the first,—that is to say, the octave of the fifth, and the double octave of the third —which produced the sensation of the *perfect major chord*. Rameau, availing himself of this experiment, made it the basis of a system, the structure of which he explained in a *Treatise on Harmony*, which he published in 1722. This system, known under the name of *System of Fundamental Bass*, had a prodigious currency in France, not only among musicians, but among people in general. From the moment that Rameau had adopted the idea of making certain physical phenomena the source of all harmony, he was obliged to have recourse to forced inferences; for all harmony is not included in the perfect major chord. The perfect minor chord was indispensable; and he imagined some sort of tremulous motion of the sonorous body, which, according to his idea, produced this chord to an attentive ear, but in a manner less distinct than the perfect major chord. By means of this arrangement, he had only to add to, or take away from, the sounds of the superior or inferior third of these two perfect chords, in order to find a great part of the chords then in use; and, in this way, he obtained a complete system, in which all the chords were connected together. Though this system rested on a very frail basis, it had the advantage of being the first to exhibit something like order in the phenomena of harmony. Rameau had, too, the merit of being the first to perceive the mechanism of the inversion of chords, and therefore deserves a place among the founders of the science of harmony.

By this factitious production of chords, he destroyed the relations of succession, which are derived from their tones, and was obliged to substitute, for the laws of those relations, the rules of a fundamental bass, which he formed of the low sounds of the primitive chords—fanciful rules, which could only have a forced application in practice.

At the time when Rameau produced his system in France, Tartini, a celebrated Italian violinist, proposed another, which was also founded upon an experiment of vibration. By this experiment, two high sounds, vibrating in thirds, produced another low sound, which was also the third of the lower one of the two, which again produced the perfect chord. Upon this, Tartini had established an obscure theory, which Rousseau, though he did not understand it, preferred to that of Rameau, but which never had any success. Systems of harmony had become a sort of fashion. Everybody had one of his own, and found somebody to puff it. In France, there appeared, almost at the same time, those of Ballière, of Jamard, of the Abbé Roussier, and many others, which are now deservedly forgotten.

Marpurg had attempted to introduce the system of Rameau into Germany, but without success. Kirnberger, a celebrated composer and a profound theorist, had just discovered the theory of prolongations, which explains, in a satisfactory and natural manner, some harmonies, of which no other theory can give the law. At a later period, Catel reproduced, in France, this same theory, in a simpler and clearer manner, in the *Treatise on Harmony*, which he composed for the Conservatory of Music; and, if I may be permitted to speak of my own labours, I will say, that I have completed this same theory, by an explanation of the mechanism of substitution, and of the combination of this same substitution with prolongations and alterations.

From this theory have sprung harmonies of a new class, with which the art has been enriched; but this is not the place to enter upon explanations on this subject.

CHAPTER XI.

OF ACOUSTICS.

Acoustics is a science, the object of which is the theory of sound. It differs from music in this respect, that it has no relation to the laws of the succession of sounds, of which melody is the result, nor to those of their simultaneousness, which regulate harmony. The examination of the phenomena manifested in the vibration of sonorous bodies, of different kinds and of different dimensions, and the results of these phenomena on the sense of hearing, constitute the domain of acoustics—a word derived from a Greek verb signifying *to hear*.

Percussion, friction, and other modes of producing sound, when applied to sonorous bodies, produce in the air around them a certain oscillating motion, which is called *vibration*. When this vibration is exceedingly slow, the sound is not appreciable by the ear; it only produces upon this organ the effect of noise; but, if it becomes rapid to a certain degree,—say sixty-four vibrations in a second,—we hear a sound of a very low tone. The tone rises as the number of vibrations becomes greater in a given time; but, beyond a certain limit of rapidity, the sound ceases to be audible.

It was for a long time believed that the air alone possessed the degree of elasticity which is necessary to convey sound to the ear; but it is now known that liquids, and some solid bodies, have the same property, and even propagate sound with more rapidity than the air.

In all treatises on physics, this principle is laid down —that the air in vibration is the real sonorous body, and the result of the following experiment is given as a demonstration of this principle. If a bell, with a mechanical apparatus for striking, be placed under the receiver of an air-pump, the ear hears the sound as long as the receiver is filled with air; but, as the air is withdrawn by the pump, the sound grows weaker, and ceases altogether as soon as the air is entirely withdrawn, though the bell may still be struck. This experiment is less conclusive than it appears to be at first; for, besides that sound may be transmitted to the ear by other elastic bodies as well as the air, no account could be given of the difference of bells,—that is to say, of the different qualities of sounds,—if the sonorous bodies did not possess in themselves sonorous qualities, which are modified by their manner of producing sounds. In this respect, as in many others, the science of acoustics is yet very imperfect.

A string, whether of metal, silk, or catgut, fixed firmly at one end, and stretched at the other by a weight or a peg; a thin blade of metal; a plate of wood, metal, or glass, of whatever form; a tube into which the air is introduced; a bell, etc.,—are sonorous bodies, the vibration of which produces sounds of different qualities. Within about thirty years, acoustics have been enriched by a multitude of observations on the phenomena produced by the sonorousness of these bodies; these observations have not been without their use in the improvement of certain instruments, and have given rise to the invention of others. There is reason to believe that we shall hereafter obtain still more satisfactory results, from the investigations pursued by several persons of great scientific attainments.

The imperfection of apparatus for experiments, and the want of care and exactness in performing them, have introduced a great many errors into the science of acoustics, which are the more serious, because the mathematicians, taking assertions without sufficient proof, as the basis of calculation, and considering them as demonstrated truths, have drawn from them consequences which seem to be in direct opposition to other facts, which are proved in the practice of music. The following is an example. Supposing it to be absolutely true, that a sonorous body, the length of which is exactly half that of another, makes twice as many vibrations in a given time, and produces a sound which is the exact octave of the other,—they have taken the number 1 to represent the larger, and 2 to represent the less of the two sonorous bodies. Admitting, also, that the exact fifth of the sound of the larger sonorous body would be produced by another body of two thirds its dimensions, the fourth by one of three quarters the size, the major third by one of four fifths, the minor third by one of five sixths, the minor sixth by one of five eighths, the major sixth by one of three fifths, and so of the other intervals,—they have expressed the relations of all the intervals of the scale by the following proportions:—

The major tone C to D is as 9 to 8; the minor tone D to E is as 10 to 9; the major third C to E is as 5 to 4; the major third D to F is as 6 to 5; the exact fourth C to F is as 4 to 3; the exact fifth C to G is as 3 to 2; the major sixth C to A as 5 to 3; the minor sixth E to C as 8 to 5; the major semitone C to D flat as 16 to 15; the minor semitone C to C sharp as 25 to 24; and the difference between C sharp and D flat as 81 to 80.

From all this it would result, in the execution of music, that musicians ought to make the D flat higher than the C sharp, while they do exactly the contrary; for the musicians feel that C sharp is an ascending relation, and that D flat is a descending one. Practice is here in opposition to theory. Some theorists, considering the relation of which we have just spoken as a fact resulting from the organization of musicians, have said that this fact did not destroy the theory, which could not be erroneous; others have declared that the musicians do really make D flat, thinking it C sharp, and *vice versa;* which, if it were true, would destroy the whole system of musical sounds. We ought to add that d'Alembert, and Professor Charles, and Messrs. de Prony and Savart, and some others, struck with the weight of the objection, have confessed that facts hitherto unknown may possibly overthrow the calculations believed to have been exact, and that the theory of the true relations of musical intervals is perhaps yet to be discovered.

The tuners of keyed intruments, placed, without knowing it, under the influence of these relations, experience some difficulty in checking their inclination to raise too high the upper sounds of certain intervals —a tendency which would lead them to make other intervals false, in relation to which the same laws are not so obvious. The result of the pains which they take to correct this tendency of their ear, is generally expressed by the word *temperament*. Several different formulas have been devised for the adjustment of this temperament, and perhaps we shall some day arrive at the conviction, that they are all the result of an imperfect theory of musical sounds. I believe it is possible to prove to a demonstration, that the tuning of instruments is according to the direction and progress of music, in certain harmonic states, and that this tuning cannot now be the same as it was at the beginning of the seventeenth century.

From what has been said, it appears that the science of acoustics is not yet established, and that, on the most important subjects, we are still left to conjecture.

CHAPTER XII.

OF THE ART OF WRITING MUSIC—COUNTERPOINT—CANONS—FUGUE.

In poetry, as in some of the arts of design, composition presents itself to the imagination of the poet, or of the artist, under the form of a simple idea, expressed as it is conceived,—that is to say, without complication of elements. It is not so in music. In this art, every thing is complicated; for to compose is not merely to imagine agreeable melodies, or to find the true expression of the different sentiments which affect us, or to make beautiful combinations of harmony, or to dispose of the voices in an advantageous manner, or to invent fine effects of instrumentation; but it is do all this at once, and many other things besides. In a quartet, in a chorus, in an overture, in a symphony,—each voice, and each instrument, advances in its own peculiar manner; and the combinations of all these movements constitute the music.

From all this, we may form some opinion of the complicated character of that operation of the mind which we call *composition*, and of the studies necessary to be pursued, in order to overcome the obstacles of so difficult an art.

There was a time when it could not be said that musicians composed: they merely arranged sounds. This period includes nearly three centuries,—that is to say, from the end of the thirteenth to about the year 1590. A few miserable popular airs, and the chants of the church, were the only melodies with which they were acquainted; and it was not uncommon to see the same air of this kind used as the common theme of twenty different compositions, and applied indifferently to every kind of words. No traces of expression, of enthusiasm, of passion, or of elevation, are to be remarked in the crowd of masses, motets, glees, and madrigals of that day—a peculiarity the more remarkable, as it was precisely at that time that the excitement of the imagination was the most vehement in religious ideas, in philosophy, in poetry, and in painting; that the genius of man was raised to the greatest heights, and that his passions were developed with the greatest force. But, free from every shackle, the thought of the poet could, in an instant, create sublime beauties, as did Dante, without being arrested by the difficulties of material art; taught by that which was before his eyes, the painter could not fail to perceive that the imitation of nature should be the object of his labours; roused by the ills which overwhelm humanity, the philosopher, the jurist, and the theologian, had only to give loose to their indignation, in order to speak with eloquence of liberty, of law, and of religion. In all these, as I have remarked, the ideas are simple; genius marks out the road, and science follows. In music, it was the reverse. It was necessary, first, that the musicians should employ themselves in creating the material resources of their art; but, in seeking these means, they deceived themselves, and imagined that they were making progress towards their object, while they were only preparing to enter upon the road which was to conduct them thither.

Their error was an advantage; for it required nothing less than all the perseverance of their efforts to arrange in order the chaos of varied forms of which the connexion of sounds is susceptible. What combinations of harmony are to be found in the works of these old masters! and what skill in the management of difficulties! Accustomed as we now are to make use of processes which they have taught us, we see in their compositions nothing but scholastic subtilties; but those who laid the foundations of this science were men of genius.

An almost barbarous word, which for a long time has had only a traditional signification, serves to express the operation of writing music according to certain laws; this word is *counterpoint*. It seems to derive its origin from the circumstance, that, in some particular notations of the Middle Ages, music was written with points, the respective distances of which between several voices were called *point contre point* (*punctum contra punctum*, *point against point*), or, by contraction, *counterpoint*. Musicians by profession call one who teaches the art of writing in music a *professor of counterpoint;* others give him the name of a *teacher of composition:* this last form of speech is incorrect, as one does not learn to compose. If counterpoint was formerly the art of arranging points against points, it is now that of combining notes with notes. This operation would certainly be long, fatiguing, and destructive of all inspiration, if the composer, by means of studies well directed in his youth, had not become familiar with all these combinations, so that they should be nothing more to him than are the rules of grammar, of which no one thinks in writing or speaking. That which we call *science* in music is not a true science, except so far as it has become a habit, which does not distract the imagination.

In whatever manner the idea of the composer may be directed in the arrangement of voices, or of instruments, he cannot perform any more than five different operations, which are,—1, to give to each part notes of equal duration; 2, to make the duration of the notes of one of the parts shorter by half than those of another; 3, to reduce them in one part to a fourth of the length of those of another; 4, to connect the notes by syncope in one part, whilst another proceeds according to the time of the measure; 5, to mingle together these different kinds of combinations, including accidental points and various ornaments. The analysis of these different combinations has furnished five kinds of counterpoint, or studies, which are called *simple counterpoint of the first, second, third, fourth, and fifth kind.* These lessons are founded on a given or selected air, and are commenced, ordinarily, by writing for two voices, then for three, four, five, six, seven, and eight. The greater the number of the voices, the more complicated are the combinations. If we are writing for three voices, for example, we can put a single note for one of them, two notes of equivalent length for the second, and four for the third; and, if we are composing for four voices, we can add the syncope, etc. It is easy to conceive that studies of this description, frequently repeated, will teach us to foresee all cases, to overcome all difficulties, and this without effort, and almost without reflection. It is a common opinion that an educated musician writes with more calculation than one who has never studied the science; but this is an error. I think, even, that the contrary is true, and that, all circumstances considered, he who is called, in derision, *a learned musician*, if truly worthy of the title, writes less painfully than one who, having never studied, may, every moment, be arrested in his progress by unforeseen difficulties.

Simple counterpoint, of which we have spoken above, is the basis of every composition; for it is applied at every instant, and under all circumstances: we cannot write even a few measures correctly without it; and he who speaks of it with the greatest contempt, makes use of it—as Mons. Jourdain did of prose—without knowing it. It is not so with what is called *double counterpoint*, which is founded upon certain circumstances of limited extent. A dramatic composer may write a great number of operas without having occasion to make use of it; but in instrumental music, and in the music of the church, this kind of counterpoint is frequently employed. In writing *simple counterpoint*, the composer attends only to the immediate effect of the harmony; but, in *double counterpoint*, he must know, also, what that harmony would become if it were reversed,—that is to say, if the upper parts should become the bass, and *vice versa;* so that the operation of his mind is, in reality, double.

When the counterpoint is susceptible of inversion in three different parts, we give it the name of *triple counterpoint;* if it is susceptible of inversion in four parts, it is called *quadruple counterpoint.*

Inversion may be produced in several ways. If it consists in a simple change of octave between the parts,—that is to say, if that which was in the lower part passes to the higher, and reciprocally, without changing the name of the notes,—this susceptibility of inversion is called *double counterpoint in the octave.* If the inversion may be produced on the octave of the fifth, whether above or below, the composition is called *double counterpoint in the twelfth;* and, lastly, if the arrangement of the harmony is such that the inversion may take place to the octave of the third above or below, it is a *counterpoint in the tenth.* The double counterpoint in the octave is much more satisfactory to the ear than the two others, and it is also in more general use.

When a composer undertakes to develope a subject, a phrase, a theme, and to present it under all forms—as Haydn and Mozart have done in their quartets and symphonies, Handel in his oratorios, and Cherubini in his beautiful masses,—the double counterpoint offers immense resources, for which nothing can be substituted; but, in dramatic music, in which such a development of the same musical idea would injure the expression, and substitute a pedantic affectation in the place of truth, this counterpoint would not only be useless, on many occasions, but frequently even injurious. Taste and experience must guide the composer in this respect.

Thus far, we have seen that the science was composed of only useful or necessary objects. We are now to consider it in its abuses. What, indeed, shall we say of those queer arrangements of sounds which are called *retrograde counterpoints*, that is to say, advancing backwards; *counterpoints by contrary movement*, in which the voices move in opposite directions; *retrograde contrary counterpoints*, or turning the book upside down; *inverse contrary counterpoints*, which are still more complicated? All this, I repeat, is an abuse of the science. The ear suffers from the trammels fastened by the musician upon himself, and from which he can derive no real advantage. These idle subtilties exist only for the eye. It must not be supposed, however, that it is these musical logogryphs which have given to people in general their prejudices against the science; for it is a long time since they have ceased to make a part of the customary music, and have been consigned to the dust of the schools. They never had much credit; some pedantic masters of the sixteenth and seventeenth centuries being the only ones whom we can accuse of having attempted to substitute them for the true science. It was these musicians who invented such absurdities as the *jumping counterpoint*, in which the voices were prohibited from the use of the adjoining notes of the scale; the *bound counterpoint*, in which every kind of interval of the third, fourth, etc. was prohibited; the *obstinate counterpoint*, which admitted only of a single passage constantly repeated by one voice, whilst the others proceeded as usual; and a thousand other follies, which it would take too much time to enumerate.

The public and the musicians have done justice to this degradation of an art, the true design of which is to excite the feelings, and not to produce enigmas.

Certain conventional forms, which are called *imitations*, *canons*, and *fugues*, are, however, very useful, and do not partake of the discredit which attaches to those of which we have just spoken; and I would almost venture to say that we obtain from them grander, more majestic, and more varied effects, than from all the other combinations of music. Those who have heard, in the Royal Institution of Religious Music directed by Mr. Choron, the compositions of Palestrina, of Clari, and of Handel; those who have assisted, in the King's Chapel, in the execution of the beautiful masses of Cherubini;* those, lastly, who recollect the effects of the symphonies of Haydn, Mozart, and Beethoven, and who have not forgotten the magic power of the overtures of *The Enchanted Flute* and of *Don Juan*;—all such persons, I say, will understand me, when they are informed that these beautiful creations have for their foundations those same conventional forms to which genius has given life. These forms must now be explained.

In analysing music, we sometimes meet with certain phrases the character of which is more distinct than that of others, and which possess the advantage of being capable of frequent repetition, whilst they contribute to augment the general effect of the piece. But if the same voice, or the same instrument, were always employed in thus repeating the phrases, they

* These two musical establishments have unfortunately been suppressed, since the first edition of this book appeared.

would become monotonous and tiresome: it is therefore desirable to make the phrase which we wish to repeat pass from one part into another, and even, for the sake of greater variety, to transpose it sometimes a fourth, fifth, or octave, higher or lower. The principal phrase, when thus conducted from one part into another, and varied in its position, takes the name of *imitation;* because the voices or instruments mutually imitate each other; and it is called imitation in the fourth, fifth, or octave, according to the degree of elevation in which it is made. As an example of imitation which is known to everybody, the reader is referred to the scene of the shades, in Rossini's opera of *Moses,* in which the phrase of the accompaniment passes alternately from one instrument to another.

The imitation is free in this — that it is not always made with exactness from the beginning to the end of a phrase. But there are some kinds of imitations which are more rigorous, and extend not only through the whole phrase, but even through the whole of a piece; these take the name of *canons.* This kind of music was formerly very much in vogue in society; canons were sung at table, the words of which were almost always burlesque. Everybody knows that which begins with these words — *Frère Jacques, dormez-vous?* They were all made upon this model. Piccini was the first who introduced canons upon the stage, in his opera of *La Buona Figliola.* They have since become of frequent use; Rossini and his imitators have put them into almost all their works; but their canons differ from that of Martini in this respect —that they limit themselves, almost always, to making the principal phrase an agreeable air, neglecting altogether the subordinate parts; whereas the canon of Martini, like those of all the masters who have known how to write this kind of music, is composed of as many phrases as there are voices, which serve mutually for accompaniment, as they pass alternately from one part into the other. In order to write canons of this kind, our musical studies must have been thorough—a thing which is no longer practised in Italy. Cherubini has composed many canons, which have a fine effect, and are of great purity of style.

The imitation of canons may be made like the free imitation, beginning with the fourth, fifth, octave, and even with any of the intervals: this is what is meant by the words which we frequently see written upon the music — *Canon à la quarte*, *canon à la quinte inferieure*, etc. The voice which commences the canon is called the *antecedent;* that which imitates it takes the name of *consequent.*

Sometimes the canon is double; that is to say, we meet with those canons in which two parts commence at the same time, two different airs, and these are followed by two other parts, which imitate them. There are also some canons in which the imitation is made by a *contrary movement*, which signifies that which is done in ascending, by one of the voices, is done in descending, by that which imitates, and *vice versa.* In the ancient schools of music, they made a multitude of canons, in which they imposed strange rules upon themselves, like those of which I have spoken on the subject of counterpoint, and even more singular ones still: for example, it was necessary that all the semibreves, or white notes of the *antecedent*, should become crotchets, or black notes, in the *consequent*, or that the black notes should be suppressed, and the white ones only left, etc.

The masters of these schools had a practice of challenging each other by sending canons composed in these queer forms, the secret of which they kept. They wrote them upon a single line, in order that their adversaries should be obliged to seek the solution of them, and purposely enveloped them in as many difficulties as they could. They were a kind of riddles, in which each one strove to shew his skill and ingenuity. The master who should refuse such a challenge, or fail to discover the solution of the canon, would lose his reputation.

But as, in every kind of combat, there are rules which cannot be broken, there was one in the challenges of canons, which obliged the author of an enigmatical canon to accompany it with some device, to aid in its solution. The books of the old masters of the sixteenth and seventeenth centuries have transmitted to us a collection of these devices, of which the following are specimens:—

Clama ne cesses, or *otía dant vitia*, indicated that the consequent ought to imitate all the notes of the antecedent, by suppressing the rests.

Nescit vox missa reverti, or *semper contrarius esto*, or, finally, *in girum imus noctu ecce ut consumimur igni*, indicated that the consequent ought to imitate the antecedent by a retrograde movement. Observe that, in this last device, all the letters, taken backwards, form the same words as when read from left to right.

Sol post vesperas declinat, signified that, at each repeat, the canon should be lowered one tone.

Cæcus non judicat de colore, indicated that the black notes of the antecedent were to be converted into white notes in the consequent; and so of others.

All these subtilties scarcely tended to the object of the art; but they were according to the taste of those days of pedantry.

Imitation may take the form in which the phrase recurs at intervals, being sometimes interrupted, in order to be afterwards taken up: in this case, we give it the name of *fugue*, which comes from *fuga* (flight), because, in an imitation of this kind, the parts seem to fly from each other, at the returns of the subject. The fugue, when it is well made, and managed by a man of genius, like John Sebastian Bach, Handel, or Cherubini, is the most majestic, the most energetic, and the most harmonious, of all musical forms. It cannot be successfully employed in dramatic music, because its progress requires a development which would injure the interest of the scene; but in instrumental music, and especially in the music of the church, it produces admirable effects, of a character altogether peculiar. The magnificent Hallelujah of Handel's *Messiah*, and the fugues of Cherubini's masses, which every one may have heard at Paris, are models of this kind of beauty. It must be acknowledged, however, that these beauties are of a sort which we cannot relish until after having become accustomed to them, because the complication of their elements demands an attentive and a practised ear. We may apply to them the line of Boileau,

C'est avoir profité que de savoir s'y plaire.

Fugue has not always had the form which it bears at the present day; but, like all other branches of the musical art, it has been slowly brought to its present degree of perfection. The different parts of which it is now composed, are the *subject*, the *counter-subjects*, the *response*, the *exposition*, the *episodes* or *diversions*, the *modulated returns*, the *strettes*, and the *pedal*.

The phrase to be imitated is called the *subject*. This phrase is ordinarily accompanied by others, which form with it a *double counterpoint*,—that is to say, which are susceptible of inversion in such a manner, as to change their position, by passing alternately from the lower voices to the higher, and from the latter to the former; these phrases of accompaniment are called *counter-subjects*. When the fugue is written for four voices, or for four instrumental parts, there is ordinarily a *counter-subject*, in which case it may be both rich in harmony and free in its movements. Sometimes the composer employs two counter-subjects, in which case it is said that the *fugue* has three subjects. Such a fugue is more difficult to make; but it is less interesting, more scholastic, and has less variety.

The imitation of the subject is called the *response*. This response cannot be exactly like the subject, because, if the latter modulates from any key to an analogous one, it is necessary that the response should bring back the ear from this new key into the original key; for it is precisely this shifting from one key to another that constitutes the interest of the fugue. The inverted progress which one makes in the response, in regard to the subject, renders a slight change of interval necessary; and this is called *mutation*. It is remarkable that we judge of the skill of a musician by the address with which he seizes the point of the response, where it is necessary to make the mutation, in a given subject. Of a hundred musicians educated in a good school, there is not a single one who would not make this mutation at the same place; whilst those whose studies have been ill-directed are never sure of succeeding in doing it as it should be. This is a test of their knowledge; so that, when we say of the author of a fugue, that he *has failed in the response*, we can add nothing more contemptuous.

The *exposition* is composed of a certain number of returns of the subject, and of the response, after which come the *episodes*, which are commonly composed of imitations formed of fragments of the subject and of the counter-subject. These episodes give variety and modulation to the fugue. When the composer thinks that he has sufficiently extended the developments of his subject, he goes back to the original key, and makes what is called the *stretta*, or *strettes*,—a word which comes from the Italian *stretto* (close), because these *strettes* are imitations, in a more lively style, of the subject and of the response. This part of the fugue is the most brilliant, and that to which the composer can give the greatest effect. When the subject is favourable, there may be several *strettes*, which become more and more lively. They are terminated ordinarily by a *pedal*, in which all the riches of harmony are united.

Rousseau has said that *a fine fugue is the barren masterpiece of a good harmonist.* We were not sufficiently advanced in music, in the time of Rousseau, to appreciate a fine fugue, and that writer never had an opportunity to hear one.

It was not until about the commencement of the eighteenth century that fugues were made on the plan which I have just explained. Up to that period, there was nothing but the *fugued counterpoint*,—that is to say, counterpoint in four, five, six, or seven parts,—the subject of which was taken from the psalms and hymns chanted in the church, with imitations and canons. This kind of fugued compositions is designated by the name of counterpoint *alla Palestrina*, because a celebrated composer, named Palestrina, who lived in the sixteenth century, carried the style of it to the highest point of perfection. In this kind of music, seemingly so dry, and so little favourable to inspiration, Palestrina succeeded in producing so much majesty, a sentiment of religion so calm and pure, that he seems to have met all these scientific difficulties with ease, and to have been entirely occupied in giving an appropriate expression of the sacred text. When his subjects are performed with the perfect traditional execution of the Sistine chapel, the impression which they leave cannot be equalled by any other, in reference to grandeur of proportion. At the time when this master wrote, music had not been thought of as a dramatic resource. In our days, this demand for the dramatic is carried into every thing, and even into the music of the church. Great beauties of a particular kind result from this; but it seems to me that, in point of propriety and the elevation of the religious sentiment, the fugued counterpoint of Palestrina has greatly the advantage.

From what has been said, we may form an idea of the mechanism of scientific compositions, and of the advantage which may be derived from them. If I have succeeded in making myself understood, many amateurs will renounce their prejudices against the science, and will acknowledge that it is ridiculous to require musicians to be ignorant in order to write well. If the art of writing music is sometimes infected with an air of pedantry, it is not the science which ought to be blamed, but the ill-constructed minds that make use of it. And observe that the science never appears so, except in the hands of musicians who are not really learned. This science, to be true, must become a habit, so that its possessor need make no effort to recal it; which cannot take place, unless it has been studied in youth; for it is too late to think of reforming, by science, bad habits, which have once been contracted. When the early studies of a composer have been ill directed, the more natural talent he has, the less he is able to correct his faults, when he is no longer young; and, if he obstinately persist in the attempt, he loses the qualities which he derives from nature, becomes dull, and at last, pedantic.

CHAPTER XIII.

OF THE USE OF THE VOICE.

To whatever degree of perfection an instrumentist may arrive, it will always be difficult for him to exercise over popular masses a power equal to that which results from the human voice, when directed by a proper sentiment, and perfected by proper studies. There is no need of giving proof of a great skill in the mechanical part, in order to excite lively and powerful emotions, by means of the voice; harmony, even, is not necessary; unison is sufficient. I shall refer, on this point, to one of the most astonishing effects which can be witnessed: it is that of four or five thousand children, belonging to the charitable institutions in London, who, on a particular day in the year, in St. Paul's cathedral, sing in unison, with simplicity and purity. The greatest musicians, and, among others, Haydn, have declared that the finest music which they had ever heard did not approach the prodigious effect which arises from the blending of these infantine voices in the most perfect unison which can be imagined.* There is something attractive and sympathetic in this effect; for persons whose sensibility is the least expansive have not been able to restrain their

* Observe that this unison is perfect, precisely because there are so many voices; for, among them all, there is an attraction of sound, so that individual imperfections of tone are lost in the formation of one homogeneous sound.

tears. To this example of the power of voices in unison, we may add others drawn from dramatic works. It is proper to remark, however, that these effects succeed only with great masses, and that, generally, harmony offers greater resources.

Choruses in a great number of parts were in use in the sixteenth century, particularly in Italy; at a later period, they thought of dividing these voices into several choirs of four parts each, and of placing in the large churches several organs to accompany these choirs; but, besides the difficulty of giving unity of execution to such complicated music, the effect obtained from it rarely corresponded with that which was anticipated. At length, it was perceived that well-written choruses of three or four really separate parts have more strength, exactness, and even harmony. The use of choruses in four parts has therefore generally prevailed. The kinds of voices which enter into their composition are the *soprano*, or upper; the *contralto*, or high counter; the *tenore*, which in France was formerly called the *taille;* and the *basso*, or bass.

The part of the contralto was sung formerly in Italy by eunuchs, whose quality of voice has something penetrating in it which nothing else can furnish. But, as the custom of mutilating men in order to make singers of them was never established in France, the place of the contralto has there been supplied by the high counter, a kind of voice which is scarcely met with, except in Languedoc, and particularly in the neighbourhood of Toulouse. The same cause has almost entirely banished from music both the eunuchs and the high counters; that cause is the French revolution, which, having put us in possession of Italy, has abolished the barbarous practice of mutilation, and, having overthrown the governments of the cathedrals, has deprived the inhabitants of Languedoc of the musical instruction which they had been in the habit of receiving.

From the almost total disappearance of these useful kinds of voices, considerable embarrassment has arisen in the arrangement and execution of choruses. The experiment of supplying the place of eunuchs by the voices of women in contralto, has not been successful, because these voices fail in the low notes; and the employment of tenors to take the place of the high counters has not been more so, because the music written for the latter is found to be too high for the former. This double difficulty has determined several composers to write their choruses of four parts, for two female voices, *soprano* and *mezzo soprano*, *tenor*, and *bass*. By this means, the harmony is made full, without going beyond the limits of the voices: the tenor is only elevated two or three notes above the strict limits to which it was formerly confined.

To avoid impoverishing the upper part by dividing it into two, Cherubini thought of writing in some of his masses choruses in three parts, composed only of the soprano, tenor, and bass, and has drawn the finest effects from this arrangement, in spite of its apparent poverty; but it requires all the skill of a master like him to surmount the difficulties of this kind of composition, and to produce such effects with means so limited.

Rossini and his imitators, moved by the desire of

filling their harmonies, have taken another course in regard to choruses: it consists in writing them almost always for five or six parts, namely, two basses, two tenors, and two trebles. This apparent abundance, however, is nothing more than real sterility; for the intermediate voices double every moment the same notes and the same movements. Such a method is applicable only to choruses, the harmony of which, without movement, is designated by the name of *harmonie plaquée* (plated harmony), and is in fact the same which is in use in this school. It attracts the multitude by its seeming fulness; but cultivated and delicate ears are continually disturbed by its imperfections.

The employment of voices, in the distribution of the parts at the theatres, is always made, in Italy, in a manner the most proper to obtain the best possible effect in concerted pieces. Thus we find, in almost all Italian works, two basses, one or two tenors, one *prima donna contralto*, or *mezzo soprano*, and a *soprano*, which, by the union of their voices, present the most effective combination of harmony. It is not so in France, where it is almost always the poet who selects the actors, in reference to physical qualities, or others, which have no relation to music. The practice, also, which we have of distinguishing the lines of characters by the names of the actors who have severally distinguished themselves in them, encumbers our theatres with voices of the same kind, because these characters differ from one another only in slight particulars, of no importance to the music. Thus we have our Ellevious, Phillippes, Gavaudans, Laruettes, and Trials, who were lovers or buffoons, and whose voices were all tenors. All these characters have their duplicate performers, so that tenors abound in our great theatres, whilst there are only one or two basses. Now, this last kind of voices being appropriated to the characters of fathers or tutors, it follows that, if there are no personages of this kind in a work, the composer is obliged to write the music for tenors and trebles. With these limited means, one may make pretty couplets, romances, or agreeable airs, and duets, but never good concerted pieces. There is no harmony in the voices. Such is the cause of the small effect of most of the *finales* in our comic operas, and of the inferiority, in this respect, of the French to the Italian music. Vocal harmony is a source of charming effects, but it cannot be obtained by means of voices of the same kind.

In Italy, as in France, we find a sort of bass voice, known by the name of *bariton:* it holds the middle ground between the lower bass and the tenor, and produces a very good effect, when employed in its true character; but, in our theatres, they obstinately persist in making a tenor of it. Martin, Solié, and Lays, who had this kind of voice, have done much to effect a change in this respect; and we seem now to be returning to more sound ideas, and to feel the necessity of confining the voices within their natural limits.

The art of writing properly for voices, and so as to favour the singers, is better known among the Italian than the French or German composers. The cause of this difference is to be found in the study of singing, which enters into the first education of composers in Italy, whilst it is absolutely neglected by the French and Germans. Without speaking of the advantages of the Italian language, which are indisputable, we find in Italian vocal music something easy and natural in the arrangement of the phrases, in the character of passages, in their connexion, and in the analogy of the poetical with the musical rhythm, which is favourable at once to the emission of the voice, and to the articulation of the throat and the tongue. These advantages are but rarely met with in the French music, and more rarely still in the German; the latter being frequently loaded with modulations which render the intonations very difficult. The ease of the Italian singing was formerly attributed to the narrow circle of its modulations and forms; but Rossini has shewn, in his works, that this circle may be enlarged without depriving the vocal part of any of its advantages. It is probable that the popularity which his music has acquired in France will contribute to improve our system of vocal music; but to render the reform complete, the concurrence of the poets and the musicians will be necessary, as I shall shew hereafter.

There is one point to which the Italian composers direct their whole attention, in order to avoid fatiguing their singers; it is the degree of elevation, in which they maintain the voices. In their music, each kind of voice runs through an extent at least equal to that which is given to it in the French music; but passages requiring a great extent of voice, either high or low, are very rare, and the voice ordinarily remains in its medium; whilst in the scores of French music, we meet with pieces, which, without running through a great extent, cause the singer much fatigue, by remaining a long time upon notes which are unfavourable to the voice. The works of Grétry furnish many examples of this defect. A treble singer will rise without fatigue to the most elevated sounds of her voice, as C or D, whilst it will be very painful for her to sing a long time upon E, F or G. It is the same with tenor voices, which are divided into two sorts of sounds, very distinct from each other, namely, *the sounds of the breast*, and *the sounds of the head*, the latter of which are sometimes designated by the name of the *mixed voice*.* It requires much art in the singer to smooth as much as possible the passage from the sounds of the breast to the mixed voice, and from the latter to the former, so as to make the difference of the quality of tone imperceptible. This change takes place in the majority of tenor voices, between F and G. It is plain that, if the composer makes the part dwell on these notes, he will cause the singer a fatigue injurious to the development of his powers, and which is much more difficult than it would be to rise to the highest sounds of his head voice. Accidents frequently happen to singers, for which they are much less blameable than the composer.

There are some intervals which the voice cannot take without much difficulty, and which the singer approaches with timidity, because it is very difficult to hit them with precision. These intervals are the

* Bennati has demonstrated, in his *Researches into the Mechanism of the Human Voice*, (Paris, 1832, 8vo.,) that the true name of these sounds should be the *laryngian*—a name which would indicate the manner in which they are formed.

minor and augmented fifth, the major fourth or *triton*, the diminished fourth, and the augmented second. The passing from the one to the other of the notes which form these intervals, is not natural to the movements of the throat, and the singer is consequently obliged to make preparations for them, which there is no time to do, in rapid passages. If any circumstances render it necessary for the composer to make use of these intervals, it ought to be done by means of notes of some length.

It is not the articulation of sounds alone which may present obstacles to the accuracy of the singer. If an impression has been made upon his ear by a harmony foreign to the note which he is about to attempt, it will cause him to give it with a degree of uncertainty. For example, if he is about to sound C♯, and if the chord which precedes that note contains C♮ in the other vocal parts, or in the accompaniment, the recollection of this C♮ will occupy the ear of the singer, so that he will take the C♯ with timidity, and rarely with precision. These successions of sounds, which have no connexion with each other, are called *false relations*. The ancient composers of the Italian school carefully avoided them. They are sometimes met with in modern music.

The selection of words, also, has much influence upon the emission of the sounds of the voice; and the art of the composer consists in placing certain passages or notes only upon syllables which facilitate their execution. A particular passage or note, which would give a great deal of trouble to the singer upon one syllable, becomes easy upon another. When we write music for French words, it is the more necessary to be upon our guard, as to this point, because our language abounds in uncertain and nasal syllables, which turn the sound from its natural course. For example, we can never give sounds of a good quality to the syllables, *on*, *an*, *en*, *ein*, *vif*, etc., nor articulate them easily with the throat. It is necessary, therefore, when syllables of this description occur in lyric poetry, that the musician should place them in the middle of the voice, and that he should avoid placing them upon passages or notes which are sustained.

CHAPTER XIV.

OF INSTRUMENTS.

NATURE has established many diversified gradations and qualities of voice; and art has gone much farther in the fabrication of instruments, which were originally constructed in imitation of the voice. *Sound*, as we know, is only the vibration of a sonorous body, communicated and modified by the air. But what a variety in these modifications!

What a difference between the nature of the sound of a bell, and that of instruments in which the sound is produced by the breath, by keys, by a bow, by snapping a string, or by friction! And, in each of these grand divisions, how numerous are the shades of difference in the quality of the sounds! Still all is not done, and every day new discoveries and new improvements open new paths, where further discoveries remain to be made, and new improvements to be introduced.

The most ancient instruments mentioned in history are stringed instruments played by snapping, such as the lyre, the cythara, and the harp. The monuments of antiquity afford us numerous models of them; but their forms are different and characteristic among different nations. Thus the lyre and the cythara belong particularly to the Greeks, the inhabitants of Asia Minor, and the Romans: the harp seems to be the allotment of the inhabitants of Upper Asia, of Egypt, and of the north of Europe.

Fable, which is mingled with the whole history of the Greeks, ascribes to Mercury the invention of the lyre, which originally had only three strings. The number of these strings was afterwards increased, but was never carried beyond *seven*, which made the lyre a very limited instrument, since it had no fingerboard like our guitars, by means of which the sounds of these seven strings might be modified, and they consequently could only produce seven different sounds. Hence the musician could not change his key without changing his lyre. The varieties of the lyre were distinguished by the uames of *cythara*, *chelys*, and *phorminx*. These instruments were played sometimes by snapping the strings with the fingers, but more frequently with a kind of hook, called a *plectrum*, which proves that only one of the strings could be made to sound at the same time.

The origin of the harp is enveloped in obscurity. We find it in India, in Egypt, upon the most ancient monuments, among the Hebrews, in Italy, among an ancient people named *Arpe*, among the Scandinavians, and in ancient England, without being able to discover whether all these nations had received it by communication, or invented it simultaneously. The use of the harp, in the ancient nations of India and Egypt, raises a presumption that the Greeks and the Romans were acquainted with and made use of it; but the name which we give to it is not to be met with in any of the writers of antiquity. It is generally believed that the *trigone* or *sambuque* was nothing more than a harp. A learned commentator upon the poems of Callimachus has proved that all the instruments with oblique strings, such as the *nablum*, the *barbitos*, the *magade*, the *psalterium*, and the *sambuque*, of which mention is made in the Holy Scriptures and in the writings of antiquity, were varieties of the harp, and of Phœnician, Chaldaic, or Syrian origin. As to the Romans, it is believed that the instrument which they called *cinnara*, was nothing more than a harp, and its name only a translation of *kynnor* or *kinnar*, which, in the Hebrew text of the Bible, is the name of David's harp. The number of strings to the ancient harp was originally thirteen; but this number was afterwards increased to twenty, and even to forty. These strings were made of catgut, like those of our harps, as appears from a Greek epigram in the *Anthology*. The people of antiquity do not appear to have had any knowledge of steel or brass wires; but several authors assure us that they made use, in the beginning, of flaxen strings — a fact which it is difficult to believe, inasmuch as strings of that description could produce only a dull sound, if any at all.

The harp, at first, had no means of modulation, because it was impossible to put a sufficient number of strings upon it to represent all the sounds which correspond to the notes expressed by the sharps and flats. It was not until about the year 1660 that it was first thought of, in the Tyrol, to add hooks to the instrument, in order to raise the tone of the strings, when it was necessary; but the necessity of employing the hands to move the hooks was very troublesome, and an instrument-maker of Donawerth, named Hochbrucher, in the year 1720, invented a contrivance for moving them by the feet, which was thence called a *pedal*. Though very imperfect, the pedals were useful. But the difficulty of moving the feet at the same time with the hands, to which the performers were not accustomed, threw many obstacles in the way of the inventor. In 1740, the pedal harp was not yet known in France, but was introduced there by a German musician of the name of Stecht. Hochbrucher, a nephew of the instrument-maker above mentioned, and a good harpist for his time, brought the use of the pedal to perfection about the year 1770. But it was Naderman, an instrument maker of Paris, who gave to the mechanism of the harp with hooks the entire perfection of which it was susceptible. The principle of this mechanism being, however, still defective, and subject to many accidents, Sebastian Erard determined to supply its place by a mechanism better contrived, in which a fork was made to pinch the strings, without drawing them out of the perpendicular line, as was the case in the harp with hooks. The success of his invention led him afterwards to complete the improvements of which the harp was still in want, by giving to each of its strings the power of producing three tones, namely, the flat, natural, and sharp, which he effected by means of a mechanism having a double movement. It does not seem possible to add any thing to these harps, which possess every desirable perfection.

I have remarked that, among the Greeks, stringed instruments played by snapping, and having a finger-board upon which the strings may be pressed in various places, in order to modify their tones, were not known; but the Egyptian monuments offer some examples of this kind of instrument, which might induce us to believe that this people were somewhat advanced in music. The origin of stringed instruments played by snapping, and having fingerboards, appears to be found in the East. The *wina* of India, which consists of a bamboo body, attached to two large gourds, and which is mounted with several strings, which are pressed on bridges with the fingers, appears to be the type of these instruments; but it is especially the *coud* or *luth* of the Arabs, imported into Europe by the Moors of Spain, which has served as a model for all the instruments of this kind; for these iustruments are only varieties of it, more or less complicated in their structure.

The body of the luth, convex on the back, and flat on the other side, has a broad fingerboard, furnished with ten frets for the fingers, in order to vary the sounds. It is mounted with eleven strings; nine of which are double, three tuned in unison, and six in octaves. The first two, or *chanterelles*, are single. This instrument is difficult to play, and requires much study. It was formerly cultivated with success. Berard, in Germany, and two musicians named Gualtier in France, made themselves celebrated by their performances on it in the seventeenth century. From the name of *luth* has been formed the word *luthier*, which, at first, signified a maker of lutes, but which has since been applied to all the manufacturers of stringed instruments, and even to those who make wind instruments.

An imitation of the lute, of much more considerable proportions, and mounted with a greater number of strings, was formerly called an *archilute*. Of all the instruments of this description, the latter has the greatest volume of tone; but the great size of its fingerboard, which rendered it very inconvenient for the player, has caused its use to be abandoned.

The *theorbe* was also a kind of lute, which had two fingerboards, parallel to each other. The smallest was similar to that of the lute, and bore the same number of strings; but the second, which was much larger, sustained the last eight strings, which served for the bass.

Two other kinds of lute were very much in use about the commencement of the eighteenth century. The first of them was called the *pandore*. It had the same number of strings, which were tuned in the same manner; but, instead of being made of catgut, they were of metal. Another difference was also to be remarked in its form. Instead of being convex, the back of the pandore was flat. The other instrument of the lute kind was the *mandore*. It had only four strings, which were tuned from fifths to fourths. The highest string was sometimes lowered a note in order to obtain other chords. This was called playing *with the string lowered*. These two instruments have long been out of use.

Lastly, there is a small instrument, which belongs to the tribe of lutes, called the *mandolin*. The body is round, like the lute, but the fingerboard bears more resemblance to that of the *guitar*, of which I shall speak presently. The mandolin is held in the left hand, and the sounds are produced by means of a quill, held between the thumb and forefinger; but it is necessary that the forefinger should be always below the thumb, without pressing the quill. The four strings of this instrument are tuned in unison with those of the violin. In Italy, there are mandolins with three, and others with five strings, which are variously tuned, according to the caprice of the player. The *calascione*, or *colascione*, a little instrument, with a very long neck, used by the Neapolitans, is a peculiar kind of mandolin, which is also played with a quill. It is commonly mounted with three, but sometimes with only two strings.

The whole family of lutes has disappeared from the music of Europe, and is found only in the East, where they make a great figure in concerts. In the sixteenth and seventeenth centuries, they held the first place in what were called *chamber concerts (musica da camera)*, and were also used to accompany the madrigals, ballads, table songs, and others, which were always sung in several parts. All the concerts, represented in the paintings of Titian, Valentin, and other ancient masters of the Italian school, exhibit these collections of stringed instruments, played by snapping, together with singers. Though the quality of tone of these instruments had very little brilliancy, they also made a part of the orchestras, in the beginning of the opera. We have an example of this use of them in the musical drama entitled *Il San° Alessio,* composed by Stephen Landi, in 1634. The instrumentation of this work was composed of three distinct parts—of violins, of harps, of lutes, of *theorbes*, of bass viols, and of harpsichords, for the continued bass. Such an orchestra, at the present day, would be very dull, but the effect of it would be original.

The guitar appears to have originated in Spain, though it is found in some parts of Africa. It has been known in France since the eleventh century, at which time it had the name of *guiterne.* It is almost the only one of all the stringed instruments played by snapping, and with fingerboards, which remains in use. The body of the guitar is flat on both sides; it is furnished with six strings, and its fingerboard is divided by frets, for the placing of the fingers. In France, Germany, and England, the art of playing upon the guitar is carried to a very high point of perfection. In these later times, Sor, Aguado, Huerta, and Carcassi, have made it a concerto instrument, and have succeeded in executing upon it very complicated music, in several parts; but, in Spain, the native country of this instrument, it is used only to accompany the *boleros, tirannas,* and other national airs, and the performers play upon it instinctively, by striking the strings, or rattling them with the back of the hand.

All the researches which have been made, in order to discover whether the people of antiquity had any knowledge of instruments played with the bow, have been fruitless, or rather they have almost demonstrated that instruments of that description were wholly unknown to them. It is true that there is a statue of Orpheus holding a violin in one hand and a bow in the other; but a close examination shews that the violin and bow are the work of the sculptor who restored the statue. Passages also are cited from Aristophanes, Plutarch, Atheneus, and Lucian, in which it is pretended that there is proof of the existence of the bow among the Greeks; but the slightest examination is enough to put all these pretended proofs to flight.

There is no doubt that instruments having a sound-board and neck (or fingerboard), and strings elevated upon a bridge, and put in vibration by a bow, had their origin in the West; but at what time, and in what part of Europe they were invented, is a question not easy to decide. In Wales, we find an instrument nearly square in its form, having a fingerboard and strings elevated upon a bridge. This instrument, which seems to have existed in that country from the most remote antiquity, is called *crwth (crooth)*, and is played with a bow. In England, it is regarded as the parent of the different kinds of viols and of the violin.

The Gothic monuments of the Middle Ages, and

particularly the entrances of the churches of the tenth century, are the most ancient, in which we find representations of instruments of the kind which we call *viol;* but we should still be in a state of uncertainty concerning the divisions of this kind of instruments, if the manuscript of a treatise on music, composed by Jerome of Moravia, in the thirteenth century, had not removed all doubts in this respect. From this treatise we learn that viols were divided into two sorts of instruments—the *rubebbe*, and the *viole*, or *vielle*.*

The rubebbe had only two strings, which were tuned in fifths; the viol had five, tuned in different ways. These instruments had not precisely the form of our violins and violas. The sound board, or front, and the back of it, were not separated, as in the latter, by the intermediate part, which we call *eclisses*. The back was round, like that of the mandolin, and the sound board was glued upon its edge. At a later period, these rubebbes and viols underwent divers modifications, and gave birth to the different kinds of *viols*, namely, the *viol*, properly so called, which was placed on the knees, mounted with five strings; the *treble viol (pardessus de viole)*, which also had five strings tuned to the fifth of the *viol;* the *bass viol (basse de viole)*, which was mounted sometimes with five and sometimes with six strings, called by the Italians the *viola da gamba*, in order to distinguish it from the other kinds, which they frequently designated by the name of *viola da braccio*; the *violone*, or large

* The vielle here referred to had no resemblance to the instrument which now goes by that name, which, in the ancient French language, was called the *rote*.

viol, which was placed upon a pedestal, and which was mounted with seven strings; and the *accordo*, another kind of *violone*, which was mounted with twelve strings, and sometimes even with fifteen, several of which were sounded at once, and made harmony at every stroke of the bow. The *violone* and the *accordo* had fingerboards divided by frets, like the lute and the guitar; and, on account of their great size, could only be played upon by the performer standing. There was still another kind of viol, called the *viol of love (viole d'amour)*. Its size was nearly the same with that of the treble viol. It was mounted with four strings of catgut, attached as in the other instruments, and four others of *brass*, which passed under the fingerboard, and which, being tuned in unison with the strings of catgut, gave out sweet and harmonious sounds, when the instrument was played in a certain manner. This is a more modern instrument than the others.

Towards the fifteenth century, it seems that in France the viol had been reduced to a smaller size, in order to form from it the *violin*, as it exists at the present day, and to limit this instrument to four strings. What induces the belief that this improvement was made in France, is the fact that the violin is indicated in the Italian scenes of the end of the sixteenth century, under the names of *piccoli violini alla Francese* (little violins of the French fashion). The violin has four strings, tuned by fifths, E, A, D, G. It is used for the upper part. The superiority of the sounds of the violin over those of the viols soon obtained it the preference, and it came into general use. Skilful instrument-makers sprung up in France, Italy, and Germany, and from their workshops there came excellent violins, which are still very much sought after by the *virtuosi*. Amongst these instrument-makers we may remark Nicholas and Andrew Amati, of Cremona, at the end of the sixteenth century; Antony and Jerome Amati, sons of Andrew; Antony Stradivari, a pupil of the Amatis; as well as Peter Andrew Guarneri and Joseph Guarneri; James Steiner, a Tyrolese, also a pupil of the Amatis; and several others. The violins of these skilful artists have been sold since for prices varying from *a hundred louis* (about ninety pounds) to *six thousand francs* (about two hundred and fifty pounds). At this day very good imitations of them are made, and some that, by their exact resemblance to the older instruments, deceive skilful connoisseurs. These imitations do not cost more than three hundred francs (about twelve pounds).

Of all the ancient viols, the only one which has been preserved is that called *viole*, *alto*, or *quinte*. Its number of strings has been reduced to four, which are tuned a fifth lower than those of the violin. This instrument takes that part in the orchestra which corresponds to the contralto voice in a chorus.

The bass viol, a difficult instrument to play, and the sounds of which were somewhat dull, has disappeared, in order to give place to the violoncello, less attractive, perhaps, for solos, but more energetic and suitable for the purposes of the orchestra. It was introduced into France in the reign of Louis XIV., by a Florentine named John Balistini; but it was not finally substituted for the bass viol until about the year 1720.

The *violone* and the *accordo*, which were used in orchestras to play the bass of the harmony, had the defect of all viols, namely, that of producing only sounds which were dull and void of energy. As music acquired more brilliancy, it became necessary to think of means to give more strength to the bass. For this purpose, the *contrebasso* was constructed in Italy, in the beginning of the eighteenth century. This instrument, which is now the foundation of orchestras, was not adopted in France without considerable difficulty. The first contrebasso was introduced into the Opera in 1700, and was played by a musician of the name of Montéclair. In 1757, there was but one of these instruments in the orchestra of this theatre, and that was used only on Friday, which was the principal day of this exhibition. Gossec added a second. Philidor, a French composer, introduced a third into the orchestra, for the first representation of his opera of *Ernelinda;* and the number of these instruments has been gradually increased to eight. The contrebasso is strung with three large strings, which sound an octave below those of the violoncello. These strings are three in number in the French instruments, and are tuned by fifths; the German and Italian instruments are mounted with four strings, tuned by fourths. This last plan is preferable, as it renders the instrument more easy to play.

The third kind of stringed instruments is that in which the strings are put in vibration by means of a key. These instruments are of two kinds. The first is derived from the imitation of lutes and other instruments, the strings of which were snapped with a quill, or with a piece of tortoiseshell. The imitation was made by mechanical contrivance, and had the advantage of offering means of combining a greater extent of sounds than could be done on any of the varieties of the lute. The first instrument of this kind that was made was the *clavicitherium*, which had strings of catgut, put in vibration by means of pieces of leather, operated upon by the keys. The *virginal* was also an instrument with strings and keys. It has often been said that the name of this instrument was a compliment to Elizabeth, queen of England, who played on it, and was very fond of it. But this is an error. The virginal was in existence as early as 1530, and had the same name. The *clavecin*, or harpsichord, was also already invented at that period. This instrument, the largest of the kind, had almost the form of our long pianos. It often had two keys, which might be played together, and which struck two notes at a time, tuned in octaves. The strings of the harpsichord were put in vibration by strips of wood terminated with a piece of quill or leather, and which were raised by touching a key. The end of the quill or leather gave way and fell down as soon as it touched the string, leaving the latter free to vibrate. The *spinet*, which was only a harpsichord of a square form, was constructed on the same principle. There were some of a particular kind, the sound of which was very soft, and, for that reason, were called *sourdins*. The harpsichord, the spinet, and the clavichord, continued in use till about 1785. The other kinds of keyed instruments were modelled upon the Oriental instruments called *canon*, and *psalterium*, or psaltery. It is known that the latter, of which great use was formerly made, was composed of a square box, on which a thin pine-board or tablet was glued. On this tablet strings of iron or brass wire were extended by means of pegs, and tuned so as to give all the sounds of the scale. The performer held in each hand a little rod, with which he struck the strings. Such an instrument was at once inconvenient and limited in its powers. An attempt was made to improve it, and thence sprung the *clavichord*, which consisted of a box of a triangular form, with a sound board and pegs, to which wires of brass were attached, and a key, which operated upon little plates of copper, by which the strings were struck. It was this instrument which afterwards suggested the idea of the piano.

The thin and sometimes disagreeable sound of the harpsichord, the spinet, and even the clavichord, had, for a long time, induced some of the harpsichord makers to seek for the means of producing more agreeable sounds; and as early as 1716, a manufacturer at Paris, by the name of Marius, had presented to the Academy of Sciences for their examination two harpsichords, in which he had substituted little hammers for the strips of wood used to strike the strings. Two years afterwards, Christoforo, a Florentine, improved upon this invention, and made the first *piano*, which has served as a model for those which have since been made; but it appears that the first attempts of this kind were coldly received; for it was not until the year 1760 that Zumpe, in England, and Silbermann, in Germany, had regular manufactories, and began to multiply pianos. In 1776, the brothers

Erard made the first instruments of this kind which were constructed in Paris; for until that time they were imported from London. The first pianos which were constructed at this period had only an extent of five octaves, and the hammers struck upon two strings tuned in unison for each note. The extent of the key-board was afterwards carried to six octaves and a half, and the number of strings to each note was raised to three, in order to give the sound more body and strength. Numerous changes, or improvements, have been made in the manufacture of pianos. Their size has been increased; their structure has undergone a thousand variations; their quality of sound has ceased to be thin and shrill, and has become soft and full. Even the form of the instrument has been greatly changed. They are now either oblong, which is the most common form in use, or larger at one end than the other, like the harpsichord; or upright, with perpendicular or oblique strings; and of many other forms, which it would take too long to mention. The English pianos, principally the grand pianos (*à queue*), have, for a long time, been unquestionably superior to all others; but instruments are now made at Paris which may vie with them in respect to their quality of tone and their structure. The German pianos, especially those of Vienna, are also very agreeable, but their tone is less powerful. Their structure is very light, and facilitates the execution of difficult passages.

From what has now been said, it follows that instruments, the principle of which consists of sonorous and flexible strings, are susceptible of much variety, and have undergone modifications of every kind, like all things else connected with music. The same may be remarked of instruments whose sonorousness is derived from the air blown into them. These instruments are divided into three principal kinds; namely: 1, flutes, which are made to sound by means of air introduced into a tube through an orifice at the side or end; 2, instruments with reeds, in which the vibrations of a flexible tongue produce the sound; and, 3, instruments with a mouth-piece, in which the sounds are formed by modifications of the motion and position of the lips.

Flutes, in some form or other, have been found among all nations which have cultivated music. India, Egypt, and China, afford varieties of this instrument, which may be traced back to the most remote times. The Greeks and Romans had flutes of different forms for most of their religious ceremonies, for festivals, marriages, funerals, etc. The flute with several pipes of different lengths, which is still to be seen in the hands of some itinerant musicians, appears to be the most ancient form of the instrument employed by the Greeks. They attributed its invention to Marsyas. After this came the Phrygian flute, which had only a single pipe, pierced with three holes, and which was played by putting one of the ends of the instrument into the mouth. The double flute, composed of two pipes, pierced with holes, and united together near a single orifice, called the *embouchure*, was held in both hands. This is the only instrument of antiquity which can induce the belief that the Greeks and Romans had any knowledge of harmony; for it is not to be presumed that the two pipes were intended to be played in unison. Some critics have thought that the two pipes of this flute were not played together, and that they were only made use of in order to pass from one mode to another. All this is very obscure. The three principal kinds of flutes, of which we have spoken, were divided into an infinity of others. The antiquaries pretend that the number of varieties exceeded two hundred.

The question has been frequently agitated, whether the ancients were acquainted with the *flûte traversière, (cross flute)*, which is the only one now made use of in regular music. Some ancient monuments, recently discovered, have solved the difficulty, by shewing, in bas-relief, a figure playing upon a flute of that description. This explains those passages in the writers of antiquity, which recognise, in many places, the difference between the *straight* flute and the *oblique* flute. The latter was nothing more than the *flûte traversière*.

Formerly, the only kind of flute used in France was the *flûte à bec*, that is, the embouchure of which was placed at one end. All the parts for the flute, which were written for the operas of the age of Louis XIV., were played with flutes of this kind. It was also called the *flûte douce*, or the *English* flute. When the *flûte traversière* was first introduced, it received the name of the *German* flute, because its use was first renewed in that country. Until about the end of the eighteenth century, this flute had no more than six holes, stopped by the fingers, and a seventh, which was opened by means of a key. Like the greater part of wind instruments, the German flute was imperfect in several notes, which failed in precision. These defects have been corrected by the addition of keys, which are now eight in number.*

These keys also enable performers to execute many passages which could not be done on the ancient flute.

The flute is naturally in the key of D; but this does not prevent it from being played in all the other keys. In military music, and in that kind of music for wind instruments, called *band* music, flutes of somewhat smaller dimensions, and in the keys of E♭, F, etc. are employed. Another kind of small flute, called the *octave*, or *piccolo*, is also used in orchestras, when the composer is desirous of brilliancy, or of producing certain peculiar effects, or imitations, such as the whistling of the wind in a tempest. The *piccolo*, which is of less than half the size of the ordinary flute, sounds an octave higher, which makes the quality of its tone shrill and frequently disagreeable. The composers of the present day have extended the use even to the abuse of this instrument.

The material of flutes is ordinarily box, ebony, or maple, etc.; but all these kinds of wood are subject to the inconvenience of becoming warmed by the breath, and thereby causing the sound of the instrument to vary. To avoid this defect, flutes have been made of glass, which were nearly invariable; but their weight, which rendered them inconvenient in execution, and their brittleness, have caused them to be

* In Germany, flutes, with as many as seventeen keys, have been made, which have a greater range of sound than the others; but this multiplicity is embarassing, and changes the quality of tone of the instrument.

given up. It has been found to be a more simple and useful remedy, to adapt to the common flute a metallic tube, which may be extended when the instrument becomes warm, and which re-establishes the just tone by lengthening the tube.

Of all the ancient *flûtes à bec*, one alone remains in use. This is the *flageolet*, which produces an agreeable effect in orchestras for the dance. This instrument was formerly very defective in point of justness, and very limited as to its means of execution; but it has been much improved, within a few years, by the addition of keys.

Of all the varieties of *instruments with reeds*, which have been in use at different periods, the *oboe*, *English horn*, *clarinet*, and *bassoon*, are the only ones which have been preserved.

The most ancient of these instruments is the oboe; which was in the hands of the minstrels as early as the end of the sixteenth century. At that period, it was a coarse instrument, of a hard and harsh tone, having only eight holes, without keys. Its whole length was two feet. It remained for a long time in a state of imperfection, which prevented it from being employed in the orchestra, except for the music of rural festivals. Keys were first added to it about the year 1690. The Besozzi, who were celebrated for their skill on this instrument, attempted its improvement; and an instrument-maker of Paris of the name of De Lusse, about the year 1780, added a key to it. Several other improvements, which have been made in later times, have carried the instrument to a point of perfection which leaves nothing to be desired. Its extent is now two octaves and a half.

The quality of the tone of the oboe, when well played, gives it a wonderful power of expression. It is capable of more force, and of more variety, than the tone of the flute. Though it is produced by a small instrument, it has much power, and frequently rises above the mass of sound of the most effective orchestras. The oboe was more employed by composers forty years ago, than any other wind instrument of a high tone. It is equally well adapted for the orchestra and for solos.

The instrument which has been improperly called the *English horn*, may be considered as the contralto of the oboe, of which it is a variety. Its size is much greater, so that in order to facilitate the playing upon it, it is necessary to make it crooked. The English horn is a fifth lower than the oboe, in consequence of the length of its tube. Its tone is plaintive, and suitable only for slow movements, romances, etc. It is a modern instrument, and was unknown sixty years ago.

The *bassoon*, which belongs also to the family of the oboe, and is the bass of that kind of instruments, was invented in 1539, by a canon of Pavia, named Afranio. The Italians call it *fagotto*, because it is formed of several pieces of wood united together like a bundle. The extent of the bassoon is about three octaves and a half; and its lowest note is the B♭ below the staff, in the F clef. The form of this instrument has undergone many modifications; but, notwithstanding the labours of many artists and skilful instrument-makers, it is far from having arrived at perfection. Several of its notes are false, and are only susceptible of correction, to a certain degree, by the skill of the artist who plays upon it. Almost all its lower notes are too low, when compared with the higher. The number of keys has been increased to fifteen, and its means of execution have been enriched accordingly; but its defects have not all been corrected. Several of the notes still have a sort of muffled tone; whilst others of them, principally in the bass, remain false. It is probable that these defects will not be overcome, until the instrument is pierced anew upon better principles and upon a new system. It may, perhaps, be necessary to change its form, and to bend the lower extremity, in order that it may become warm more readily.

The defects which I have pointed out in the bassoon, are the more to be lamented, as it is an indispensable instrument in the composition of an orchestra. It performs the office both of the tenor and bass, of the reed instruments, and binds together the different parts of the harmony. It is employed with a better effect in the orchestra, than as a solo instrument. Its tones are melancholy and monotonous when played alone.

In Germany, a contrebasso of the bassoon, called *contrebasson*, is sometimes used. This instrument is larger than the bassoon, and sounds an octave below. It is difficult to play, and requires that the performer should be of a robust constitution. Its defect is a slow articulation.

The *clarinet* is an instrument much more modern than the oboe and bassoon; for it was not invented until the year 1690, by John Christopher Denner, an instrument-maker of Nuremberg. At first it had but one key, and was very rarely used, on account of its numerous imperfections; but the beauty of its tones induced artists to attempt improvements in its construction. The number of keys was gradually increased to five; but, when arrived at this point, it still offered but few resources. It nevertheless remained in this state from 1770 to 1787, when a sixth key was added. The number of its keys was finally increased until they amounted to fourteen; but all the defects of the instrument have not yet disappeared. Besides the difficulties of execution, which still exist, several of the notes are deficient in precision and in quality of tone. It is the same with the clarinet as with the bassoon; its tube requires to be pierced anew upon a better system of acoustics. Multiplying the keys of wind instruments corrects the want of precision, but injures the quality of the tone.

The difficulties of execution on the clarinet are such that the same instrument cannot be used to play in all the keys. Those in which there are many sharps require a peculiar clarinet; and it is the same, also, in relation to keys in which there are many flats. In order to comprehend this, it should be understood, that, in proportion as the tube of a wind instrument is shortened, its tones are raised; and that they are lowered by lengthening the tube. It follows that, if the tube of a clarinet is lengthened, so that its C is in unison with B♭, it will be sufficient to make the instrument of that size, in order to enable the performer to produce the effect of the key of B♭, by playing in C; and he will thereby be relieved from the necessity of executing those notes which present difficulties to be overcome in the execution. If we continue to lengthen the tube of the instrument, so that its C sounds the same as A, the effect which the artist will produce by playing in C, will be the same as if he should play in the key of A, with three sharps in the clef. This is the explanation of the terms used by musicians: *clarinet in* C, *clarinet in* B♭, *clarinet in* A.

The clarinet was not introduced into the French orchestras until the year 1757; since which period it has come into general use, not only in common orchestras, but in military bands, in which it plays the principal part. The sound of this instrument is of great volume, full and soft, and possesses a quality unlike that of any other, particularly in its lower notes, called the *chalumeau*. In military music, for the solos, clarinets in E♭, or in F, are used, which have a sharp and piercing sound, proper for that kind of music which is intended to be heard in the open air. There is also a kind of large clarinet, a fifth lower than the clarinet in C, which possesses a concentrated quality of tone. It is called the *cor de basset*, or basset horn. It is the contralto of the clarinet. A *bass clarinet* has lately been constructed, which presents no more difficulties in the execution than the common clarinet, and which completes this family of instruments.

The third kind of wind instruments which are played with an open *embouchure*, or *mouth-piece*, includes the *horn*, the different sorts of *trumpets*, the *trombone*, the *serpent*, and the *ophicleides*.

Hunting airs were played in the first operas by the *cornet*, an instrument made in the shape of a horn, and pierced with holes. These clumsy instruments were called *cornets à bouquin* (old buck's horn). The *cor de chasse* (hunting horn) was invented in France in 1680, and was at first used only in hunting. Being carried into Germany, it was there improved, and began to be used in music. In 1730, it was used in France, but was not introduced into the orchestra of the Opera until 1757. The sounds which could then be drawn from it were few in number; but, in 1760, a German, named Hampl, discovered that it could be made to produce an additional number, by closing in part, with the hand, the open portion of the instrument, which was called the *pavillon.* This discovery opened the way to those skilful artists who devoted themselves to the study of the horn. Another German, named Haltenhoff, completed the improvement of this instrument, by adding to it a grooved sliding tube, by means of which the precision of the tones may be preserved, when they become too sharp in consequence of the warmth of the instrument.

It is in the nature of the horn to give only certain sounds in a pure, free, and open tone; the others, which are obtained by the aid of the hand, are much more dull, and are termed *stopped sounds.* But as there are some keys in which the stopped sounds are precisely those which ought to be heard the most frequently, — in which case the instrument would be without effect, — lengthening tubes, or *crooks*, have been invented, to be added to it, the purpose of which is to change the tones of the instrument, as those of the clarinet are changed, by lengthening its tube. For example, if we suppose that the horn is in C, it will be readily conceived that by adding a tube to it, which lowers C a tone, the horn will be in B♭, and all the open sounds of the key of C will then be open sounds in the key of B♭. If the added tube is longer, it will place the key of the horn in A; if longer still, it will be in G; and so on. It follows from this that the performer always plays in C, and that the added tube produces the necessary transposition.

This plan is ingenious, and would suffice for every want, if music was not modulated, or if in modulations there were time to change the transposing tube. But this is not always the case. The composer is, therefore, obliged either to suppress the parts of the horns in certain places, in which they would produce very good effects, or to write them in the stopped notes, which do not correspond to his intentions. Struck with this inconvenience of the common horn, a German musician named Stœlzel conceived the idea of adding pistons to it, by means of which he opened a communication, at will, between the column of air in the horn and that of the additional tubes, and thereby obtained open sounds in all the notes. This improvement, which has been perfected by several manufacturers of brass instruments, will, at some future period, be of great advantage, but it is not yet generally adopted. It must be admitted, however, that the fault of the pistons is, that they injure the beautiful quality of sound of the horn.

The horn is an exceedingly valuable instrument, for the variety of its powers. Both energetic and tender, it serves equally well to express the more violent passions and the softer sentiments. Equally well adapted for solos, and for the full orchestra, it may be modified in a thousand ways, but must be well understood, in order to exhibit its whole character. The art of writing parts for the horn, in such a manner as to develope all its resources, is an art entirely new, and which Rossini has carried to perfection.

The *trumpet* is the soprano of the horn, as it sounds an octave higher than that instrument. More limited than the horn, since it has none of the sounds stopped with the hand, it is not less useful in many circumstances. Its quality of tone is more silvery, clear, and penetrating, and the effects of neither of these instruments can be supplied by the other. Their union sometimes produces the happiest combinations. Formerly, the only known instrument of this kind was the cavalry trumpet; and, for many years, none other was used at the Opera. At length, improved trumpets were brought from Germany, by the two brothers Braun, about the year 1770; and since that period, the cavalry trumpet has disappeared from the orchestra. At the commencement of the present century, trumpets were manufactured of a semicircular form, which, properly speaking, were nothing more than small horns. The sound of these instruments had not the brilliancy of the others, and within a few years the ancient model has been restored.

The sounds of the trumpet are modified for the changes of key, in the same way as those of the horn—that is, by means of additional tubes.

Divers attempts had been made, within the last twenty-five years, to increase the resources of the trumpet, but without any corresponding success. At length an Englishman conceived the idea of adding keys to it, like those of the oboe or clarinet, and his experiments for that purpose were crowned with success; but it was found that he had created a new instrument, which, in the quality of its tone, had little resemblance to the common trumpet. This was an acquisition, but not an improvement. The inventor designated his trumpet with keys by the name of the *bugle horn*. This instrument, upon which melodies may be executed, as upon the clarinet or oboe, is now employed with success in military music, and even in the opera. Rossini has made a happy use of it in the first act of his *Semiramide*.

The principle of the construction of keyed trumpets being once discovered, it was soon perceived that it might be applied to other instruments of the same kind, but of greater dimensions, which should be the alto, tenor, and bass, of the trumpet. This new family of brass instruments has received the name of *ophicleide*. The extent of these different instruments is nearly that of the voices to which they correspond. Their union produces fine effects, which cannot be supplied by the other brass instruments, which have not the same means of modulation.

There is another kind of instruments, which are called *trombones*, and which are also capable of giving all the notes in open sounds, by means of a slide, which is moved by the performer, in order to lengthen or shorten the sonorous tube. This kind of instrument is divided into three voices; namely, the alto, tenor, and bass. The sound of the trombones is more dry, hard, and energetic, than that of the ophicleides; but they produce peculiar effects, unlike those of any other instruments.

This whole great division of brass instruments is put in vibration by means of a conical and concave mouthpiece, to which the performer applies his lips more or less closely, at the same time blowing, and marking the note by a movement of the tongue. This is very difficult, and requires natural aptitude as well as labour. There are some persons, the conformation of whose lips is an insurmountable obstacle to their playing well upon the horn or trumpet.

To the instruments with the embouchure, or mouthpiece, which have been mentioned, must be added the *serpent;* a barbarous instrument, which wearies the ear in our churches, but which is not equally disagreeable in military music, when united with other basses, such as the trombone and the ophicleide. This instrument was invented in 1590, by a canon of Auxerre, named Edme Guillaume. Its construction is faulty in all respects. Many of its sounds are false, and by the side of notes which are very powerful, we find others which are extremely feeble. The expulsion of the serpent from the churches will be one step towards good taste in music.

The *organ* is the largest, the most majestic, the richest in the variety of its effects, and the finest of all wind instruments. It has been said that it is a machine rather than an instrument; and this may be true; but however it may be described, it is not the less certain that it is one of the noblest inventions of the human mind.

Some passages to be found in the writers of antiquity, and particularly in Vitruvius, have put the commentators to the torture, to discover what these writers understood by the *hydraulic organ*, the invention of which they attribute to Ctesibus, a mathematician of Alexandria, who lived in the time of Ptolemy Evergetes. All that the commentators have said only serves to prove that they were completely ignorant of the subject in question. In all probability, we shall never know what was the mechanism of this hydraulic organ. As to the *pneumatic* organ, namely, that which is put in vibration by the action of the air, which is also said to have been known to the ancients, without any better evidence than some obscure passages in their poets, it is probable that it was nothing more than the rustic instrument of the Scotch and the Auvergnese, which we call the *cornemuse*, or bagpipe.

The most ancient organ of which mention is made in history, is that which the Emperor Constantine Copronymus sent, in the year 757, to Pepin, the father of Charlemagne. This was the first which appeared in France. It was placed in the church of St. Corneille, at Compiegne. This organ was very small, and portable, like that which was constructed by an Arab named Giafar, and which was sent to Charlemagne by the Caliph of Bagdad.

A Venetian priest, named Gregory, appears to have been the first who attempted the building of organs in Europe. In 826, he was employed by Louis the Pious to make one for the church of Aix-la-Chapelle. The art of organ-building made very slow progress; and it seems not even to have begun to be developed until the fourteenth century. Francis Landino, surnamed *Francesco d'egli Organi*, on account of his skill upon the organ, made many improvements in its construction about the year 1350. In 1470, a German named Bernard, who was an organist at Venice, invented the pedals.

The organ is composed of several ranges of pipes, some of which are of wood, or of a mixture of tin and lead, called *stuff*, with open mouths, like the flute played at the end; and the rest of which have in their mouthpiece tongues of brass or *reeds*. These pipes are placed upright, upon the end in which their mouthpiece is, in holes, which are made in the upper part of certain wooden boxes, called *wind-chests*. Large bellows distribute the wind into tubes, which communicate with the interior of the wind-chests. To each range of pipes is attached a plate or rod of wood, which is also pierced with holes, at distances equal to those of the wind-chests. This plate or rod is called the *register*. It is arranged in such a manner as to move easily, when it is drawn out or pushed in by the organist. If the register is pushed in, its holes do not correspond to those of the wind-chest, in which the pipes are placed, and consequently the wind cannot enter into the pipes; but if it is drawn out, the holes will perfectly correspond, and the air may be admitted into the pipes. Then, when the organist places his finger upon a key, the latter, as it sinks down, draws a little rod, which opens a valve corresponding to the hole in the register, the wind enters, and the pipe of the note gives the sound which belongs to that note. If several registers are drawn out, all the pipes in them, which correspond to the note touched, will sound at the same time. If the pipe is a flute, the sound is produced by the vibration of the column of air in the pipe; if it is a reed-stop, the sound results from the beating of the tongue, which breaks the air against the walls of the mouth of the pipe.

Besides the variety of sounds, which arise from this difference of principle in their production, the organ has others, which are the result of the different forms and sizes of the pipes. For example, if the pipe of the note which corresponds to C, in the F clef, below the staff, is a flute pipe of eight feet in height, we give it the name of *open flute*. This stop, throughout the entire extent of the key-board, is in unison with the different voices, included within the same extent; namely: the bass, the tenor, the contralto, and the highest soprano. The height of the pipes diminishes as the notes rise. If the largest pipe is only two feet in height, and is of the flute kind, we give it the name of *prestant*, that is to say, excellent, because this stop has the clearest sound, and is the least liable to get out of tune. It is an octave higher than the open flute. If the pipe of the lowest note is only one foot in height, it sounds two octaves above the open flute; the stop composed of this range of pipes is called the *flageolet*. A flute stop, the low C of which has a pipe eight feet in height, sounds an octave lower than the flute of four feet. There are stops of sixteen and even thirty-two feet. When the space, which the builder has at his command, is not sufficient to allow him to make use of pipes of so great dimensions, an ingenious expedient is resorted to, which consists in closing the extremity of the pipe, opposite the mouthpiece; in which case, the column of sonorous air, not finding any vent, is forced to descend and issue from a small opening called the *lumière*, and in this manner, running twice the length of the pipe, it sounds an octave lower than if it issued immediately from the upper extremity of the same pipe. This kind of flute stop is called *bourdon*. When the largest pipe, in a stop of this description, is four feet in height, it is called a *bourdon de huit* (bourdon of eight feet); when eight feet in height, it is a *bourdon de seize* (of sixteen feet). Among the flute stops, there is one made of stuff, the pipes of which are terminated by smaller pipes, called *chimneys;* others have the form of two inverted cones, placed upon one another; each of these stops has its peculiar quality of sound. The pipes of the reed stops, called the *trumpet*, *clarion*, *bombarde*, *vox humana*, have the form of an open inverted cone. The pipes of the *chromorna*, another reed stop, are in the shape of long cylinders. The pipes of these stops may be varied at pleasure, according to the fancy of the organ builder.

We find in the organ a kind of stop, the idea of which is very singular, and the effect of which is a mystery. This stop, which is generally designated by the name of the *mutation stop*, is divided into the *furniture*, or *mixture*, and the *cymbale*. Each of these stops is composed of *four*, *five*, or *six*, and even *ten* pipes for each note. These pipes, which are of a small size and high sound, are tuned to the third, fifth, or fourth octave, double third, etc., so that each note gives the perfect chord several times repeated. It follows, therefore, that the organist cannot give several notes in succession, without giving rise to successions of major thirds, fifths, and octaves. But this is not all: if the organist plays a chord, each of the notes which compose it gives rise to a perfect chord, doubled or tripled; so that, it would seem, the result must be a frightful noise; but, by a sort of magic, when these stops are united with all the flute stops of two, four, eight, sixteen, and thirty-two feet, open or stopped, there results from this mixture, which is called the *full organ*, a combined effect of the most majestic and the most surprising character. No other combination of sounds, or of instruments, can give an idea of it.

Besides the solos of flute, oboe, clarinet, bassoon, and trumpet, which may be executed on the organ, the play of this instrument may be divided into three great effects, which are—1, the union of all the flute stops, which is called *fonds d'orgue;* 2, the union of all the reed stops, which is called the *grand stop*, or *grand choir;* and 3, the *full stop*.

A grand organ has ordinarily four or five key-boards for the hands, and one for the feet, which is called the *pedal key-board.* The first key-board belongs to a small, separate organ, the name of which is the *positif* (or choir organ). The second is commonly that of the great organ, and may be united to the first to play the two organs together. Sometimes a third is added, called the key-board of the *bombarde*, upon which the most powerful reeds stops are played. The fourth key-board is used for solos; it is called the key-board of *recitation.* The fifth is designed to produce the effect of an *echo.* The pedal key-board enables the

organist to play the bass when he wishes to make use of his left hand in executing the intermediate parts.

It had been a matter of regret, for a long time, that the organ, with all its means of variety and power of effect, was destitute of *expression*,—that is to say, of the means of gradually increasing and diminishing the force of its sounds. Some of the German and English builders at first thought of the expedient of trap-doors, which, being opened or closed by means of a pedal, permitted the sound to be produced with force, or concentrated it in the interior of the instrument. But this kind of expression had the inconvenience of resembling a long yawn. Before the revolution, Sebastian Erard undertook to construct an organ piano, in which the sounds were made expressive, by the pressure of the finger upon the keys: he had completely succeeded, when the troubles of the revolution broke out, and put a stop to his further progress. Since that time, an accomplished amateur, by the name of Grenié, conceived a plan of rendering the organ expressive by means of a pedal, the pressure of which, more or less strong, should give more or less force to the sounds. He demonstrated the success and value of his invention, at first in some small organs, and afterwards in instruments of a larger size, in the Royal Academy of Music, and in the church of St. Cœur, at Paris. This organ has the most beautiful effect. Erard has carried the organ to the height of perfection, in an instrument built by him for the King's Chapel, in which he has united the expression of the pedal upon the two key-boards of the great organ, to that produced by the pressure of the finger upon a third key-board. In this state, the organ is truly the most beautiful, majestic, and powerful instrument in existence, and may be called a masterpiece of the human mind.

The most celebrated organ-builders are—in France, the Dallerys, Clicquot, Messrs. Erard and Grenié; in Italy, Azzolino *della Ciaja* of Sienna, the Troncis of Pistoia, Eugene Biroldi, Jean-Baptiste Ramaï, the Serassis of Bergamo, a Dalmatian priest named Nanchini, and his pupil, Callido; in Germany, John Scheibe, Godfrey Silbermann, John James and Michael Wagner, Schrœtker, Ernest Marx, Gabler, J. G. Tauscher, and the Abbé Vogler. The last is distinguished by his *system of simplification*, the object of which is to free the organ from the mutation stops.

The cylinder or barrel organs, used by the itinerant musicians, and the *serinette* (or bird organ), are constructed upon the same principles as the great organ. A cylinder, pricked with brass points or pins, stands in the place of an organist, and moves the keys. The art of pricking or noting these cylinders is called *tonotechny*.

In these later times, the action of compressed air has been employed to establish a new class of instruments; the plan of which consists in causing the air to act by a very small orifice, opening gradually upon very thin metallic plates, which vibrate as the air strikes them, and produce sounds that grow louder as the action of the air is increased. These instruments were invented in Germany but a few years since. Their varieties are called the *physharmonica*, *eoline*, *eolodion*, etc. They have not power enough to produce any effect in large halls, but are very agreeable in the parlour. Mr. Dietz, a piano-maker of Paris, has improved this method of producing sounds in an instrument which he has called the *aerophone*.

The effect of these instruments is analogous to that of the *harmonica*, the principle of which is friction. An Irishman, named Puckeridge, appears to have been the first who thought of uniting a certain number of drinking glasses, of tuning them by varying their sounds by filling them with different quantities of water, and of drawing sounds from them by rubbing their edges with the fingers slightly moistened. The celebrated Dr. Franklin made some improvements upon this discovery, principally in suggesting a process for the making of proper glasses for producing pure tones. The instrument, thus improved, was brought to the continent, and two English ladies, sisters, the Misses Davis, gave it a reputation by their talent in playing upon it. The *harmonica* has since been improved by being constructed of glass bells, crossed by an iron axis, and put in motion by a wheel. A key-board of a peculiar kind causes a little leather ball, which supplies the place of a finger, to rub the edge of the bells, and in this manner the performer is able to execute regular pieces of music, and to make chords upon the harmonica. The glassy tone of this instrument is injurious to the health, as it excites the nervous system too strongly.

Several instruments of friction have been made in imitation of the *harmonica;* the most celebrated of which is the *clavicylinder*, which the natural philosopher Chladni exhibited at Paris, about the year 1806. Though the inventor of this instrument has kept its construction a secret, it is believed that it consisted of a series of metallic cylinders, operated upon by bows, which were set in motion by a crank, and were brought in contact with the cylinders, by means of the keys of a key-board.

It remains for me to speak of the last and the least important kind of instruments; namely, those of percussion. These are the instruments, the forms and use of which are known with most certainty, from the representations of them on the monuments of antiquity. They are divided into two principal classes—the *sonorous* and the *noisy*. Among the *sonorous* instruments of percussion, which were in use in Egypt, Greece, and Rome, must be placed the *sistrum*, which consisted of an elliptical rim of brass, crossed by sonorous rods, which were made to sound by being struck with a little stick; the *cymbals*, formed of two sonorous plates, which were struck against each other; and the *crotales*, or little bells. Only one instrument of the *noisy* kind is to be remarked in the ancient paintings and bas-reliefs. This is the tambour with bells, which we call the *tambour de basque*, or tamborine. It was played upon, as at the present day, either by striking it with the hand, or by shaking it.

Modern music admits of a great number of instruments of percussion. Among those which are sonorous, we observe the *triangle*, which takes its name from its shape, and consists of a steel rod, which is struck with a piece of iron. This little instrument, which originated in the East, produces a pretty good effect in certain pieces, when it is not too freely used. It unites well, in military music, with the other sonorous instruments of percussion. The *crotales*, or little bells, and the *cymbal*, came also from the East, where the best are made. These instruments were formerly used only in military music; but Rossini and his imitators have transferred the use, or rather the abuse of them to the theatre, together with the most noisy of the instruments of percussion, the stunning *great drum*, the only proper place for which is at the head of a troop of soldiers, to mark the step.

Among the noisy instruments of percussion, the *timbals*, or kettle drums, are distinguished from the others by the power of varying their sounds, and of being tuned. The kettle drums consist of two bowls of copper, the tops of which are covered with a skin which is stretched upon an iron rim, tightened by screws. Each drum gives a different sound, and these sounds are modified by tightening or loosening the iron ring. The two drums are tuned commonly to the fifth or the fourth of one another; but there are some cases in which this order is inverted. Though the tone of the drum is not easily perceived, yet an attentive ear will discern it, when the instrument is well tuned.

Two other instruments of the same kind are used in military music; the one is the drum, properly so called, which is merely noisy, and serves to mark the rhythm of the step of soldiers; the other is the large drum, which has a longer body than the other, and gives a lower and softer sound. They are sometimes introduced into the common orchestras.

In the foregoing description of musical instruments, I have omitted some varieties, which had but a short existence, and can only be considered as fancy instruments. I ought not, however, to pass over in silence those of this description, which have had for their object to solve two difficult problems; namely, to enrich music with effects on a new plan, and to furnish composers with the means of preserving their improvisations. I shall speak of instruments which unite the key-board with the bow, and of melographic pianos.

It is more than a century since the first attempts were made to give to keyed instruments the power of sustaining their sounds, like instruments played with the bow. About the year 1717, a manufacturer of harpsichords at Paris attempted to solve the difficulty, in an instrument which he called the *viol-harpsichord*, because it resembled a viol placed upon a table, was played with a wheel instead of a bow, and because its sound was similar to that of a viol. This instrument was approved by the Academy of Sciences; but it seems that a long time elapsed before any one thought of perfecting the invention. About the end of the eighteenth century, a mechanic of Milan, by the name of Gerli, introduced into several concerts and churches an instrument which had the form of a harpsichord, and which was mounted with strings of catgut, played upon by *bows of hair*, according to the account given in the Italian journals of the time.

At the exhibition of the products of industry, which took place at the Invalids in 1806, Schmidt, a piano-maker of Paris, presented an instrument, which had the form of a long square box, having at one extremity a key-board, with the mechanism of the ordinary piano, and at the other another key-board, designed to give motion to little cylindrical bows, which produced sounds from strings of catgut. The sounds obtained by this mechanism had the defect of resembling those of the viol.

Several other attempts have been made with more or less of success. A mechanic, named Pouleau, about the year 1810, made an *orchestrino*, which was of the same kind as the instrument of Schmidt. Its sounds were agreeable, but weak. The Abbé Gregory Trentin afterwards constructed a *violin-cembalo* (or violin-harpsichord), which was of the same kind. The *sostenante-pianoforte*, invented by Mr. Mott of Brighton, and the *plectro-euphone*, exhibited at Paris, in 1828, by the Gamas of Nantes, were also similar. The principles by which Dietz has constructed his instrument are more conformed to what observation teaches concerning the sounding of instruments played with the bow, than those which were adopted by his predecessors. Finally, Dietz has come as near as possible to the solution of the problem, in his *polyplectron*, which he made known at the same time. The *polyplectron* is capable of producing a great number of very pretty effects; but they are the effects of a peculiar instrument, rather than imitations of the violin and other instruments played with the bow.

The idea of constructing a harpsichord, or piano, by means of which the improvisations of a composer might be preserved, has considerably occupied the attention of several mechanics. An Englishman, by the name of Creed, was the first who wrote, in 1747, a tract, in which he undertook to shew the possibility of this invention. It is asserted also, that a monk, by the name of Engramelle, about the year 1770, made an instrument of this kind, the success of which was complete; but the explanations which are given of it are very obscure, and of a kind to give rise to doubts concerning the truth of the facts. On the other hand, John Frederick Ungher, counsellor of justice at Brunswick, in a German work, printed in 1774, has claimed the invention of the instrument attributed to Creed, and proved that he had previously made a similar one.

In the month of August 1827, Mr. Carreyre made trial, before the Academy of the Fine Arts of the Institute, of a *melographic piano,* which consisted of a clock movement, which unrolled, from one cylinder to another, a thin plate of lead, on which were impressed, by the action of the keys of the piano, certain peculiar signs, which might be translated into the ordinary notation, by means of an explanatory table. After the experiment, the plate of lead was removed, to make the translation, and a commission was appointed to report; but, as no report has ever been made, it is probable that the translation was not found to be exact. At the same time, Mr. Baudouin read before the Academy a paper, accompanied with drawings, concerning another melographic piano; upon the merit of which the Institute has not yet pronounced. It follows from all this that the problem yet remains to be solved.

In the rapid sketch above given of what relates to instruments and their manufacture, the reader may have been struck with the prodigious fruitfulness of imagination manifested in all these inventions. Will things remain stationary in this respect, or not? This is doubtful. The imagination of man will always be active, but it may be doubted whether there will be produced hereafter effects greatly superior to those which are now obtained. All the distinguished men, who have employed themselves in the construction of instruments, have sought to make improvements in them, by a more severe application of theoretical principles; but, in practice, the results have not been such as they expected, either from unknown causes, or from their not having taken the necessary precautions. Theory is sometimes found in opposition to practice. For example, the principles of the sounding of vibrating surfaces, demonstrate that violins, violas, and basses, are constructed on arbitrary rather than scientific rules; but in the application of these principles, no one has yet been able to make instruments as good as those which were made by rules the foundation of which is unknown. The same thing may be remarked of pianos. Time alone will shed light on these mysterious circumstances.

CHAPTER XV.

OF INSTRUMENTATION.

Instrumentation is the art of employing instruments in the manner best adapted to derive from them the greatest possible effect in music. This art may be learned with time and experience; but it requires, like every other branch of music, a particular talent, and a certain instinctive presentiment of the result of combinations. A composer, in arranging his music, or in making what is called *the score*—that is, a union of all the parts which are to concur in the general effect,—would write only at random, if he had not present to his mind the qualities of the sounds of each instrument, their accent, and the effects which result from their partial or entire combination. Sometimes, it is true, the composer obtains effects which he did not foresee; and, in other cases, those which he strives to produce, do not succeed; but, if skilled in his art, he generally attains the end which he proposes in the arrangement of the instrumentation.

This faculty of foreseeing, by means of the intellectual powers alone, the effect of an orchestra, of which one is arranging the instrumentation, as if that orchestra were actually playing, is not the least of the marvels of music; it is nevertheless what always takes place, when a composer conceives any piece whatsoever; for the melody, the voices which accompany it, the harmony, the effect of the instruments, every thing, in short, is conceived at one gush, if the musician is born truly worthy of the name. As to those who imagine these things only in succession, we may be assured that their musical conceptions will always remain within narrow limits. Such was Grétry, who had a genius for dramatic expression and for happy melodies, but who, being but a second-rate musician, could never conceive, at once, the whole idea of a piece; whereas Haydn, Mozart, Beethoven, Cherubini, and Rossini, never failed to conceive, at a single attempt, the effects which they wished to produce.

There is a kind of knowledge, which is not less useful to a composer; it is that of the peculiar resources of each instrument, of the passages which may be executed on them, and of those which would present insurmountable difficulties. This kind of knowledge may be easily acquired, either by an examination of scores, by the lessons of a master, or, better still, by studying some of the instruments themselves. The pains taken by the composer, to put nothing into a part which an artist cannot execute with ease, will be advantageous in the performance of his music.

It is rare to make use of a single instrument of each kind in instrumentation. The clarinets, oboes, bassoons, horns, and trumpets, are generally employed in couples; but a part is sometimes written for a single flute, when it should be united with the clarinet or oboe parts. Sometimes the horns are four in number; but, in that case, the parts are written for two in one key and two in another. In pieces which require brilliancy and strength, two trumpet parts are added to the horns. The trombone is never employed alone. It is common to unite together the alto, tenor, and bass trombone. The general plan of wind instruments, in an overture, or other great dramatic piece, is composed of two flutes, two oboes, two clarinets, two or four horns, two trumpets, three trombones, and two bassoons. Two drums are almost always added.

Two parts for violins, one or two parts for violas, and for the violoncello and contrebasso, comprise all the stringed instruments for a symphony, and for every other kind of music for a full orchestra. The number of performers to each violin part is undetermined. It may be eight, ten, twelve, and even twenty. The parts for the violas, violoncello, and contrebasso, admit also of a number of performers.

Mozart, Haydn, and some other distinguished composers, changed the plan of instrumentation for their pieces; sometimes they employed only the oboes and horns for the wind instruments; at other times, the flutes and clarinets took the place of the oboes; and, again, the richest resources of the orchestra were combined. Happy contrasts of effects resulted from this variety. In the new school, the whole powers of the orchestra are always combined, in order to obtain the greatest possible effect, whatever may be the character of the piece. Each part in the composition, taken by itself, is more brilliant, thanks to this profusion of resources; but a certain monotony is the inevitable consequence of the uniformity of this system. Unhappily, it is with this defect, as with the abuse of noise,—it has ended by becoming a necessary evil.

The ear which is accustomed to this luxury of instrumentation, though frequently fatigued by it, finds every piece of music feeble without it. Nothing is more fatal to enjoyment than to weary the senses, by strong impressions too long continued, or too often repeated: to the palate of an epicure, exhausted by spices and pepper, simple and natural food is tasteless.

The accompaniments of a piece of well-written music are not confined to the support of the melody by a dependent harmony; we frequently observe in them one or two plans, which seem, at first sight, to be at variance with the principal melody, but which, in reality, concur with it, in the formation of a whole, which is more or less satisfactory. These plans of ornamented accompaniment may disturb an uncultivated ear, but they complete the pleasure of the educated musician and the enlightened amateur. Sometimes they are the most important part of the piece, and the voices become to them, as it were, an accompaniment. This may be observed in those Italian comic airs, which are designated by the words *note and word*, and in choruses. In these cases, it is necessary that the style of the accompaniment should be graceful and pensive, or lively and exciting. The works of Mozart, Cimarosa, and of Paisiello, contain charming things of this kind. Amongst the French works, the operas of Boieldieu are filled with this kind of animating accompaniments.

The brass instruments, such as horns, trumpets, trombones, and ophicleides, have acquired an importance which they did not formerly possess. Méhel and Cherubini began this revolution. Rossini has completed it, and extended the use of these instruments, by a great number of combinations and effects, which were previously unknown. These effects, when employed with moderation, will add much to the power of music, under certain circumstances, in which the use of the ordinary means is insufficient.

Having thus glanced at the rich combinations of effects, the use of which has been pushed even to an abuse, within a few years, the following questions arise; namely, independently of the creations of genius, what is now to be done to multiply and improve those effects, for which there is so general and strong a desire? and can we expect to obtain new ones by a mere increase of noise? No; for the sensations produced by noise are sure to be followed quickly by fatigue. On the other hand, there might perhaps be much difficulty in bringing back the public to the simplicity of the orchestras of Cimarosa, and of Paisiello; for much more genius would be requisite to induce us to take this retrograde march, than to conduct us to the point where we now are. What therefore remains to be done? It seems to me that the course may be pointed out. The following are my ideas on the subject.

Variety, as we know, is the thing most desired, and the most rarely attained, in the arts. The means of obtaining the best effect from an orchestra would therefore be to introduce this variety into the instrumentation, instead of adopting a uniform plan for each piece, as has always been done. All the operas of the seventeenth century have nothing but violins, violas, and bass instruments of the same kind, for their accompaniment. In the beginning of the eighteenth century, the accompaniments consisted of violins, basses, flutes, or oboes. The resources were successively increased, but the forms of instrumentation remained the same, so long as the system was in vigour. In our days, it is rare to find an air, a duet, or even a ballad, which is not accompanied by parts for two violins, alto, violoncello, contrebasso, flutes, oboes, clarinets, horns, trumpets, bassoons, kettle drums, etc.

What a source of monotony is this obstinate perseverance in the production of the same sounds, the same accents, and the same associations? Why should we not, with means much more developed, give to each piece a particular physiognomy, by means of the difference in the quality of instruments? We should have airs, duets, ballads, and even quartets, accompanied by string instruments of different kinds, or by a single one, such as the violoncellos, or altos and violins; and the plan of using these instruments might be divided into two kinds; one of which should consist of sustained sounds, and the other of divided sounds. We might also employ flutes or clarinets alone; oboes with English horns and bassoons; combinations of the brass instruments, such as common trumpets, keyed trumpets, horns, ophicleides, and trombones. This variety, which I propose, might be exhibited not only in different pieces, but even in the course of a single scene. A union of all the resources should take place in the important situations, in the *finales*, etc., and would have the greater effect, as it would be more rare.

All this, it may be said, is not genius. I know it; and it is fortunate that it is not; for, if there were any processes for the manufacture of good music, the art would be little worthy the attention of minds of a high order. But why should we not offer to genius, without which one can do nothing, all the resources which experience or reflection can suggest? Why limit its domain? Reduce Mozart and Rossini to the quartet of Pergolese, and they would still find beautiful melodies and elegant harmony, but they could not produce those powerful effects which you admire in their compositions. How is it possible to suppose the existence of *Don Juan*, and *Moses*, with nothing but violins, altos, and basses? No doubt the fine effect of those compositions is the result of a strong orchestra, and of the genius which has put it in action.

The great masters of the ancient schools have also invented effects of another kind, by the use of means much more simple; and for this reason, I think these means should not be renounced. I wish every thing should be used; the rest may be left to talent. Every body has observed that, at the theatre, pieces without accompaniment always please, when they are well sung; and this effect is a natural consequence of a change of means, independent even of the more or less happy manner in which the composer employs them. Let the same process be attempted in regard to instrumentation, and we shall get rid of that weariness which never fails to be felt towards the end of the representation of a long opera, however beautiful it may be.

CHAPTER XVI.

OF THE FORM OF PIECES IN VOCAL AND IN INSTRUMENTAL MUSIC.

Music, whether vocal or instrumental, has various objects, which denote natural differences in the form of the pieces. There are four great divisions of vocal music: namely, 1, sacred music; 2, dramatic music; 3, domestic music; and, 4, popular airs. Instrumental music is divided into only two principal kinds: namely, 1, orchestra music; and, 2, domestic music. These characteristic kinds are subdivided into several particular classes.

In the music of the church, we find entire masses, vespers, motets, *Magnificat*, *Te Deum*, and litanies. Masses are of two kinds; namely, *short* and *solemn*. A *short mass* is one in which words are scarcely repeated at all. In this kind of mass, the *Kyrie*, the *Gloria*, the *Credo*, the *Sanctus*, and the *Agnus Dei*, which are its principal divisions, form a piece of short duration. It is not the same with the *solemn* or *high mass*, which is sometimes so much extended as to require two or three hours for its performance. In masses of this description, the *Kyrie*, the *Gloria*, and the *Credo*, are divided into several pieces, which are suggested by the nature of the words. For example, after the introduction of the *Credo*, which is ordinarily in the grand style, come the *Incarnatus est*, which should be solemn; the *Crucifixus*, the character of which is sad or melancholy; and the *Resurrexit*, which is filled with animation and joy. The solemn masses of Pergolese, of Leo, of Durante, and of Jomelli,* were not so extensively developed as those of the present day. The reason of this difference lies in the conception of the music of the church. The old masters thought that this kind of music ought to be grand or solemn; but they never thought of making it dramatic. Our modern composers, Mozart and Cherubini, for example, have conceived the music of the church in a manner entirely dramatic, which requires much more development, as it becomes necessary to describe a great number of contrasts indicated by the sacred words.

When the churches were frequented by the higher ranks, during almost the whole length of the services on festivals and Sundays, as was the custom about fifty years ago, vespers were frequently written in music; but since the churches have been less attended, composers have ceased to employ themselves in this sort of music, which required much labour. The *Magnificat*, which made a part of these vespers, is given up, as well as the litany. The *Te Deum*, which serves for occasions of public rejoicing, and the motets, are the only separate pieces of church music on which composers still labour. The extent of these pieces depends upon the fancy of the musician.

In the usages of the Catholic church, there are only two modes of singing the prayers; namely, the *plain-chant* (or simple chanting), and the solemn music.

* Neapolitan masters, who wrote about the middle of the eighteenth century.

The plain-chant, as it is performed in the French churches, is horribly disfigured by bad execution; and the use of the solemn music is every day becoming more rare, so that an ear of any delicacy is constantly liable to be torn in pieces by the braying of the singers, who neither comprehend the words which they pronounce, nor the music which they execute. It is a pity that we cannot, in imitation of the German Protestant churches, introduce into ours a kind of simple and easy music, which may be sung by the people without any other accompaniment than the soft stops of the organ. In a common music of this kind, there would be more of religious devotion, and more satisfaction to the ear. It would have the further advantage of improving the taste of the people, and of banishing the habit of those shocking cries, which render the popular singing odious to a delicate ear.

The *oratorio*, in Italy, Germany, and England, makes a part of the religious music; but, in France, it belongs only to the concert-room, for it is never performed in the churches. When the French composers undertook works of this kind, they always produced them at the sacred concert. Händel, the celebrated German musician, who passed the greater part of his life in England, has composed several magnificent works of this kind, upon English words: of which the *Messiah*, *Judas Maccabeus*, *Athalia*, *Samson*, and the cantanta of *Alexander's Feast*, are particularly mentioned as models of the most elevated style. Whatever may be the future progress of music, Händel will always be regarded as one of the finest geniuses by whom the art has been illustrated.

The kind of music which is the most generally known, is that of the theatre. Everybody undertakes to judge of dramatic music; everybody speaks of it; and none, even of those who are the least versed in the art, are ignorant of its technical terms. But everybody does not know the origin and the variations of the different pieces which enter into the composition of an opera. It will be proper, therefore, to go into some details upon this subject.

Music had been reduced to the symmetrical forms of counterpoint, applicable only to the music of the church and of the parlour, when a number of Italian literati and musicians, among whom we distinguish Vincent Galileo, Mei, and Caccini, conceived the idea of a union of poetry and music, in order to revive the dramatic system of the Greeks, in which poetry was sung. Galileo produced, as the first attempt of this kind of pieces, the episode of the *Count Ugolino*, which he had set to music. The reception which this first essay met with determined the poet Rinuccini to compose the opera of *Daphne* (about the year 1590), which was set to music by Peri and Caccini. This work was followed by *Euridice*, and both had great success. Such was the origin of the opera.

The most important part of these works consisted of recitals, which were sometimes in measure and sometimes without. These recitals took the name of *recitative*. The movement of these ancient recitatives was less lively and less distinct than that of our operas; it was a languid style of singing, occasionally without measure, rather than true recitative; but, for the times, it was, nevertheless, a remarkable innovation, since nothing which had preceded its invention could have given any idea of it.

In the opera of *Euridice*, the second one written, one of the personages sings Anacreontic stanzas, which may be considered as the origin of what is called an air. This piece is preceded by a short prelude. The movements of the bass follow those of the voice, note for note, which gives a heavy character to the piece, but which produces a remarkable difference between this and the recitative, in which the bass frequently sustains its notes. In other respects, the model of the airs of the opera existed before in the popular melodies which had been known time out of mind. Airs took a form somewhat more settled in a musical drama of Stephen Landi's, entitled *Il Santo Alessio*, which was composed and represented at Rome in 1634. The air, which is found in the first act of this work, on the words *se l'hore volano*, is remarkable, not only for the rhythm of the first phrase of the melody, but also for a passage of somewhat extended vocalization upon the *volo;* but, like all the airs of the seventeenth century, it has the fault of containing changes of measure, and of passing alternately from triple to common time. A monotonous form characterizes all the airs of this epoch; they are all cut into couplets like our vaudevilles and ballads. The same custom is found also in all the operas of Cavilli, who composed more than forty, and particularly in his *Jason*, which was represented at Venice in 1649. By a singular arrangement, all the airs of this period were placed at the beginning of the scenes, and not towards the close, as in modern operas.

In the last half of the seventeenth century, the fashion of the airs was changed, and the most skilful composers adopted one which was the most opposed to reason, and the most unfavourable to dramatic effect that could be imagined. These airs began with a slow movement, which was terminated in the key of the piece; then came a lively movement, conceived in a style of scenic expression; after which they returned to the slow movement, which was repeated entire. The least part of the fault of this repetition was, that it destroyed the musical effect just produced by the *allegro;* for it often resulted in a musical absurdity: as for example, in an air of the *Olympiad,* in which Megacles, being determined to separate himself from Aristea, whom he loves, in order to resign her to Licidas, his friend, addresses the latter in the following touching language:—

> Se cerca, se dice:
> L'amico d'ovè?
> L'amico infelice,
> Rispondi, mori, etc.

That is, "If she seek you, and say, '*Where is your friend?*' answer, '*My unhappy friend is dead.*' Ah! no: do not give her so much pain for me; answer only, with tears, '*He is gone.*' What an abyss of misfortune! to leave her whom I love, to leave her for ever, and to leave her thus."

All the composers who have written music upon these words, have not failed, after the lively and dramatic movement on the words *what an abyss of misfortune,* to return coldly to the beginning, and again to take up the slow movement of the words *if she seek*, etc., as if it were possible that Megacles should suddenly become calm after such an explosion of passion. Jomelli was the first who perceived the necessity of ending by the four last lines.

The use of this style of *airs* lasted until the time of Piccini and Sacchini. Many of them were also written in the course of the eighteenth century, composed of a single movement only, very slow and very much drawn out. Such pieces, with all their merit, could not succeed now, when we have become habituated to rhythms more or less rapid and distinct. Simple *cavatinas*, of short duration, can alone be written in this manner.

Among the forms of airs which have had the most success, the *rondeau*, which consists of several repetitions of the first phrase, in the course of the piece, holds the first place. Its invention appears to belong to an Italian composer, of the name of Buononcini, who lived at the commencement of the eighteenth century. At a later period, Sarti, another renowned master, conceived the idea of the *rondeau* in two movements, of which he gave the first example, in the air, *un amante sventurato*, written by him at Rome, for the singer Millico, and which had a prodigious success.

A composer of the finest genius, by the name of Majo, who died too soon for his own fame, gave the first example of an air, in a single *allegro* movement, without repetition, in one which begins with the words *Ah! non parla.* This style of air has had more success in France than in Italy, for almost all the airs of the French operas of the old masters are in this form.

Paisiello, Cimarosa, Mozart, Paër, and Mayer, have written many airs of a mixed character, composed of a slow movement followed by an *allegro*, some of which are masterpieces of impassioned or comic expression. The style of these airs seems to be the most favourable to musical effect. Rossini has adopted another arrangement, which consists in making the first movement an *allegro moderato*, followed by an *andante* or an *adagio*, and terminating the piece by a movement which is lively and strongly marked by rhythm. This would be a good plan for effect, if it did not give too much extent to the pieces, and thus weaken the dramatic action. A movement, growing gradually more and more rapid, is an almost infallible means of reviving the attention of an audience; and the imitators of Rossini, without his genius, frequently make use of it to conceal the poverty of their ideas. It is with these styles of airs, as with the means of instrumentation; we may make use of them to advantage, provided the theme be not stereotyped and presented always in the same manner. All the arrangements of airs above spoken of are admissible, if we know how to employ them properly; and the result of their mixture ought to be a variety which no longer exists, and the want of which is felt more and more every day.

A sort of little air, which is called a *couplet*, when its character is gay, and a *romance*, when it is melancholy, belongs originally to the French opera. At first, the comic opera, as it appeared at the fairs of Saint Laurent and Saint Germain, was nothing more than what we now call the *vaudeville*. The couplets constituted the whole of its materials. This little kind of music, springing from the ancient French taste for songs, is yet very much in favour, and is frequently abused by those composers who are solicitous to please the popular ear. In condemning this profusion of little pieces, however, I am far from rejecting the use of them altogether. Couplets and romances, which require talent and taste on the part of the musician, have the advantage of not retarding the scenic march, like a grand air, and are, at the same time, equally susceptible of agreeable and elegant melodies. All the difference between them consists in their relative extent. Couplets and romances have the further advantage of varying the forms of the airs. The Italian composers have felt the possibility of drawing a good effect from them, and, in their operas within a few years, have introduced romances, which have always been well received, even by the Italians. The romance of *Otello* must be placed at the head of these pieces.

Next to the air, the kind of piece which is most commonly found in the music of the theatre, is the *duet.* Its forms have undergone nearly the same variations as those of the airs. The first example of a duet, is found in the drama of *Il Santo Alessio*, of which I have already spoken; but it is in the Italian comic opera that we find it the most frequently employed. The ancient Italian serious operas contained only a single one, which was always placed in the most interesting scene. At the present day, there is scarcely an opera written, which does not contain several duets, of a comic, serious, or mixed character.

The Italian composers now seem to measure the merit of duets by their display. They are always of the same pattern, that is, the three everlasting movements; and these composers would think themselves disgraced by writing a short and graceful duet, like those in the *Marriage of Figaro*, and *Don Juan*, on the airs *Crudel*, *Perche fin ora*, and *La ci darem la mano*. It will be necessary, however, to make use sometimes of this style of pieces, which, whatever may be said, are more dramatic than the greater number of the long pieces which have succeeded them.

The trios of the opera have their origin in Italy, like all concerted pieces. It is in the comic opera that Logroscino, a Venetian composer, made the first attempt of this sort, about the year 1750. He was surpassed in his effects by Galuppi, another Venetian composer; but it was Piccini, especially, who, in his *Buona Figliola*, carried what are generally called *concerted pieces*, to a very remarkable degree of perfection. The *finale*, which is nothing more than a highly-developed modification of this kind of composition, also became necessary for the termination of acts. It is well known what interest Paisiello, Cimarosa, and Guglielmi, succeeded in giving to this part of the music. The famous septet of *Roi Théodore* was an immense stride in the art of throwing interest into lyrical scenes composed of a number of characters. Mozart afterwards completed this great musical revolution by his wonderful trios, quartets, sextets, and finales, in the *Enchanted Flute*, *Don Juan*, and *Marriage of Figaro*. Rossini has not added anything to the form of concerted pieces; but he has made improvements in the details of rhythm, of the vocal effects, and of instrumentation.

The ancient French composers did not perceive the utility of great combinations of voices, which perhaps would not have been within the comprehension of their audiences. Besides, the subjects of the comic operas were too slight, and the number of their characters too small, to allow of this kind of composition. Philidor, nevertheless, seized the opportunity afforded him by the opera of *Tom Jones*, to make a good quartet. Monsigny, whose knowledge of music was limited, but who possessed a very lively imagination, and much sensibility, in his *Felix*, or the *Enfant trouvé*, made a trio, which, if not very good, was at least very expressive.

As to the serious French opera, Gluck, who settled its form, introduced into his composition nothing but recitative carried to its highest perfection, choruses, and airs, but rarely duets, and scarcely ever trios, quartets, or concerted pieces. The somewhat complicated forms of this kind of music began to be naturalized in France by the labours of Méhul and Cherubini. Conceiving the developments of the lyric scene upon a grander plan than their predecessors, these two great musicians applied the improvements of the Italian opera, modified by the peculiar qualities of their genius, to the French musical drama. Their productions had somewhat more energy than those of Paisiello and Cimarosa; they even amplified the richness of the harmony of which the German school had given the model; they made discoveries in instrumentation, by which Rossini has since profited; and, finally, they were more observant of dramatic exactness; but their melodies are not so happy, and they sometimes make the merit of their music consist more in its arrangement than in its inspiration. Whatever may be our opinion of the kind of music which they have adopted, it cannot be denied that they have rendered great service to the progress of their art.

They it was who introduced grander proportions into music than the French had been accustomed to, and who wrote true concerted pieces, and true finales, worthy the attention of the educated musician and the man of taste. Their example opened the way for other skilful composers, who have succeeded them; and it is the glory of Boieldieu, Catel, Auber, Hérold, and others, that they have received their counsels and followed their example. Boieldieu is particularly distinguished by the grace, elegance, and spirit, which he has had the skill to unite with the forms of music.

One of the qualities by which the French school is most distinguished, is, that it has produced excellent choruses. Rameau was the first who gave brilliancy to the French operas, by the beauty of this kind of composition. If his merit is inferior to that of Händel in richness of learned forms, and in modulation, it cannot be denied, at least, that he has given great dramatic force to the choruses of his operas. Besides, the learned forms of the choruses of oratorios, and the fugues with which they are filled, are not suitable for the stage; for the attention should not be diverted from the principal object, which is the dramatic interest. Since Rameau's time, an immense number of French choruses have been written by Gluck, Méhul, Cherubini, and others of the same school.

This portion of the opera was formerly its weakest part in Italy, because the Italian audiences attached no importance to it. Paër and Mayer were the first to give to the choruses that brilliancy which they ought to have in dramatic music. Rossini succeeded them, and enriched this part of the drama with forms of melody before unknown to it; and the result has been to produce new effects, to which the Italians were not accustomed, but which had the greatest success. The choruses of Weber are arranged in a picturesque and dramatic manner.

The overture of an opera, which the Italians call the *sinfonia*, is considered by some persons as an important part of the music of a drama, and by others as of trifling consequence. The first which enjoyed any reputation in Italy, was the overture to the opera of *Frascatana*, by Paisiello. The overture to the *Iphigénie en Aulide*, by Gluck, had a prodigious effect, when heard for the first time, in 1773, and has since continued to excite admiration, by the mixture of majesty, confusion, and pathos, with which it is filled. The overture of *Démophon*, by Vogel, is also very fine in its opening, and through the whole of the first part; but the end is unworthy of the beginning. Two other overtures have also had much reputation in France—those of the *Caravan* and of *Panurge*, both composed by Grétry. They contain phrases of happy melody, but are so ill constructed that they do not deserve their reputation. Without plan, distinct character, or harmony, their success was only to be ascribed to the unformed taste of the French public. Cherubini has composed several overtures of very remarkable merit, which have become classical, in almost all the concerts of Europe, and are performed with equal success in England, Germany, and France. The most beautiful are those of the *Hôtellerie Portugaise*, and of *Anacreon;* the plan, style, and instrumentation of which are equally admirable.

Among pieces of this kind, that which is considered to be the most beautiful, in whatever point of view it may be examined, is the overture to the *Magic Flute* —an inimitable masterpiece, which will for ever be the model of overtures, and the despair of composers. Every thing is united in this fine work—breadth and magnificence in the opening; novelty in the themes; variety in the mode of reproducing them; profound science in the plan and in the details; striking instrumentation; an interest constantly increasing, and a conclusion full of fire. We may also mention, as models of dramatic interest, the overtures of *Egmont* and of *Prometheus*, by Beethoven. Rossini, in his overtures of *Tancredi*, *Otello*, the *Barbier de Seville*, and of *Semiramide*, has multiplied the happiest melodies, and the most attractive effects of instrumentation; but he has shewn, also, that the finest genius is not always able to make the best use of the happiest ideas. Every piece of instrumental music is, in fact, commonly divided into two parts. The first exhibits the ideas of the author, and modulates into a key relative to the principal key; the second part is devoted to working out these ideas, to a return into the primitive key, and to a repetition of certain passages of the first part. The development of ideas in the second part is the most difficult thing in the management of an overture: it requires preliminary studies in the science of counterpoint, and care in the combinations. Rossini cuts the Gordian knot. He does not make the second part, but confines himself to the introduction of a few chords, in order to return into the primitive key, and then repeats, almost exactly, the whole of the first part in another key. In the overture to *William Tell*, he has taken more pains, and has produced a work more worthy of his brilliant reputation.

It has been frequently said that an overture should be a summing up of the piece, and that it ought to have reference to some passages of the principal situations in it. Several musicians have adopted this idea, and, in consequence, have made a kind of *pot-pourri* of the overture of their opera. The notion seems to me to be strange. If a recapitulation of the opera be necessary, so be it; but it ought certainly to be at the end of the piece, when the hearer can perceive the merit of certain phrases, which recal to mind certain situations of the work. If, on the contrary, these phrases are heard by him before he has any knowledge of the situations, they do not recal anything to his mind, and do not attract more attention than any other phrases might do. Besides, it is well to recollect that no justly esteemed overture is written upon this plan. The overtures of *Iphigénie*, of *Démophon*, of *Don Juan*, of the *Magic Flute*, of *Egmont*, of *Prometheus*, of the *Hôtellerie Portugaise*, and of *Anacreon*, are really dramatic symphonies, and not *pots-pourris*.

Though the overture belongs to instrumental music, I have thought proper to speak of it in connexion with the musical drama. I return now to what concerns the form of vocal pieces.

In the sixteenth and seventeenth centuries, there was a true music for the private concert, which consisted of a sort of vocal pieces, in four, five, or six parts, which were called *madrigals* and *songs*. The use of this kind of music has diminished since the opera has become sufficiently interesting to draw the attention of amateurs. The airs of the opera have insensibly taken the place of what was called the *music of the chamber*, and the latter has almost entirely disappeared. All of it, which has been preserved, are the *canzonette*, in Italy; the *lieder*, in Germany; and the *romances* for one or two voices in France. These different pieces participate of the national taste stamped on the other parts of the music of each of these nations: thus the taste of the Italians for beautiful and embellished melodies may be observed in the *canzonette;* the *lieder*, or German songs, are distinguished by a remarkable frankness of style united with an instinctive feeling of profound harmony; while the French *romances* shine particularly by the dramatic or intellectual character of the words. The name of *nocturnes* is sometimes given to the romances for two voices.

These little pieces occasionally have a prodigious vogue, when first brought out, and their authors enjoy, for ten or twelve years, a brilliant drawing-room reputation, which they lose by the infatuation of the public for the next new comer. A musician, now become celebrated for a higher kind of composition, Boieldieu, wrote charming romances, which were very fashionable; after him came Garat, then Blangini, then Madame Gail, to whom Romagnesi succeeded; Beauplan enjoyed a moment's fame; and, at present, Labarre, Panseron, and Masini, are all the rage.

Instrumental music is divided into several branches, which are all included under two principal kinds—1, concert music; and, 2, chamber music.

The *symphony* holds the first rank in concert music. It derives its origin from a certain kind of instrumental pieces, which were formerly called, in Italy, *ricercari da suonare,* and in Germany, *partien,* and which were composed of songs varied, airs for the dance, and of fugues or fugued pieces, designed to be performed by viols, bass viols, lutes, theorbes, etc. When these pieces went out of fashion, their place was supplied by pieces divided into two parts, of a movement somewhat lively, followed by another piece of a slower movement, and by a rondeau, which derived its name from the repetition of its principal phrase. The first symphonies were composed only of two parts for violins, one for the alto and one for the bass. A German musician, by the name of Vanhall, began to improve the symphony, by adding two oboes and two horns. He was imitated by Toelsky, Van Malder, and Stamitz. Gossec added parts for clarinets and bassoons to the other instruments, and the addition of the *minuet* and *trio* increased the number of pieces which already existed in the symphony. The minuet derives its name from the measure, in triple time, in which it is written. It was formerly almost of as slow a movement as the dance of which it bears the name; but the time of it has been gradually quickened, and Beethoven has, at last, made it a *presto*. It is for this reason that he has dropped the name of *minuet*, and substituted that of *scherzo (badinage)*. I have not been able to discover the meaning of the word *trio*, which is given to the second part of the minuet. It may be that it comes from the composer's sometimes suppressing one of the instruments in this second part.

One can hardly pronounce the name of symphony without awakening the recollection of Haydn. This great musician so much improved the plan and the details of this kind of music, that he is, in some sort, the creator of it. The history of the progress of the genius and talent of that astonishing man, is in itself the history of the progress of the art. His first works proved his superiority over his contemporaries; but they were much inferior to those which subsequently issued from his pen. If we keep in mind the fact that these works were always adapted to the skill of the performers, by whom they were to be executed,—a skill which Haydn himself excited and in part created,—we shall be able to conceive, without difficulty, what profound talent was necessary to produce those masterpieces, with the limited means at his command. If the knowledge of the performers of Haydn's time had been equal to what now exists, he would have left nothing for his successors to do. The principal talent of Haydn consists in making the most of the simplest idea, working it out in a manner the most learned, the richest in harmony, and the most unexpected in its effects, without ever ceasing to be graceful. He is distinguished also by the directness and clearness of his plan, which is such that the least educated amateur can follow out its details with as little difficulty as the most skilful musician. Mozart, who is always impassioned, and always excited by deep feeling, shines less than Haydn in the development of the subject of his symphonies; but in the exquisite sensibility with which he was so abundantly endowed, there is a power of emotion which always carries away the audience, and excites their sympathy.

Beethoven, whose talent was for a long time misunderstood in France, now reigns supreme in the symphony. Bolder than the two great artists whom I have just mentioned, he never fears encountering the greatest difficulties, and frequently achieves a happy triumph. His genius carries him to the highest regions, and no one has a better knowledge of the effect of instrumentation, in which he has made many discoveries; but he is frequently fantastic and peculiar, sometimes incorrect, and seems rather to extemporize than to follow any settled plan. In fine, he shares the fortune of all men of genius, by occupying the attention, rather with the beauties of which he is prodigal, than with the faults which disfigure them.

Quartets, quintets, sextets, etc., are mere diminutives of the symphony, and designed to take its place in private concerts. Haydn, Mozart, and Beethoven, are also the masters of this kind of miniature symphony, in which they frequently display such talent, that we forget the limited extent of the means which they employ. The same qualities which they have infused into their grand symphonies, are found in their quartets.

Boccherini, a man who lived poor, isolated, and unknown, in Spain, has also cultivated this kind of music, and particularly the quintet, with a rare felicity of inspiration. Not having sufficient communication with the world to be informed of the progress of music and the variations of taste, he composed during a period of nearly fifty years, without renewing his musical sensations by hearing or reading the works of Haydn or Mozart; he drew every thing from his own mind, and hence the independence of manner and style, the originality of ideas, and the charming simplicity, which characterize his productions. We may, perhaps, wish for more learning, more richness of harmony, and something less of antiquity, in the forms of the music of Boccherini, but not for more true inspiration.

The *sonata*, for a single instrument, or for several united, is also a sort of symphony. Its name comes from *suonare*, which signifies to play upon one or more instruments. This word was formerly applied to none but stringed or wind instruments. In speaking of keyed instruments, they used the word *toccare*, from whence has been formed the word *toccata*, which signifies *a piece to be touched*. For nearly a century, however, the term *sonata* has been applied to all pieces of this kind, for whatever instrument they may be composed.

Like the symphony or the quartet, the sonata is divided into several pieces, consisting of a first movement, an adagio, and a rondeau; sometimes, but rarely, a minuet is added. Sonatas accompanied by one or two instruments, ordinarily take the name of *duets* or *trios*. Sonatas are sometimes composed for the piano, to be executed by two persons. The four hands embrace the whole extent of the key-board, and fill up the harmony in a rich and interesting manner, when these pieces are written by a skilful composer.

The best sonatas for the piano are those of Charles Philip Emanuel Bach, Haydn, Mozart, Beethoven, Clementi, Dusseck, and Cramer. The fugued sonatas of John Sebastian Bach, for the harpsichord and violin, are masterpieces. Krumpholtz has been for the music of the harp what Clementi was for that of the piano, that is to say, the model of those who have since written for the instrument. An uncommonly elevated style and striking effects of harmony are the qualities for which this composer is distinguished. Corelli, Tartini, Locatelli, and Leclair, are at the head of the authors who have composed the best sonatas for the violin. Francischello and Duport are distinguished for the composition of sonatas for the violoncello. In regard to sonatas for wind instruments, there are but few which deserve to be mentioned. Generally, the music for these instruments remains in a state of manifest inferiority. A composer of talent might acquire reputation by placing this kind of music upon a level with the pieces which have been written for all the other instruments. There are only one or two beautiful things, by Mozart and Beethoven, of this kind. Krommer has also written music for wind instruments, which produces some effect; and Reicher has since produced the best works of this kind that are known in France.

For some years the sonata has fallen into discredit. A certain frivolousness of taste, which has invaded music, has substituted, in the place of the serious forms of this kind of pieces, a lighter sort of works, called *fantasies*, *airs with variations*, *caprices*, etc. The fantasy was originally a piece in which the composer abandoned himself to all the impulses of his imagination. It had neither plan nor order. The inspiration of the moment, art, and even science, though carefully concealed, constituted the fantasy, as Bach, Händel, and Mozart, made it. But this is not what we now understand by that word. In no composition can there be less of fantasy than in those pieces which have that name at the present day. Every thing in them, art and science excepted, is regulated, measured, and arranged, upon a plan which is invariably the same. To hear one modern fantasy, is to hear the whole. They are all made upon the same model, with the exception of the principal theme, which, however, is not even original, since it almost always consists of the melody of a romance, or of an air from some opera. As a fantasy always terminates by variations upon the theme, the *air with variations* does not differ from it. It is not possible that disgust and satiety should be slow to follow the abuse made of these forms of composition; we shall then return to music more real in its character, and art will again enter upon its legitimate domain.

These melancholy fantasies and monotonous variations have also usurped the place of the *concerto*,—a sort of piece which is not without fault, but which has the advantage, at least, of shewing the talent of the artist on an extensive scale. *Concerto*, an Italian word, which formerly signified *a concert*, or an assemblage of musicians, who executed divers pieces of music (*academia* is the word now used), was originally written *concento*. In the seventeenth century, the name of *concerto* began to be given to pieces composed for the purpose of exhibiting one principal instrument, which the others accompanied; but it was not until about the time of Corelli, a celebrated Roman violinist, that this kind of piece became fashionable. It is generally believed that another violinist, named Torelli, who preceded Corelli by some years, gave to the concerto the fame which it retained until about the year 1760. The concerto, when it was accompanied by a double quartet of violin, viola, and bass, was called *concerto grosso*, or grand concert. The *concerto grosso* contained passages of *tutti*, in which all the instruments were employed; but another kind of concerto, called the *concerto da camera*, contained only one principal part, with simple accompaniments. Originally, concertos were written only for violins; but they have since been composed for all the instruments, and sometimes with accompaniments of full orchestra.

The concertos for the violin, composed by Corelli, Vivaldi, and Tartini, were formerly celebrated; they are so still in the school, and deserve the respect of artists, by their greatness of thought and dignity of style. Stamitz, Lolli, and Jarnowich, though not wanting in merit, had not the ability to sustain the elevated character of the concerto. The object of their efforts was to satisfy the public by agreeable compositions, and it must be acknowledged that they frequently succeeded. The first of these violinists, who was born in Bohemia, and enjoyed a great reputation at the court of Manheim, about the year 1750, reduced the number of the pieces of which the concerto was composed, to two—namely, a first piece and a *rondeau*, each of which he also divided into three solos, intermingled with *tutti* passages. The rondeaus of Jarnowich had much success. At last came Viotti, who, without producing anything new in regard to the form of the concerto, shewed such powers of invention, in melody, in embellishment, in the form of his accompaniments, in harmony, and in modulation, that he soon threw his predecessors into oblivion, and left his rivals without the hope of competition. Viotti did not shine by his learning: his studies had been moderate; but the richness of his imagination was such, that he was not under the necessity of considering how to economize his ideas. He composed much more by instinct than by reflection; but that instinct guided him, as by miracle, and made him hit right, even in harmony.

Concertos for the harpsichord were not attempted until a long time subsequent to the first compositions of the same kind for the violin, and concertos for wind instruments not until a still later period; but they were both mere imitations of the settled forms of the concerto established by Stamitz. These are precisely the forms, nevertheless, which seem to me to be wrong, and wearisome to an audience. How is it that we still remain attached to so defective a style as that of those concertos, where the first *tutti* brings out exactly the same phrases as the first solo?—where the same modulation follows from the tonic to the dominant, in order to return afterwards to the tonic, and recommence the same strain?—where those solos, which are nothing more than a development of the same ideas, are constantly reproduced, with no other change than that of the key?—where the interminable cadences, multiplied for the purpose of giving notice to the audience when to applaud the performer, contribute to render the piece more monotonous?—and, finally, where the last piece reproduces nearly the same plan, and all the defects of the first allegro? It is high time to seek for means of avoiding these faults, and to give up these ready-made frames for all sorts of subjects. The fancy of a composer should be free. His ideas ought not to be fitted to a form, but the form to the ideas.

There is another kind of instrumental music, which may be considered as a branch of sacred music: I mean pieces for the organ. The immense resources of this instrument invite the genius of the organist to variety; and, besides, the diversity of forms of worship, and of the ceremonies of each, occasion the employment of many different styles. For example: in the Protestant churches, the organist ought to be able to accompany the hymns and choral pieces by a harmony rich in effect and in modulation. He ought also to possess a fruitful imagination for the preludes to the hymns, and be able to vary them with elegance, and without neglecting science, or sinning against the majesty of the temple. The fugue, the true foundation of the art of playing the organ, should be familiar to the artist; and, finally, he should possess a knowledge of the ancient styles, and be able to make the best use of them in favourable circumstances. Germany has produced a prodigious number of great organists. Since the time of Samuel Scheidt, who lived at Hamburgh, in the commencement of the seventeenth century, and who possessed talents of the first order, there have appeared Buxtehude, Reinken, John Sebastian Bach, Kittel, and others, whose compositions, in all the different kinds of organ pieces, will, for a long time to come, be considered as models of perfection.

The art of the Catholic organist is still more extended. The necessity of well understanding the plain chants, both Italian and French, as well as the different modes of accompanying them, whether by placing them in the bass or in the upper part; the art of treating the masses, vespers, *Magnificat*, hymns, chants, and *Te Deum*, according to the importance of the festivals, the offertories, and other great pieces, the fugues or the fugued style;—all this, I say, belongs to this branch of the art, the difficulty of which is understood but by few. According to the common prejudice, an organist is a vulgar artist, to whom little attention is given; but, in reality, an organist who possesses all the qualities of his art, ought to stand upon a level with the most renowned composers, for nothing is more difficult, or more rare, than to meet with such a combination.

It is manifest that the inventory of the Catholic organist should be much richer than that of the Protestant. After Frescobaldi, and a small number of

Italian and French organists, who have left fine works, we find nothing more. Unhappily, there is not a single situation of organist in France which offers sufficient means of living. It is not astonishing, therefore, that the emulation of artists should not be excited, and that the art of writing for the organ should degenerate more and more. It is doubtful whether this art will ever revive, if talent cannot hope for an honourable existence by it.

In the sketch, which has been given, of the forms of pieces of music, some secondary kinds have been omitted, because they are only divisions, or rather slight modifications, of more important kinds; but nothing essential has been forgotten.

PART III.

OF EXECUTION.

CHAPTER XVII.

OF SINGING, AND OF SINGERS.

When a singer, endowed with a fine voice, with intelligence and feeling, and who has devoted several years of his life to bringing out, by study, the qualities nature has given him; — when, I say, this singer comes to try for the first time, in public, the effect of those advantages which seem to assure him success, and suddenly finds his hopes disappointed, he accuses the public of injustice, and the public treats him as ignorant and presumptuous. In this case, both parties are in the wrong; for, on the one hand, he who is not familiar with his own powers, but by the effect which they have produced in the school, is not in a condition to make a proper use of them in the presence of a numerous assembly, and in a large hall; and, on the other, the public is in too great haste to judge by its first impressions, having neither sufficient experience or knowledge to discern the good which is mingled with the bad, nor to take into account the circumstances which may prevent a favourable exhibition of the singer's talents. How often does the public itself revise its own judgments, for want of having passed them at first with a proper knowledge of the case! So many things are to be attended to in the art of singing, that, without having made it a particular study, or having learned by reflection and experience in what it consists, it is very difficult to judge of a singer, at the first hearing, either in regard to his merits or his defects.

In order to sing, it is not enough to possess a fine voice; though this gift of nature is an invaluable advantage, which no degree of skill can possibly supply. But one who possesses the art of regulating his voice with firmness, and understands the management of its powers, sometimes produces a better effect, with an inferior voice, than an ignorant singer can do with a fine one.

The delivery (or *placing of the voice*) consists in adapting as perfectly as possible the motions of respiration to the emission of sound, so as to bring out the power of the latter, as much as the quality of the organ and the conformation of the chest will admit, without carrying it to that degree of effort which makes the sound degenerate into a cry. When there were such things as good schools of vocal music in Italy, the delivery of the voice *(la mise de voix)*, as it was called by the singers of that day, was a study of several years; for people did not then think, as they do now, that accomplishment is instinctive. The following anecdote will enable us to form an idea of the pains bestowed both by masters and pupils on this study.

Porpora, one of the most illustrious masters of Italy, conceived a friendship for a young pupil, and asked him if he had courage to persevere with constancy in the course which he should mark out for him, however wearisome it might seem. Upon his answer in the affirmative, the master noted, upon a single page of ruled paper, the diatonic and chromatic scales, ascending and descending, the intervals of third, fourth, fifth, etc., in order to teach him to take them with freedom, and to sustain the sounds, together with *trills, groups, appogiaturas,* and passages of vocalization of different kinds.

This page occupied both the master and scholar during an entire year, and the year following was also devoted to it. When the third year commenced, nothing was said of changing the lesson, and the pupil began to murmur; but the master reminded him of his promise. The fourth year slipped away, the fifth followed, and always the same eternal page. The sixth year found them at the same task, but the master added to it some lessons in articulation, pronunciation, and, lastly, in declamation. At the end of this year, the pupil, who still supposed himself in the elements, was much surprised, when his master said to him, "Go, my son; you have nothing more to learn; you are the first singer of Italy and of the world." He spoke the truth, for this singer was Caffarelli.

This mode of instruction is no longer pursued. A pupil who places himself under the care of a master, only goes to him to learn such an air or such a duet; the pencil of the master traces some features, some ornaments; the unfledged singer catches what he can, and immediately ranks himself with the first artists; so that we have no more Caffarellis. There is not now in Europe a single school in which six years are given to teaching the mechanical part of singing. It is true, in order to devote so much time to this branch, the pupils must be taken in extreme youth, and the unfavorable chances of the change of voice may suddenly render useless the labour of several years. The voice of eunuchs did not present the same inconveniences, and it had, besides, the advantage of a natural position; so that these unfortunate beings were the most perfect singers that the world has ever seen. If it is a triumph for the cause of morals that humanity no longer tolerates these disgraceful mutilations, it is a calamity for the art to be deprived of these admirable voices. We cannot form an idea, at the present day, of such singers as Balthazar Ferri, Severino, Farinelli, and others, who flourished in the first half of the eighteenth century. Crescentini, who terminated his career as a singer at the court of Napoleon, and who is now professor of singing at the Royal College of Naples, is the last virtuoso of this beautiful Italian school.

Next to the voices of eunuchs, those of women have the least to fear from the change. The only effect of the approach of womanhood is a certain attenuation of quality, which ordinarily lasts two or three years, after which the voice regains its brilliancy, and acquires more purity and smoothness than it possessed before the change.

From eighteen to thirty, women enjoy all the beauty of their voices, when the gifts of nature have not been injured by badly-directed studies.

A remark has already been made concerning the chest voice, and the mixed or head voice of men. The latter not being possessed by women, they are enabled to rise with more facility than tenors. But if they are destitute of the advantage of the head voice, they have at least that of more equality. The voices of women are naturally less well placed (*posées*) than those of men. We generally observe in them a sort of little dull hissing, which precedes the sound, and which gives rise to the habit of taking the note a little flat, in order to carry it afterwards to its true sound. Masters are not sufficiently attentive to the correction of this fault. When the habit of it has been contracted a year or two, the evil is without remedy. The rarity of very pure voices in women adds to their value. Madame Barilli was endowed with one; Madame Damoreau possesses the same advantage.

The most useful training, in the art of singing, especially for the female sex, is that of the respiration, which is shorter in women than in men. This is the reason that they often take breath in the wrong place, so as to change the effect of the musical phrase, or to injure their pronunciation.

I have made use of the terms *to carry on the sound*, *trills*, *groups*, *appogiaturas*, *fioritures*, etc. It is proper that I should explain their signification.

If two sounds follow each other in such a way that there is a separate articulation of the throat upon each one of them, and each disconnected from the other, the effect is called *detached* or *staccato*. The articulation of two sounds, which are made by uniting the first to the second, by a connexion of the throat, is called *port* of the voice. *To carry on the sound* is to unite one sound to another by a movement of the throat.

The *trill,* which is frequently but improperly called a cadence, is the alternate and rapid passing from one note to the neighbouring note. It is one of the most difficult effects to produce in the art of singing. Some singers have the trill naturally in their oices; others acquire it only by a long and painful labour.

The *group* is a rapid succession of three or four sounds, which serves as a sort of embroidery to notes, which the singer believes to be too simple for the effect of the song. The group is a useful ornament; but certain singers are too prodigal of it, and give it at last an air of vulgarity.

The *appogiatura* is an ornamental note, which is sometimes joined to a written note, and takes the half of its length. It may be taken above or below the real note. The taste and discernment of the singer must guide him in the choice of this ornament.

Fioritures is a word which means, in general, all kinds of ornament, and, in particular, certain passages composed of diatonic or chromatic scales, of passages in thirds, ascending or descending, etc. They are indispensable in singing, but they must not be abused. The merit of the greater number of singers of the existing school is almost confined to the talent of executing *fioritures* with rapidity. Formerly the composer wrote the air plain, and left the selection of these *fioritures* to the singer—a circumstance which added to the variety of the music; for all the performers not being guided in the same manner, they chose their embellishments according to the inspiration of the moment, so that the same piece was almost always presented under a different aspect. When the schools of vocal music began to decline, the singers were less capable of choosing for themselves the ornaments suitable to each kind of piece; and the thing came to such a point, that Rossini found himself obliged, almost always, to write the *fioritures* with which he desired to embellish his melodies. This method, at first, had a pretty good result, which was to disguise the weakness of the singers, by making them repeat a lesson; but, in the end, it had also the inconvenience of rendering the music monotonous, by presenting it always under the same aspect; and, further, it accustomed the singers no longer to take the trouble to seek for new forms of ornaments, since they found them already made to the extent of their means of execution. This finished the ruin of a school of which there are now no traces remaining.

The mechanical part of singing, even the most perfect, is an indispensable part of the merit of a good singer; but it is not all. The most successful delivery of the voice, the best-regulated respiration, the purest execution of the ornaments, and what is very rare, the most perfect intonation, are the means by which a great singer expresses the sentiment which animates him; but they are nothing more than means; and he who should persuade himself that the whole art of the singer is comprised in them, might sometimes give his audience a degree of tranquil pleasure, but would never cause them to experience vivid emotion. The great singer is one who identifies himself with the personage whom he represents, with the situation in which he is placed, and the feelings which agitate him; who abandons himself to the inspiration of the moment, as the composer should do in writing the music which he performs; and who neglects nothing which may contribute to the effect, not of an isolated piece, but of a whole character. The union of all these qualities constitutes what is called *expression*. Without expression, there never was a great singer, however perfect the mechanical part of his singing might be; and expression, when it is real, and not merely laboured acting, has often obtained pardon for an incorrect performance.

The celebrated singers of the eighteenth century were not less renowned for their power of expression than for the beauty of their mechanical performance. Some things are related of them which would appear almost fabulous at the present day. Everybody knows the story of Farinelli, whose touching voice and expression cured the king of Spain, Philip V., of an attack of melancholy, which threatened his reason. The anecdote of Raff, who saved the life of the Princess Belmont, put in jeopardy by a violent fit of grief, by causing her to shed a torrent of tears, also attests the vast power of expression possessed by these great singers. Senesino, a singer of extraordinary merit, forgetting his part, in order to embrace Farinelli, who happened to sing an air with a miraculous perfection; La Gabrielli, affected even to the exhibition of the most lively emotion, upon hearing Marchesi sing a *cantabile;* and Crescentini, causing Napoleon and all his court to shed tears in Romeo and Juliet,—are also proofs of the power of expression which these divinities of song possessed. At moments, when Madame Malibran avoids exaggeration, and exhibits true expression, combined with irreproachable execution, she gives us an idea of this sort of merit; but, if I may judge of the others by Crescentini, whom I have heard, these singers maintained, during the whole of a part, that perfection which Madame Malibran exhibits only at intervals.

The French singers have never possessed that union of qualities which has been admired in the Italians. One alone, endowed with a warmth of feeling, with a winning playfulness of imagination, and with a delicate taste, approached them nearly in certain respects, and possessed peculiar qualities, which, in another department of the art, made him one of the most astonishing singers that ever lived. This singer was Garat. No singer was more happily organized, and no one ever had more comprehensive ideas of the art of singing. The thoughts of Garat were always ardent, but he knew how to regulate them by art and reason. An air, or a duet, according to this great singer, did not consist in a succession of well-performed or even well-expressed phrases; he wanted a plan, a gradual progress, which led to great effects at the proper moment, and when the excitement had reached its crisis. He was rarely understood, when, discussing his art, he spoke of the plan of a vocal piece, and musicians themselves were persuaded that his ideas were somewhat exaggerated on this subject; but when he joined example to precept, and, to demonstrate his theory, sung an air, with the different colouring which he could give to it, they then comprehended how much of reflection and study were necessary to arrive at perfection in an art, which, at the first view, seems destined only to procure enjoyment for the ear.

One of the most invaluable qualities of Garat was the beauty of his pronunciation; it was not merely a perfect clearness of articulation,—a sort of merit which is indeed rare,—but was in him a powerful means of expression. It is but justice to acknowledge that this quality belongs more to the French school of vocal music than to any other; and in it Gluck laid the foundation of the style which he adopted for our Opera. In the pronunciation of the French language there is a degree of energy, which is not favourable, perhaps, to the soft and graceful emission of the voice, but which makes it very proper for dramatic expression. Unhappily, some of the actors at the Opera, such as Lainé and Adrien, have abused this peculiar character of the French language, and have caused this dramatic expression to degenerate into excess. In their manner of scanning the words, the voice came out only by fits, and with an effort, so that the sounds produced were often very disagreeable cries. In the manner established at the Opera, there was no appearance of a regulated delivery of the voice, or of vocalization, nor a single trace of what is called in Italy the *art* of singing. It was, if you will, musical declamation; but those who limited their art to this declamation could not pass for singers. Garat alone could pronounce in a dramatic manner, without departing from the beautiful traditions of the true school of vocal music, and could give to his singing a great dramatic expression, without neglecting any of the resources of vocalization.

The state of the French singing differs in some respects from that of the Italian. A pure and sonorous voice, a clear and regular pronunciation, and a dramatic expression, were all that was required of the French singers for a long period. An unreasonable prejudice had made embellishments and ornament considered as unsuited to our language. The Comic Opera has been insensibly freed from the obstacles which this prejudice had placed in its way; but the Opera had always resisted. The latter has at last yielded to the dominion of fashion, and its progress has been rapid in the new style. It is matter of congratulation, that the time has arrived when lyric declamation no longer interests an audience, whose taste has taken another direction, since it has become accustomed to the Italian music.

Still, care must be taken not to run from one extreme into another. It is well to preserve the peculiar physiognomy of the music of any country. Servile imitation is never a conquest. A reasonable use of ornaments in the French style of singing is necessary; its excess would be injurious. In our theatrical habits, there is a very proper desire to exclude those pieces so out of place, which have no object but to exhibit the flexibility of a voice. Let us admit embellishments and every kind of ornament, but let us not banish our dramatic forms, to which nothing is wanting but more elegant and graceful melodies. Especially let us not lose the traditionary knowledge of that beautiful recitative, in the style of Gluck, the merit of which is so well appreciated by the Italian composers of the present day, that they endeavour to approach it as nearly as they can.

There is one point to which the authority which has thus far directed the arts in France, has not as yet given sufficient attention: I mean the preparation and preservation of singers. What I call the preparation of singers consists in the selection of persons and their education in respect to health. If the persons selected to be educated as singers presented themselves with voices entirely formed, and safe from those physical revolutions which modify individuals in their youth, nothing would be easier than to make this selection. But it is not so: out of one hundred individuals who have a pretty voice in their infancy, ninety will lose it at the period of change, or will recover it only in a moderate degree when it has lost its quality; and among the ten who have been more favoured by fortune, we are not always certain of meeting with a single one who unites to the excellence of his organ a sufficient degree of deep and lively feeling to become what may be justly called a *singer*. This sentiment manifests itself in infancy in such a manner as to be readily perceived by a master who possesses the qualities necessary to the exercise of his art. Two sounds are enough to indicate it. But will the pupil in whom it is discovered be one of those who preserve their voice? This is a question which cannot be settled by any external sign. This uncertainty was the cause of the mutilation of individuals of the male sex.

Discouraged by a great number of fruitless trials

made with children of the male sex, none are admitted into the public schools of vocal music but adults, with whom there are not the same risks to be run. But here a new difficulty presents itself; one which is greater, because it is without remedy, and almost without exception; which is, that the individuals who arrive at the age of puberty without having laid a foundation for their musical education by long studies, scarcely ever become musicians, either in regard to the reading of music at first sight, or to the feeling of the rhythm. Whatever may be the beauty of the voice, its flexibility, or quality, and however just the feeling both of intonation and expression, possessed by a singer who commenced his musical education after the period of early youth, he will never be anything more than an incomplete artist, whose execution will offer no security, because he will be guided only by a sort of instinct, which may frequently be at fault.

Placed between two kinds of difficulties, equally formidable, it is necessary that the government, which defrays the expense of the musical education of singers, should neglect no chance of success, and run many risks of pure loss, in order to obtain some happy results. But it is not necessary to rely entirely upon chance, in order to procure persons for trial; for we might be a long time deceived in our hopes. The following method should be adopted:—

Experience has demonstrated that voices, like vineyards, are, in general, distributed in France, by districts. Picardy furnishes finer basses and in greater number than any other province; and almost all the fine basses which have shone at the Opera, and in the other musical establishments, were from that province. Tenors, and particularly those which are called *high counters* or *counter-tenors*, are to be met with in greater number in Languedoc, and especially in Toulouse and its environs, than in any other part of France. The voices of this kind in that country are of singular beauty, and the chance of preserving them, after the change, is much more favourable there than elsewhere. Lastly, in Burgundy and Frenche-Comté, the female voices have more extent, and a purer quality, than in all the other provinces. Without seeking to explain this singular circumstance, it is sufficient to establish it, in order to be convinced of the necessity of seeking, in the different parts of France which have been above mentioned, the children who are intended for the profession of singers, and to confide the selection of them to the care of an enlightened man, who should have a due sense of the importance of his mission. There is no doubt that, by means of precautions of this kind, we may obtain, at the end of seven or eight years, a certain number of good singers, the want of which is felt more and more every day.

In order to supply this want of singers, pupils whose musical education has scarcely been commenced are brought upon the stage. This ruinous method is practised not only in France, but in Italy. A singer brought forward in this manner remains in mediocrity all his days, for want of the employment of two or three years in perfecting his studies; and thus talents are fruitlessly dissipated, which might have furnished durable resources. Governments which constitute themselves the protectors of the arts, ought to put an end to this deplorable evil. In a word, it is not enough to prepare singers. They must also be preserved; and this requires care of more than one kind. The method formerly pursued by Lainé, Adrien, and all those masters who were called *professors of lyric declamation*, had for its inevitable effect to destroy the voices in the very beginning, by their ignorance of what concerns the delivery of the voice, and vocalization, and still more by the exaggerated efforts which they required of pupils whose physical constitution was scarcely formed. The emission of the sound never being made in a natural manner, and the strength of the lungs being constantly exerted, the most robust voices were unable to resist the fatigue of a labour for which the Herculean strength of Adrien had been insufficient. Thus, for several years, voices which were free and of good quality, and which had not been procured without much difficulty, were destroyed before they were able to leave the Royal School of Music. This evil at length disappeared, with the music which gave birth to it, and with the professors who were charged with the teaching of it. But all is not yet done.

The care which the preservation of the voice requires ought to commence from the moment of its first emission. Now, it is to be remarked that, besides the art of singing, there is a preliminary part of music, called *solmization*, which is designed to form skilful readers, by the execution of certain progressive exercises upon all the difficulties of time and intonation. The study of these exercises is made ordinarily in childhood, under the direction of masters who, for the most part, are strangers to the art of singing. No care is taken, either in the composition or in the selection of these exercises, in reference to the extent of voices; so that it almost always happens that children are made to sing out of the limits which nature has assigned to them. The efforts which they are obliged to make to reach the high sounds which they are made to sing, very soon destroy the foundation of the voice, and strain the fibres of the throat. When this is once done, there is no remedy. All the art in the world cannot give such children smoothness of voice, for they have lost it for ever. Add to this, that the precautions necessary to take in the beginning, to deliver the sound with the respiration, not to respire too frequently, and not to weary the chest by retaining the breath too long,—all this, I say, is completely unknown to the majority of the masters of *solfeggio*. After two or three years' practice, they succeed in forming good readers of music; but they have, in the mean time, destroyed or injured the voices of their pupils; and in this state they deliver them to the professors of the vocal art, all whose skill can never restore to these poor young people that which they have irretrievably lost.

The following suggestions will furnish a mode by which this evil may be corrected. The reading of music is independent of the art of singing; and it is therefore useless to unite in study two things which are naturally separated. The instructions of the professor of solfeggio, if limited to teaching the pupil to read music, by merely naming the notes, without singing them, and to dividing with exactness all the times of the measure and all the combinations of the notes, would surely be sufficient to attain the end proposed in this preliminary study. In regard to intonation, to which the ear must be accustomed, this ought to be the business of the professor of singing, who should prepare his pupils for it with the proper precautions. From the first moment that a child attempts to emit sounds with the voice, he should be forewarned against the *errors* of a bad method, and every thing should concur to make the best possible use of the original capacities of the organ.

Let it not be believed, in conclusion, that I am here broaching a new theory of the division of musical studies; for it was thus that the study was conducted in Italy, when the art of vocal music was cultivated there with success. Experience, as well as reason, proves the necessity of this division of musical studies. The interest of the masters of solfeggio would perhaps suffer something by it, for they are willing enough to be considered as professors of singing. I do not doubt that time will effect this important improvement in musical studies, which, for several years, have been making great progress in France.

CHAPTER XVIII.

OF INSTRUMENTAL PERFORMANCE.

§ 1. *Of the Art of Playing on Instruments.*

INSTRUMENTAL performance is naturally divided into the individual and collective. It is composed of the art of playing on individual instruments, and of combining the performances of a certain number of persons, so as to produce an united effect in time and sentiment. It is proper to treat separately of each of these things.

Instruments, as is commonly known, are divided into five principal kinds: the *first* is composed of instruments played with the bow; the *second*, of instruments played by snapping the strings; the *third*, of instruments with key-boards; the *fourth*, of wind instruments; and the *fifth*, of instruments of percussion. Each of these kinds of instruments requires peculiar qualities, to be well played; thus instruments played with the bow demand especially a delicate ear, to produce precision of tone, which is formed by pressing the fingers upon the strings, and much suppleness of arm, for the management of the bow. Good execution, upon instruments played by snapping the strings, cannot be attained without great strength of finger, to resist the impression of the strings, and to obtain a fine tone. Instruments with key-boards, in which the intonations are already made, require length, suppleness, activity, and strength of fingers. In order to acquire skill upon wind instruments, the same accuracy of ear is requisite, as for stringed instruments; and, besides, the faculty of moving the lips with facility, of modifying their pressure, and of regulating the force of the breath,—qualities which collectively constitute what is called the *embouchure*. As to instruments of percussion, it seems, at first view, that any robust man ought to possess the necessary qualities for playing on them; yet great differences are perceptible between different drummers, though they may have had the same education. To play the drum, the performer must possess a certain suppleness of wrist, and a certain power of touch, which it would be impossible to analyse, but which are not the less real.

In the enumeration of qualities necessary to play well upon instruments, I have not mentioned sensibility or imagination, which are elements of all talent, because we were considering none but physical qualities. In vain would a pianist or oboeist be endowed with the most exquisite sensibility, if the fingers of the one were stiff or feeble, and the lips of the other thin and dry; they could no more become great instrumentists, than could the best made man become a singer, if he had no voice.

The playing of bowed instruments, as the violin, alto, violoncello, and contrebasso, is composed of two distinct parts; the *fingering* and *the management of the bow*. The fingering (or *touch*) is the art of forming the intonations by the pressure of the fingers upon the strings against the upper part of the neck or finger-board. This pressure, which shortens the vibrating length of the string, more or less, cannot produce pure sounds, unless it is very energetic, for a string does not vibrate in a satisfactory manner, except when it is very firmly fixed at its points of attachment. It is, consequently, necessary that a violinist or violoncellist should press the fingers with much force upon the strings, notwithstanding the painful sensation which this exercise produces in the commencement of his studies. Sometimes the ends of an artist's fingers become armed with a sort of callus, or hardening of the skin, by the long use of his instrument. No inconvenience, however, seems to result from this, as to the production of sound.

Another important point in fingering is precision—that is, the art of placing the fingers upon the strings in such a manner as to render the intonations just. All violins, or violoncellos, are not of the same dimensions; certain makers having adopted larger forms for these instruments than others. Now, the spreading of the fingers to form the intonations is always in proportion to the length of the neck of the violin, alto, or violoncello; for it is evident that the length of the string is in proportion to the dimensions of the instrument. The greater the length, the greater must be the spreading of the fingers to pass from one sound to another; the less the distance, the more the fingers must be brought together. A delicate ear promptly informs the performer of the faults which he commits against precision; but this is not enough: to play just always, he must be provided with a certain power of address, and must have had long practice on the sounds. There are different degrees in the manner, of playing *just* or *false*. An approximation to justness is all to which ordinary instrumentists ever attain; absolute precision is the lot of but a very small number of artists. This is especially difficult to acquire in what are called *passages of double string*. In these passages, which produce the effect of a union of two voices, the bow touches two strings, and produces at the same time two intonations, which are the result of a combination of the fingers of the left hand. Besides the necessary influence of the fingers upon precision of tone, it appears that the bow has also an influence depending upon the manner in which it strikes the string, and that, as the position of the left hand is fixed in a precise way, for each sound, the intonation may be higher or lower, according to the mode of pressure with the bow. The celebrated violinist Paganini, at least, ascribes the extraordinary precision of his playing to this power of the bow.

The action of the fingers of the left hand upon the strings affects only the justness of the intonations and the purity of the vibrations. The quality of the sounds, as more or less soft or loud, more or less hard or mellow, is the result of the management of the bow by the right hand. This management, which, in appearance, is nothing more than alternately drawing and pushing the frail implement upon the strings, is excessively difficult. Experience has shewn that a perfect correspondence cannot be effected between the movements of the bow and those of the fingers, without reducing, as much as possible, the action of the arm which directs the bow, in such a manner that the wrist may act freely and without stiffness. If we examine the movements of a skilful violinist, nothing seems more easy than this independence of the wrist; but many years' study are necessary to acquire it. This is not all: the *drawing* and the *pushing* of the bow are susceptible of a multitude of combinations, which also have their difficulties. Sometimes several sounds flow from the same stroke of the bow, which requires much skill in the use of the arm; on other occasions, all the notes are made in a rapid movement by a number of strokes of the bow equal to that of the notes, which requires an entire correspondence between the movements of the fingers of the left hand and those of the right hand; other combinations present successions of sounds alternately united and detached; and, finally, there are successions of notes, which are detached in rapid movement by a single stroke of the bow, drawn or pushed. This last kind of passage, which is called *staccato*, requires a peculiar skill.

The artist must not confine himself to the mastering of these mechanical difficulties; the art of modifying the quality of the sounds must also be an object of his studies. It was formerly thought that a good execution could only be obtained by means of a very stiff bow; because, the effects being but slightly varied, nothing more was required of the instrumentist, than that his playing, in which almost all the sounds were detached, should have breadth and freedom. To obtain this necessary stiffness, a bow was devised in the shape of a convex curve, almost exactly like an arc of a circle, of which the hair formed the chord. It was afterwards perceived that a flexible bow was more proper than a stiff one to produce a rich and pure sound; and the rod was consequently made straight again, and subsequently in the form of a concave curve, which it now bears. Artists now modify the slight tension of their bow, by means of a screw, according to the quality of their playing, and the passages with which they are familiar. By means of this flexible and light bow, the effects which may be produced upon the violin or the violoncello are of many kinds. Near the bridge, the strings are so firmly supported, that the bow cannot put them in a state of complete vibration, without great difficulty; and the sounds which they produce, when touched at that spot, are somewhat nasal, resembling those of the viol. If the bow is removed a little from this point, the strings produce a sound of great volume, but somewhat disagreeable, and even harsh, which, however, has a good effect in detached passages which require force. The nearer the bow approaches the finger-board, the more mellow, but the less powerful, the sounds become. The bow is sometimes used over the finger-board, and in this position the sounds become very soft, but at the same time are deadened. In proportion as the bow is removed from the bridge, the performer diminishes the strength of his pressure upon the strings. The inclination, more or less considerable, of the rod upon the strings also modifies the quality of the sounds. From all these facts, which have been observed at successive periods, results the inexhaustible variety of effects which a great artist is enabled to draw from his instrument. Perhaps much yet remains to be discovered, to raise the art of playing on bowed instruments to its highest perfection. Yet, in respect to the variety of effects, and the overcoming of difficulties, Paganini seems to have carried the art of playing on the violin to its utmost limits.

The violin was for a long time only a vulgar instrument, confined to the playing of popular airs and dances. It was afterwards introduced into the orchestra, where it now holds the first rank; but those who first played upon it had so little skill, that Lully complained of not daring to risk the insertion of the least difficult passages in his compositions, for fear that the symphonists should be unable to execute them. France, Italy, and Germany, had not a single school for the violin. The first who comprehended what could be done upon this instrument was Corelli. This Italian violinist lived at the end of the seventeenth and the commencement of the eighteenth centuries. His *sonatas* and *concertos* are still considered as classic models. He introduced into them a great number of passages and combinations of fingering and bowing which had never before been thought of. His successors Vivaldi and Tartini extended the range of the instrument, which he had, in some sort, created. Nardini, Pugnani, and a great number of other Italian violinists, whom it would take too long to mention, gradually improved the art of managing the bow and the fingering. Viotti finally enlarged the boundaries which had been assigned to the violin, by his prodigious execution, as well as by the beauty of his compositions, in which novelty and grace of melody, expression, breadth of proportion, and brilliancy, are combined. The concertos of Viotti are the finest that are known.

The German violinists have been distinguished, since the middle of the eighteenth century, by the skill of their left hand; but they draw little sound from the instrument, and their management of the bow is, in general, little developed. Italy and France possessed great violinists a long time before Germany had any which were remarkable. The first who founded a school in Germany was Benda. About the year 1790, Eck placed himself at the head of the German violinists. Fränzel, whose agreeable talent was comprised within the very smallest proportions, was also in vogue at the same period. At the present day, Spohr is considered the first violinist of Germany; and he possesses, in fact, great skill; but his execution, which is somewhat cold, never obtained much success in France, where violinists are criticised with the greatest severity.

The French violinists have been celebrated throughout Europe for more than a century. Leclerc, whose style belonged to the school of Corelli, was the first who entered the lists on equal terms with the great Italian artists. The music which he composed for the violin was a long time regarded as a classic model, and is not without its difficulties for the violinists of our days, notwithstanding the immense progress which has been made in the art of playing on that instrument. Guillemain, Pagin, and some others, who lived after Leclerc, had more grace in their playing, but less breadth of style and tone. Gaviniès, who was surnamed the *French Tartini*, was worthy of the name for the greatness of his style of playing. The art of bowing, which had been neglected in France until his time, in order to cultivate the left hand, drew his attention, and he acquired a skill in it which Viotti himself admired. The studies which he published, under the title of *Twenty-four Mornings*, will long remain as a monument of his talent.

After him commenced what may be called the Modern school, at the head of which are Kreutzer, Rode, and Baillot. The first had not pursued classical studies; but his happy organization revealed to him the secret of a sort of chivalrous style, which is brilliant, light, and full of beauty. The talent of Rode, purer and more correct, was a model of perfection. Admirable for the precision of his tones, and the art of melodious instrumentation, he was also remarkable for the rapidity of his fingering. His only fault was too little of variety in the management of his bow. The two great artists whom I have mentioned no longer exist, but as recollections which belong to the history of the art; but Baillot, their contemporary, and the living depository of all the classic traditions of France and Italy, still survives, with all the vigour and brilliancy of youth, growing greater with time, and seeming to defy, at once, the age which is passed and that which is approaching. To this great artist, especially, the glory belongs of having established in France the most brilliant violin school of Europe, not only by the pnpils whom he has educated, but by the example which he has given of an admirable mechanical skill, and the most elevated style. His variety of bowing is prodigious; but in him skill is only a means of carrying out his inspirations, which are always profound or impassioned. Baillot shews all the vigour and elevation of his talent when he performs the music of the great masters, and when his audience sympathises with his emotions. Nobody has analysed the qualities of style suited to the performance of the music of the great masters so well as he; and it may be asserted that he has a greater variety than any other violinist; for in the same evening he will perform the quartets or quintets of Boccherini, Haydn, Mozart, and Beethoven; and each of these composers will have, in his hands, his appropriate character; and the hearer might almost think himself listening to different performers in succession.

To the three great artists whom I have mentioned, must be added Lafont, who, without belonging to what is commonly called a *school*,—that is, without any particular theory of the bow and fingering,—has made for himself, by the most assiduous labour, a style which is very agreeable in respect to precision and sweetness of tone.

The violinists above named have educated a great number of pupils, who have become distinguished artists, and who insure an indisputable superiority to the French orchestras.

With Paganini, a new era commenced for the violin: that of difficulties overcome. He was endowed with a nervous and flexible organization, and possessed a hand prodigiously supple, which gave him the means of executing passages which no other artist could do like him; to nature he was indebted for those advantages, and to the most determined perseverance in labour, and to some peculiar circumstances, for a skill which partook of the marvellous. Having had—so to speak—no other master than himself, he seemed to have been determined to the career he afterwards pursued, by the sight of certain works of Locatelli, an Italian violinist of the eighteenth century, who had turned his attention to the production of new effects, and whose *capriccios* seemed to have served as models for the first lessons of Paganini. Locatelli made frequent use of the harmonics; Paganini devoted himself to the improvement of these sounds, and to the production of them in all the positions and all the keys, and even to making them on two strings at once, and blending them with the common sounds of the instrument.

The fingering of the violin in certain passages is sometimes insurmountably difficult. Paganini eluded these difficulties, by varying the tuning of the instrument, so as to bring himself into the most advantageous condition for the execution of the passages which he was about to undertake. It was also by means of these varieties of tuning that he produced effects of sound which could not otherwise exist. Thus he played a concerto in E flat minor, in which he multiplied the difficulties of execution, so that it seemed almost supernatural; but the secret of this wonder consisted in making the orchestra really play in E flat minor, whilst the solo violin was tuned half a tone higher, and the performer really played in D minor. The difficulty, therefore, disappears in part, but the effect of the piece was not the less satisfactory. Paganini was the first artist who executed passages in which the left hand snapped certain of the notes whilst the bow was playing others, and who found means of playing on the fourth string entire pieces, which would seem to require the four strings of the instrument. It cannot be denied, therefore, that this virtuoso enlarged the recources of the violin; but unhappily his desire of creating applause by the difficulties of his execution, led him to an abuse of the instrument, which frequently carried him out of the domain of the art. The skill of the artist was always admirable, but the taste was not always satisfied. Be it as it may, it must be confessed that Paganini was the most extraordinary violinist that ever existed; and he also excited the most universal enthusiasm, and met with the most brilliant success.

In the new school, there is another violinist, who, though young, has acquired a great reputation by his genuine talent. This artist is De Beriot. Possessing a superb tone, a flexible and varied bow, an irreproachable intonation, and great taste, he needs only to enlarge his style, and to free himself from the somewhat narrow limits of the air with variations. His last works have shewn that he comprehends what remains for him to do, and it may be hoped that he will, sooner or later, place himself very high in the scale of violinists.

As the violin is a brilliant and powerful instrument in the solo, so the viola, or alto, seems destined to be heard in pieces of harmony, and as a part of the accompaniment. The quality of the tone of this instrument, which is plaintive and subdued, prevents it from being able to satisfy the ear for any considerable time. In the quartet, or in the symphony,

it discourses well with the other instruments; but it becomes monotonous when heard alone. It is not surprising, therefore, that few solos have been composed for the alto, and that few violinists have thought of particularly cultivating this variety of the violin. Alexander Rolla, the leader of the orchestra in the Theatre *de la Scala*, at Milan, and M. Urhan, professor at Paris, are almost the only artists who have distinguished themselves on this instrument in modern times. The fingering and the management of the bow being the same for the alto as for the violin, every master of the latter may play on the former.

It is not so with the violoncello, which is held between the legs of the artist, and which requires a peculiar fingering. The spreading of the fingers, to form the sounds, being always in proportion to the length of the strings, it is easy to see that it must be much more considerable upon the violoncello than upon the violin. It follows, therefore, that notes of the same denomination, affected by sharps, flats, or naturals, cannot be made with the same fingers, as is frequently practised upon the violin. Besides, the necessity of leaving the neck, in order to place the thumb upon the finger-board, when the performer wishes to reach the high sounds, bears no analogy to what is called *shifting* on the violin. These two instruments are also as different in regard to execution as they are in their size.

The violoncello is susceptible of as much effect in solos as in the orchestra. Its tone is penetrating, and bears much analogy to the human voice. The natural province of this instrument in solos would seem to be to produce effects of melody. The greater number of violoncellists, however, make their skill consist in playing difficult passages, because these difficulties procure them the applause of the public.

The first who introduced the violoncello into the orchestra of the Opera, was a musician of the name of Battistini, of Florence, a short time before the death of Lulli. Before his day, the bass viol (which had seven strings) was alone used both for accompanying voices and for instrumental music. Franciscello, a Roman violoncellist, was the first performer who made himself celebrated by the execution of solos. He lived about the year 1725. Two German virtuosos, Quanz and Benda, who heard him at Naples and Vienna, agree, in the eulogiums which they bestowed upon him, in placing him at the head of the most skilful artists of their time. Berthaud, who was born at Valenciennes, at the commencement of the seventeenth century, must be considered as the head of the French school of the violoncello. Among his pupils we observe the brothers Janson, Duport the elder, and, especially, Louis Duport the younger, who, to this day, has never been surpassed in regard both to beauty of tone and dexterity of bow. In elegance of style, and skill in fingering, Lamarre appears to have been the most distinguished violoncellist; but, unhappily, his playing was frequently deficient in volume and distinctness of tone, particularly upon the third and fourth strings. The French school of the present day contains several artists of much talent.

The German school is distinguished by some violoncellists of great merit. The first, in the order of time, is Bernard Romberg, whose compositions have served as a model for the concertos of the greater number of his successors. A style of great breadth and vigour was the distinguishing characteristic of his talent. After Romberg appeared Maximilian Bohrer, who has acquired a great reputation by his skill in mastering the greatest difficulties, the precision of his intonation, and the elegance of his playing. Without being so remarkable in point of execution, Dotzauer deserves to be mentioned for his compositions, which are in a very good style.

The English, who have had no violinists worthy of being mentioned, reckon among their musicians two virtuosos upon the violoncello. The one is Crossdill, who is distinguished by a broad and vigorous execution. The other is Lindley. A fine quality of tone, much dexterity of bow, and a great neatness of execution, have procured him deserved reputation; but unhappily, his playing is absolutely destitute of style, and his manner is vulgar.

The contrebasso, which is a gigantic instrument, supplied with four strings in Germany, and with only three in France, Italy, and England, is the basis of the orchestra. No other instrument can supply its place for strength and fulness of tone. The length of its strings is such, that the distance from one note to another is considerable, which obliges the performer, every moment, to change the position of his hand; so that rapid passages are very difficult of execution. It is rare that the performance on this instrument is satisfactory; for, among contrebassists, some confine themselves to playing the principal notes, neglecting those which seem to them be less necessary, and others, more exact, produce but little sound in rapid passages. The concurrent action of the fingering and the management of the bow is very difficult to acquire. The contrebasso seems intended only to fill out, by its low sounds, the plan of an orchestra; yet, in spite of its colossal dimensions, the roughness of its sounds, and the difficulties of a delicate performance, it has been played upon in a manner to create astonishment, at least, if not to charm the ear. Dragonetti, the first contrebasso of the Opera and the Philharmonic Concerts, at London, has attained a degree of skill which surpasses imagination. Endowed by nature with strong musical feeling, Dragonetti possesses a certainty in time, and a delicacy of touch, which enable him to control all the artists who surround him in an orchestra; but this is only a part of his merit. No one has carried to such an extent the art of executing difficult passages, and of managing with dexterity the unwieldy bow of his instrument. What he has done is truly wonderful. Those who have attempted to imitate him have not even approached his talent, and have only produced feeble copies.

The stringed instruments, played with the bow, of which we have spoken above, compose the basses of orchestras, and were the only ones employed in them during the first half of the eighteenth century, either for the performance of dramatic or religious music. The operas of Pergolese, of Leo, of Vinci, and of Porpora, have no other instrumentation than that of violins, violas, and basses. The accompaniments of the vocal parts, in those days, were an accessory of little comparative importance. The whole merit of the music consisted in the grace of the melodies and in the expression of the words. The wind instruments, which by the different character of their sounds contrast happily with the stringed instruments, and colour the music with a great variety of tints, had not as yet taken their place in the orchestra, or were, at least, almost unperceived, because they were employed only at distant intervals, and without good judgment. This kind of instruments has gradually acquired greater importance in the different styles of music; but violins, violas, and basses, still remain, and always will remain, the foundation of orchestras, because they possess, at the same time, the greatest degree of energy, of sweetness, and of variety of tone.

But, in order to derive from stringed instruments all the effect of which they are capable, in great orchestras, it is essential that there should be a unity in the mode of execution, — that is, that the same passages should be executed in the same manner by all the performers; that all the bows should be drawn and pushed as the same time; that the detached and the tied notes should be made at the same places; that the accents of loud and soft should be given upon the same notes; and, in a word, that there should seem to be but one violin, one viola, one violoncello, one contrebasso. There is no country in the world where these conditions are so well fulfilled as in France; and the orchestras of Paris, especially, are very remarkable in this respect. This must be attributed to the superiority of the school which exists in the Conservatory, and to the certainty of the principles which are there taught. It has sometimes been made a reproach to this school, that it casts all its artists in the same mould; but this reproach seems to me to be a eulogium rather than a criticism, in regard to the violinists of the orchestra. As to those who are called by nature to distinguish themselves in solo playing, if they are endowed with the qualities which make a great artist, — that is, an energetic feeling, and the germ of a peculiar manner,—the uniformity of the principles which they receive in a school cannot be any obstacle to the development of their natural talent. When their proper time shall come, they will always know how to shake off the trammels of the master, and will retain the advantage of a systematic management of the bow. All the foreign composers who have visited France, and particularly Rossini, have admired the French violinists.

Though France has produced several virtuosos on wind instruments, she has not the same superiority, in this class, as in the stringed instruments. Germany, in general, has the advantage of her in this respect. One of the greatest difficulties, which there is to overcome, upon this sort of instruments, is, to soften their tone and to play *piano:* the wind instruments generally play too loud in the French orchestras. The necessity of playing *piano* is, nevertheless, become so much the more imperious, since the music of the new school admits of the almost continual use of all the instruments in mass, in order to produce a variety of effect, and that these masses drown the vocal parts, unless they are extremely softened.

The wind instruments, employed in the orchestra,

by the composers of the present school, are, two flutes, two oboes, two clarinets, two bassoons, two or four horns, and two trumpets, to which are sometimes added three trombones, several ophicleides, a bugle or keyed trumpet, etc.

The most essential quality to enable one to play the flute well is a good embouchure,—that is, a certain conformation of the lips proper to convey into the instrument all the breath that issues from the mouth, without producing a sort of hissing, previous to the emission of the sound, which in the playing of some flutists, is very disagreeable. The construction of the instrument has been much improved within twenty-five years; but it is not yet perfect, and in point of precision is far from being irreproachable: the artist alone can give it the requisite justness, by a modification of his breathing, and sometimes by certain combinations of fingering. Detached notes being made by means of an articulation called the *stroke of the tongue*, it is indispensable that the artist should possess much flexibility in the organ of speech, in order to execute rapid passages with clearness, and especially that he should accustom himself to establishing a perfect correspondence between the movements of the tongue and those of the fingers.

The first flutist of any merit in France, was Blavet, director of music to the Count de Clermont. He flourished in the first half of the eighteenth century, but was inferior to Quanz, a composer at the court of Prussia, and teacher of the flute to Frederick II. Quanz was not merely a virtuoso, but a great professor. He wrote an excellent elementary book on the art of playing the flute, and commenced the improvement of that instrument by the addition of a key. Before his time it had but one. No remarkable flutist appeared, from the time of Quanz and Blavet, until Hugot, a French artist, acquired a brilliant reputation, about the year 1790, by the beauty of the tone which he drew from the flute, and by the neatness of his execution. In regard to his style, it was vulgar, like that of all the performers upon wind instruments of that age. This praiseworthy artist, in an attack of fever, escaped from his bed, and threw himself out of the window, in the month of September 1803.

No flutist had been able to remedy the principal defect of the flute, which is its monotony, when Tulou, yet a child, and a pupil of the Conservatory, manifested a peculiar genius, which was to produce a reformation in the instrument itself, in the art of playing upon it, and in the music composed for it. He was the first to discover that the flute is capable of varying its tones, and of furnishing different qualities of sound, by means of modifications of the breath. This discovery was not the result of research or reflection, but of that sort of instinct which makes great artists. The flute, in the hands of Tulou, frequently produces inflections, worthy of rivalling the human voice, which give to his playing a quality of expression unequalled by any other flutist, though other virtuosos have taken his manner for their model, at least in certain things. Drouet and Nicholson hold the first rank among the flutists of his school. The first is distinguished by a brilliant execution, and by a flexibility of tongue, more astonishing than any which had been heard before him; but his style is cold, and his playing is more like the surmounting of difficulties, than the production of true music. Nicholson is the first flutist in England, and would be a distinguished artist in any country. There are some traces of bad taste in his playing, and particularly in his compositions; but his execution is neat and brilliant, his quality of tone pure and full, and his skill in passing from one sound to another by insensible gradations, very remarkable.

The art of playing the oboe took its rise in Italy; and from a coarse instrument, designed for the use of the shepherd, it has become the most perfect of the whole family of wind instruments. The most considerable difficulty to be overcome, in order to play well upon the oboe, consists in the necessity of retaining the breath, for the purpose of softening the sound, and avoiding the accidents vulgarly called *quaacks*, which take place when the reed alone vibrates, without causing an emission of the sound from the instrument. It is necessary, however, to take some precautions, when one plays with much softness, because the instrument sometimes *octaves*, that is, gives the octave above the sound which the performer desires to produce.

Filidori, an oboist, who was born at Sienna, and was the contemporary of Louis XIII., who heard him with admiration, is the first person mentioned in the history of music, for his talent in playing upon the oboe. A family, originally from Parma, named Besozzi, afterwards produced several celebrated artists of this kind, who flourished in Italy, Germany, and France, during the whole of the eighteenth century.

Alexander Besozzi, the eldest of four brothers, lived at the court of Sardinia, and devoted a long life to the improvement of his talent and the composition of good music for his instrument. Antony established himself at Dresden, and formed a school of pupils, who afterwards propagated his method. Gaëtan was distinguished at London, as late as the year 1793. Charles Besozzi, son of Antony, was the pupil of his father, on the oboe, and surpassed him in skill. Lastly, Jerome, son of Gaëtan, entered into the service of the king of France, 1769, and remained there until his death. A German oboist, by the name of Fischer, was the rival of the Besozzis, and attained upon the oboe a lightness and sweetness of playing before unknown. The oboe school, founded in France by Jerome Besozzi, produced Garnier and Salentin. Vogt, a pupil of the latter, is at this moment distinguished by a very remarkable power of execution; and his only fault is, that he does not sufficiently soften the tone of his instrument. Brod, a pupil of Vogt, has avoided this defect of his master, and plays with perfect lightness and taste; but he has fallen into the opposite fault, and, in playing with softness, sometimes runs into the octave.

The clarinet, an instrument the tone of which resembles neither that of the flute nor that of the oboe, is of great utility in the orchestra. Unhappily, its construction is yet imperfect, in respect both to justness and equality of tone; but these defects may be obviated, at least in part, by the talent of the artist. The German clarinetists have an incontestable superiority over the French. Some few of the latter are distinguished by a brilliant style, but they have never succeeded in acquiring the soft and velvet tone of their rivals in Germany. Prejudices of divers kinds have been in their way. For example, they make a part of their talent consist in drawing from their instrument a powerful and voluminous sound, which is incompatible with sweetness; and, further, they persist in pressing the reed by the upper lip, instead of resting it upon the lower, which is both firmer and softer. Joseph Beer, a virtuoso in the service of the king of Prussia, founded, in the last half of the eighteenth century, a clarinet school, which has sent out several remarkable artists, among whom we distinguish Baerman, who performed in Paris with much success in 1818. A soft and velvet tone, a neat and free articulation in difficult passages, and a more elegant style than any other performer on the instrument, have placed this artist in the first rank, even in Germany. Wilman, of London, is also an artist of very rare merit; and, finally, Berr, of the orchestra of the Italian Theatre, is remarkable for the fine quality of his tone and the finish of his execution.

We have already seen (chap xiv.) what are the defects of the bassoon; and whether from these defects, or some other cause, there is scarcely a bassoonist who deserves to be mentioned for superior talent. Ozi and Delcambre possessed a fine tone, but were deficient in taste; and, as to difficulties, they retained the instrument within narrow limits. A Hollander, by the name of Mann, had a more remarkable talent for a flowing and easy style, and for neatness of playing, but he did not try to make himself known, and remained in obscurity. The reformer of the bassoon has not yet appeared. In France, the bassoonists have a tone which is agreeable enough, but destitute of strength. It is not so in Germany, where the tone generally, has more of roundness.

The instruments of brass are very difficult to play, particularly those the intonations of which are modified by the movement of the lips, as the horn and the trumpet. This difficulty is so great upon the horn, that it has been found necessary, for the majority of performers, to limit the extent of the scale of sounds, which they are required to perform. An artist who plays with facility the low and medium sounds, cannot attain to the high sounds, and *vice versa.* The considerable dilation of the lips, which is necessary for the first, is incompatible with the contraction by which the others are executed. Besides, the embouchure varies, in the opening at its orifice, according to the gravity or the acuteness of the sounds of the instrument. For low sounds, a wide embouchure is requisite, and for high sounds, it is necessary that it should be much less opened. These considerations have led to a division of the horn into the *first* and *second horn*, which Dauprat, professor in the Conservatory, has more properly named the *alto* and *bass horn*, because the diapason of the instrument, when thus divided, bears some analogy to the contralto and bass voices. The artists who play the part of the alto cannot play that of the bass, and *vice versa.* Besides these two divisions of the horn, there is another, which has received the name of *mixed horn*, because it participates of the first two, without reaching the low extreme of the one or the high extreme of the other. This division is the easiest for the acquisition of a neat and sure execution, because it is equally removed from the inconveniences of a too great dilation or contraction of the lips. The horns of the orchestra are always ranged in one or the other of the first two categories; but some solo performers have adopted the third. This last is the least esteemed, because it is limited to a small number of notes, and because it is easier than the others. Frederick Duvernoy, who enjoyed a great reputation, twenty-five years since, made use of the mixed horn. He never went beyond the extent of an octave of the medium.

After the difficulty of making the sounds with neatness, and that of executing with facility and volubility, there is none greater than that of equalizing the strength of the open and stopped sounds. The latter are almost always subdued, while the others are round and brilliant. No artist appears to have possessed this important quality of evenness of tone in so great a degree as Gallay; who, in this particular, has so much skill, that it is very difficult to distinguish these two kinds of sounds in his playing. He is a model for young horn players.

After Hampl, the first horn player who acquired celebrity, appeared Punto, his pupil, who was born at Teschen, in Bohemia, about the year 1755. This artist, whose true name was *Stich*, which signifies *pricking* (*punto*, in Italian), had an admirable talent for obtaining fine tones from the horn, in the high notes, and for the execution of embellishments and trills, as correctly as a violinist could do upon his instrument.

He constantly made use of a silver horn, which, he said, possessed a purer quality of tone than those of brass. Lebrun, a French-horn player, in the service of the king of Prussia, was the rival of Punto, and excelled him in the art of playing gracefully upon his instrument. He was the first who conceived the idea of making use of a conical pasteboard-box, pierced with a hole, to give the effect of an echo. Several other French-horn players have been distinguished for particular qualities. I have mentioned Duvernoy and Gallay. We may also add the name of Dauprat, who, in his capacity of professor, has much improved the school of the horn in the Conservatory.

In the orchestras, we frequently observe that it happens to the horn players to fail in their intonations, and to make what is vulgarly called a *quaack*. These accidents almost always arise from a neglect on the part of the artist to remove the water which collects in the tube by means of the breath. The least drop is sufficient to arrest the air in its passage, and to prevent the articulation of the sounds. Accidents of this kind would be less likely to happen in the use of horns with pistons.

The trumpet, an instrument of the same kind as the horn, is also very difficult to play; and the faults of the performer are more readily perceived, because its sounds are more acute and penetrating. It is particularly difficult to play with softness and purity. The French artists who play upon this instrument have not the skill of the Germans, nor even of the English. Among the Germans are the Altenburgs, father and son, who were virtuosos of the first order, and many others, who execute passages of singular difficulty, with softness and precision. Some of the works of Händel contain parts for the trumpets, which are so difficult that we can hardly conceive it possible to play them, and which induce the belief that, in his time, there must have been in England a trumpet player of extraordinary talent. At the present day, Mr. Harper is remarkable for the art of modifying the softness and strength of the sounds, for the precision with which he executes difficult passages, and for the happy conformation of his lips, which permits him to rise without difficulty to the highest notes.

The brass instruments, the intonations of which are modified by mechanical means, as the keyed trumpet, the ophicleides and trombones, have also their difficulties; but they have the advantage of not exposing the performer to fail in producing the notes. The continual motion of the slide of the trombones, and the opening of the keys of the bugle-horn and ophicleides, joined to their great diameter, prevent the water from being condensed in them, and thus destroying the vibration of the air within the instrument. In order to play well upon these instruments, it is merely requisite to be a good musician, to have firm lips and a robust chest. There are some artists who distinguish themselves by the execution of difficult passages on the trombone; but these performances are singular rather than useful in the orchestra, which is the proper place for this instrument.

Hitherto, I have spoken only of execution upon those instruments which are united into a collection more or less numerous in large or small orchestras;

and it remains for me now to speak of those which are most frequently played by themselves, as the organ, piano, harp, and guitar.

When the difficulties to be encountered in the art of playing upon the organ, and particularly a large organ, are enumerated, it is not easy to conceive that any one can be found possessing the qualities requisite to overcome them. In fact, besides that this art is composed, first, of the free articulation of the fingers, and of rules for the fingering, as for the other instruments with key-boards,—that the difficulty of fingering is complicated by the resistance of the keys, which sometimes require the strength of a weight of two pounds each to make them yield under the finger —it is necessary that the organist should learn to move his feet with rapidity, to play the basses upon the pedal key-board, when he wishes to leave the left hand at liberty to play the intermediate parts, and this double attention requires a very great effort; that he should know how to make a proper use of the various key-boards, to unite and separate them, and to pass from one to another, without interruption to his performance; that he should possess a knowledge of the effects of the different stops, and a taste for the invention of new combinations of them; and finally, that he should at the same time possess science and genius, to treat the service of the church with majesty, and to extemporise preludes and pieces of every kind. A thousand other details also enter into the duty of the organist; for example, he must not be a stranger to the knowledge of plain chant, and must be able to understand its notation, which is different from the ordinary notation; he must know the usages of each locality for the service of the church; and must be able promptly to remedy any temporary accidents which may happen to his instrument.

When we consider this complication of difficulties, we are not astonished at the small number of great organists who have appeared in three centuries,—that is, from the sixteenth to the nineteenth. Italy and Germany have produced the greatest number. Among the Italian organists are Claude Merulo, who lived at the end of the sixteenth century, the two Gabrielli, his contemporaries, Antegnati, and especially Frescobaldi, who were conspicuous from 1615 to about the year 1640. Germany has produced Froberger, de Kerl, Buxtehude, Pachelbel, John Sebastian Bach, and the pupils of the latter. The greater number of these organists are distinguished for particular qualities, but there are very few who have possessed all those which have been above enumerated. John Sebastian Bach is, I believe, the only one who has exhibited this phenomenon. This great artist was one of those rare geniuses who are placed like beacons to enlighten the ages. His superiority was such, that, both as a composer and a performer, he has served as a model for all his successors, who have made their ambition consist in approaching, as nearly as possible, but not equalling his merit. The French organists have almost all been deficient in knowledge; but they have had taste in their selection of stops, and in the art of drawing the best effect from them. Couperin, Calviere, Marchand, Daquin, had no other merit. Rameau alone knew the true style of the organ, that is, the grave and severe style, which belongs to that instrument.

The piano has scarcely any other relation to the organ than that of a key-board, upon which the fingers are to be moved; and the qualities of a good pianist are not all those of an organist. The *touch*—that is, the striking of the keys by firm and supple movements of the fingers, which is indispensable to playing well upon the piano—does not resemble the touch of the organ, which should be tied rather than brilliant. One of the greatest difficulties in touching the piano consists in drawing a fine tone from the instrument, by a peculiar manner of striking the keys. In order to acquire this art, the performer must learn to restrain the action of the arm upon the key-board, and to give equal suppleness and strength to the fingers—a thing which requires great practice. A good position of the hand, and a constant study of certain passages, executed at first slowly and with evenness, and gradually increasing in rapidity, will, in the end, give this necessary quality of suppleness. This, however, is not saying that the art of drawing a fine tone from the piano is purely mechanical. It is with this, as with every other art; its principle resides in the soul of the artist, and diffuses itself, with the rapidity of lightning, even to the end of his fingers. There is an inspiration of sound, as there is an expression, of which it is one of the elements.

A fine tone and a free and easy mechanical movement are the indispensable requisites of genuine skill on the piano, but they are not the only ones. The artist must possess taste, to enable him to avoid the two extremes, into one or the other of which the majority of pianists fall, namely, that of making the merit of touching the instrument consist in the ability to produce a great number of notes in the most rapid manner possible; and that of restraining it to expression alone, which does not naturally belong to the sounds of the instrument. It is the proper mixture of these two things which makes the great pianist.

The variations of taste, which the performance of harpsichord players has undergone, may be divided into three principal epochs. The first includes the *legato* style, in which the fingers of the two hands played, in four or five distinct parts, on a plan of harmony rather than melody. This epoch ended with John Sebastian Bach, who had the finest talent of that kind which has ever existed. In order to be a skilful pianist, upon this system, it is necessary to possess a strong perception of harmony, and that all the fingers should be equally apt in the execution of difficulties. These difficulties, which are of a peculiar kind, are so great, that there are very few pianists of our days who have sufficient skill to play the music of Bach and Händel. The second epoch, which commences with Charles Philip Emanuel Bach, is that in which the pianists, feeling the necessity of pleasing by means of melody, began to quit the condensed style of their predecessors, and introduced into their style those different combinations of the scales, which, for nearly sixty years, have been the type of all the brilliant passages for the piano. The difficulties were much less in this second manner than in the first; and from that time, therefore, the merit of pianists began to consist more in expression and elegance than in the overcoming of difficulties. The head of this new school, in Germany, was the son of John Sebastian Bach, already mentioned; and after him came Mozart, Müller, Beethoven, and Dusseck. Clementi, who was born in Italy, pursued the same course, and improved the theory of the art of playing upon the piano. His pupils or imitators, Cramer, Klengel, and some others, brought this second epoch to a close. Steibelt was a pianist of the same period; but his talent, which was genuine, though his mechanical performance was incorrect, was of a peculiar character. A man of genius, he never thought of studying any master or of imitating any model. His playing, like his music, was his own. His irregularities prevented him from going to the extent of his powers; but such as he was, he was a remarkable artist. The third began with Hummel and Kalkbrenner. These great artists, preserving all that was free and judicious in the mechanical action of the preceding school, introduced into the style of the piano a new plan of brilliant passages, consisting in the dexterity of taking distant intervals, and in grouping the fingers in passages of harmony independent of the scales. This novelty, which would have enriched the music of the piano, if it had not been abused, completely changed the art of playing upon the instrument. When one step had been taken in this boldness of execution, the artists did not stop in their progress. Moschelles, in whom suppleness, firmness, and agility of finger, have been wonderfully developed by labour, did not hesitate to encounter difficulties greater than those of which Hummel and Kalkbrenner had given the model. Herz carried to a still greater height these perilous leaps and rattling notes of the new school. Like Moschelles, he obtained great success, and all the young pianists put themselves in the train of these virtuosos. One of the latter, Mr. Schunck, has even conceived passages still more singular and difficult than any which had been previously attempted. The art of playing the piano has at last become the art of astonishing, and perfectly assimilated to the art of dancing, in this respect,—that its object is no longer to interest, but to amuse. Thought is no longer anything in the talent of the pianist; mechanical execution constitutes almost its whole merit. The folly of this direction of the art has, however, already become apparent to men of correct minds and of real talent. Moschelles, who possesses more ability than any other artist in overcoming all mechanical difficulties, has come to a stand in this career; and for some time has devoted himself to the expressive style, in which he now excels as much as in the other. Kalkbrenner and Hummel have resisted the torrent. It is probable that they will find imitators, and that the art of playing the piano will again become worthy of its origin.

Among the Greeks and Romans, and in general among all the nations of antiquity, both of the East and the North, stringed instruments played by snapping held the first place; and those who played upon them with skill were regarded as most worthy of commendation among musicians. In the modern music, these instruments have lost their pre-eminence, because they are limited in their means, and are little suited to keep up with the constant progress of the musical art. The harp and the guitar are the only instruments of this kind which have survived, of all those which were in use in the fifteenth and sixteenth centuries. The music of the harp was a long time composed only of scales, and of a sort of passages called *arpeggio.* The same forms were constantly reproduced, because the construction of the instrument scarcely permitted them to be varied. Madame Krumpholz, nevertheless, contrived to make the most of a kind of music so limited, and to find means of expression in things which seemed little favourable to it. True natural talent triumphs over all obstacles. Afterwards came M. de Marin, who enlarged the domain of the harp, and attained the art of playing music upon it, of a higher kind than had ever before been written for the instrument. His manner was dignified, his playing impassioned, his execution powerful in difficulties, and if he did nothing further to enlarge the boundaries of the harp, it was because he lived too soon to enjoy the advantages presented by the harp with double movement.

The first who discovered the effect which might be drawn from this new instrument, and who had the ability to use it, was M. Dizi, a celebrated Belgian harpist, who lived a long time in London, and who has recently established himself at Paris. His lessons for this instrument, which are filled with passages of a new kind, have set the harp free from the narrow limits within which it had been previously confined. Bochsa, who came after him, never had a neat execution; but he added greatly to the importance of his instrument by the elegance and brilliancy of the style of his first compositions. He is now nothing more than an ordinary harpist, and his latest works deserve no esteem. A young French artist, M. Theodore Labarre, and Mademoiselle Bertrand, have carried execution upon the harp to the highest point of perfection to which it has yet attained. The finest tone, the most elevated style, novelty in passages, and energy, are the distinctive characteristics of their talent. A solid glory will be the lot of Labarre, if he understands his own ability, and if he has the courage to struggle against the natural monotony of his instrument.

The limited resources of the guitar are well known. It seems calculated only to sustain the voice lightly in little vocal pieces, such as romances, couplets, boleros, etc. Some artists, however, have not limited themselves to this small merit, but have sought to overcome the disadvantages of a meagre tone, the difficulties of the fingering, and the narrow compass of this instrument. Mr. Carulli was the first who undertook to perform difficult music on the guitar, and succeeded in it to such a degree as to excite astonishment. Sor, Carcassi, Huerta, and Aguado, have carried the art to a higher degree of perfection; and if it were possible for the guitar to take a place in music, properly so called, these artists would, doubtless, have effected that miracle; but to such a metamorphosis the obstacles are invincible.

§ 2. *Of Execution in general, and of Collective Execution.*

To the mere musician, music is nothing more than a mass of notes, sharps, flats, rests, and holds; to play accurately and in time, seems to him the height of perfection; and as merit of this kind is somewhat rare, it must be acknowledged that he is not altogether wrong. But what a distance from this mechanical execution, which leaves the soul of the hearer as unmoved as that of the player, to that harmony of feeling which is gradually communicated from the performers to the audience; to those delicate shades which colour the thought of the composer, shew forth its sublimity, and frequently lend it new beauties; to that expression, in short, without which music is but an idle noise!

Remarkable effect and proof of the power of talent! Suppose an orchestra, a company of ordinary singers, who, in their dull execution, leave our sensations at rest; let an ardent leader, a musician endowed with all the requisite powers of mind and body, appear in the midst of them; suddenly, the sacred fire communicates itself to these inanimate beings; the metamorphosis produced in an instant may even be such that we can hardly persuade ourselves that we hear the same players and singers. The *ne plus ultra* of musical effect takes place unless all the performers not only possess an equal skill, but also a like flexibility of organs, and a like degree of fire and enthusiasm. Such combinations have always been rare, and are only exceptions. The famous company of comedians, of 1789, offered an example of it. Since that time, Viotti, accompanied by Madame de Montgeroult, and Baillot, in a trio, played by himself, Rode, and Lamarre, at the Conservatory, have given an idea of the perfection which may be found in combinations of a few in number, but which it is very difficult to attain with choirs or full orchestras. For want of this absolute perfection, we content ourselves with that which is merely relative, since none other is known. This latter degree of perfection results, as I have said, from a union of several artists of the first order, with others less happily constituted. One who has not been so liberally endowed by nature, as to be able to communicate lively impressions to those who surround him, is at least capable of receiving them; which explains the secret of those sudden transformations which we observe in individual performers, according as they are well or ill directed.

Skill, in the mechanical part of singing or playing on instruments, is undoubtedly necessary to the attainment of a good execution; but alone it is not enough. In his sensibility, and in his enthusiasm, an artist finds the most powerful resources, for exciting those who hear him. Dexterity may sometimes astonish by its prodigies; but it is the privilege of true expression alone to touch the soul. What I call *expression* is not that grimacing which consists in twisting the arms, leaning over affectedly, moving the body, and shaking the head; a sort of pantomime of which some musicians make use, but of which they alone are the dupes. True expression is manifested without effort, by the tones of the voice or instrument. The musician who has the sentiment of it, transmits it from his soul, as by enchantment, to his throat, to the end of his fingers, to his bow, string, or fingerboard. The quality of his voice, his breathing, his touch, are stamped with it; for him, there are no bad instruments; and, for him, I would almost venture to say, there is no bad music, though he may be more sensible than another to the beauties of composition.

We should be mistaken if we supposed that there is no possible expression but that of grief or melancholy. There are tones proper to the expression of every emotion. Talent enables the performer to identify himself with the style of the piece which he is performing, to be simple with its simplicity, vehement with its passion, sparing of ornament in its severity, brilliant with embellishments in the elegant follies of fashion, and always great, even in trifles. There is no need of great or prolonged exertions to excite emotions of divers kinds: a single phrase of *cantabile*, or the theme of a *rondeau*, is enough. What do I say? The simplest note, even an *appogiatura*, properly placed, a tone, sometimes calls forth bursts of admiration from a whole audience. At the risk of being accused of exaggeration, I will even say that we have an instinct that announces the great artist by the manner in which his bow strikes the string, or his finger the key. I know not what emanation it is which then diffuses itself through the atmosphere, proclaiming the presence of talent; but we are rarely deceived. I persuade myself that I shall be understood by some of my readers.

In all countries there are persons happily constituted for art; but their number differs, according as circumstances, climate, or other causes, which it is difficult to appreciate, are more or less favourable. Thus, among performers, France has produced Garat, Rode, Baillot, Kreutzer, Duport, Tulou, and many others that might be mentioned, who rivalled the greatest artists of Italy or Germany; yet the natural character of the French nation is not favourable to music; and the flourishing state of the art among them is rather the fruit of education than of an innate taste. The French know what perfection is, and aim at it; but, though their taste is severe, they do not always obtain good results in their concerted pieces, because there is no unity in their manner of feeling. The Italians, on the contrary, are easily satisfied with mediocrity; we see them listen patiently, for an entire season, to a poor opera, ill performed, provided there occurs in the course of the representation, a *cavatina*, duet, or air, sung well enough to indemnify them for the rest. But this people, apparently so indifferent to the merit of execution, are capable of attaining to the finest effects of collective execution, by the unanimity of feeling which directs the singers and the instrumental performers. Experience proves that four or five tolerable singers, taken at random, among the Italians, and sustained by an accompanist, who could scarcely play a sonata of Nicolai, have a life, a fire, which could not be found in the same piece, executed by first-rate French singers, and accompanied by a virtuoso, though no one of the Italians could individually bear a comparison with the French. With us, there is a sort of distraction, generally opposed to that unanimity of intention, which is necessary to obtain great effects of harmony; whilst the Italians are evidently carried away by the power of the music.

It must be acknowledged that what nature has refused, education has given us. The institution of the Conservatory has given an immense impulse to the progress of music in France; not that greater talents have been formed there than existed before its establishment, for Rode, Kreutzer, Baillot, and Duport, are still the models of our young artists. But the number of skilful persons is much increased; several are dispersed in the provinces, where they have excited an emulation unknown before; and the provinces now send back in exchange to the capital the elements of new talents. The study of harmony, which has become general, begins to familiarize the amateurs with combinations which were hardly tolerated before. The organ of hearing of the performers, made more sensible by this study, seizes much more readily the meaning of the composer; and, for that reason, they give their minds to it the more, and produce it with better effect. If, notwithstanding these improvements, we frequently observe a want of unity in choirs and orchestras, and if even distinguished artists leave something to be desired in this respect, it is, it seems to me, because sufficient attention is not paid to preliminary arrangements of great importance, and because peculiar prejudices have retained in a state of inferiority essential parts, which it would be easy to improve. The objects, which, in the actual state of things, deserve the most attention, are: 1, the arrangement of the orchestras; 2, the proportions of the orchestras, both in regard to voices and instruments; 3, vocal execution in the choruses and in the pieces of harmony; 4, the accompaniment; and, 5, the unity of effect.

The orchestras of concerts and of theatrical representations are not arranged in the same manner, though the cause of the difference is not readily to be perceived.

The place of the leader, particularly, is selected in an entirely different manner, except at the Italian Theatre. It is acknowledged, on all hands, that the leader of an orchestra should have the musicians whom he directs, under his eye, and yet they persist in placing him close to the lamps; so that all the performers are behind him, and he must turn round in order to see them. At least this is the practice in the greater number of our theatres. Nevertheless, besides the advantage which there is to a leader in being able to see his subordinates, in order to watch them, to excite their attention, and to bring them back promptly to the movement, when it has undergone any change,—it is also very important for the musicians sometimes to meet the eye of the director; for the slightest motion of the head is often significant, and promptly points out an intended effect, in such a manner as to be instantly understood by everybody. Besides, it is almost impossible that an orchestra should remain indifferent or cold, when it sees its leader attentive and full of ardour. The arrangement of the Italian Theatre, and the place occupied by Grasset, nearly corresponded to the arrangement of the Theatre Feydeau, at the time when it was directed by La Houssaye. This arrangement, which places the leader towards one side of the stage, and ranges all the musicians before him, is excellent as to the instrumental part; but it seems to be less happy in what relates to the stage, because it separates the leader from the actors and the chorus singers, and obliges him to turn his head in order to see the stage. The best arrangement appears to be that which places the leader of the orchestra in front of the stage, and a little behind the centre of the musicians, as it enables him at a single glance to see both the singers and the orchestra. This has been resumed at the Italian Theatre, and it will probably be finally adopted at all the other lyric theatres.

As to orchestras for the concert, there is no doubt that the desks of the violins ought to be placed perpendicularly to the hall, the first in view of the second, the violas at the back of them, and the wind instruments with the basses in a sort of semicircle behind. The leader, placed at the head of the first violins at the left of the audience, sees without difficulty and at the same time is seen by all the musicians. The arrangement of the orchestra of the Philharmonic Concert, in London, seems to be made on purpose to prevent the performers from seeing and hearing one another. The basses are in front, the first violins behind them, the second above them, in a kind of gallery, the flutes and oboes about the centre, the bassoons in a gallery corresponding to that of the second violins and altos, the horns on one side, and the trumpets on the other; in fact, there is no unity, no plan. The leader of the orchestra, placed in front, and facing the audience, cannot possibly see the musicians whom he directs. In the matter of music, the English too often do precisely the reverse of what ought to be done.

The proportions of theatrical orchestras have been changed within a few years. The new system of dramatic music, by multiplying the brass instruments, has rendered the stringed instruments, particularly the violins, too weak. Without speaking of the orchestras of the provincial cities, this want of proportion is particularly to be remarked at the theatre of the Comic Opera, where eight first and eight second violins cannot maintain themselves against two flutes, two oboes, two clarinets, two bassoons, four horns, two trumpets, three trombones, and the kettle drums.

Whatever we may do, the most vigorous, brilliant, and varied effects will always be found in the instruments played with the bow. I am far from condemning the use of the others. They serve to colour the music; and it cannot be denied that, in spite of all the genius of the ancient composers, the want of these resources is perceptible in their compositions. Their works are rich in invention and in melody, but poor in effect. Let us not banish from the orchestras, therefore, the new means which are offered to composers; but let us shew that it is indispensable to augment the number of the violins, altos, and basses. It is not merely when they are accompanied by the whole mass of wind and brass instruments, and those of percussion, that the others appear feeble; but the impression which is left upon the ear by all this noise, when it ceases, diminishes the effect of the stringed instruments. The *pianos* appear meagre and deprived of tone, after the formidable *fortes* of the whole orchestra. Twenty-four violins, eight violas or altos, ten violoncellos, and eight contrebassos, are necessary to preserve the equilibrium with all the instruments above enumerated. Good proportions in the strength of sound of the different parts of an orchestra are indispensable to the production of satisfactory effects of execution.

There are too frequently two directions given to the

execution, when masses of voices are united to the orchestra, particularly at the theatres. Nothing is more difficult, or more rare, than a unity of feeling between the singers and the orchestral performers, especially in France, where every thing, which is not an air or a duet, is considered by the actors as an accessory of little importance. The sensation of the leader of the orchestra, his love for the art, and his skill, are sacrificed to this prejudice of the actors. In vain does he attempt to communicate the feeling which animates him to the musicians whom he directs; in vain does he desire to obtain shades and gradations of *piano*, of *forte*, of *crescendo*, of *diminuendo;* the distraction of the singers, their coldness, and their carelessness, oppose his efforts, produce at once an inequality between them and the orchestra, and end in disorder and indifference.

But what results are to be expected, when those who unite in the performance of a piece, are not animated by the same spirit? The indifference, the attention, or the enthusiasm, of the performers communicates itself to the public, and makes them indifferent, attentive, or enthusiastic; for there is a reciprocal action of the audience upon the artists, and of the artists upon the audience, which creates the charm or the torment of both. How often does it happen that a virtuoso, by a happy and unexpected tone, attracts a sudden burst of applause from his audience, feels himself, as it were, transported into a new sphere, by the effect which he produces, and discovers in himself new resources, which he had not before suspected! It is upon these occasions that music is a divine art, to which we owe the most lively enjoyments; but apart from this it is nothing. What do I say? It becomes a torment. When music does not move us, it is insupportable, and one is attempted to say, like Fontenelle to the sonata, *Que me veux-tu?* (What do you want of me?) Let those who desire to obtain success, and whose laudable ambition seeks to rise above the crowd, be themselves convinced, if they would convince others; be themselves moved, if they would move; and be persuaded that no one has ever excited in another impressions which he did not himself feel.

A singer may obtain applause in an air, cavatina, or ballad, simply by his skill in the mechanical part of singing, or by the beauty of his voice; but in pieces of harmony it is quite otherwise. In the latter, each performer loses the right of fixing the attention upon himself exclusively, and concurs in transferring it to the music, which becomes the principal object: the individuals are effaced, that the whole may be seen, and that which is lost by each particular performer is gained for the whole. The first qualities of a piece of harmony are absolute precision of tone and unity of measure. What I call *measure* is not what is ordinarily complimented with that name,—that is, a sort of near approach to it, with which performers are content, provided they come together at the beats of the time,—but a perfect feeling of time and of rhythm, which reaches even to the smallest divisions, and to the very shortest durations, without diminishing the warmth or the freedom of the performer. Precision it commonly regulated in the orchestra by careful tuning; but, in a collection of voices, it is liable to be compromised every instant, and almost with every note. Nothing is more rare than to hear a piece of harmony executed without leaving anything to be desired in this respect. The greater the number of performers, the more a want of precision is to be apprehended. In choruses, it is almost a permanent defect, especially at the theatre. There are some exceptions, however, by which we may judge of the effect, which choruses would produce, if they were always well performed. We may cite, as examples, the choruses in *Moses*, at its first representations, those in *Masaniello*, in *William Tell*, and some of those that are sung at the Italian Theatre. At the Comic Opera, there is neither care, precision, nor unity, among the chorus singers. In the Royal Institution of religious music, directed by Choron, we have heard choruses which sometimes came near perfection.

The proportions which ought to be given to voices, in choirs, have been an object of research to many chapel-masters. It is easy to see that they may vary infinitely in size. I will suppose — to take a mean number, nearly the same with that of our theatres — that the proportions are required to be given in a choir of sixty voices. In the ancient system, it would have been divided as follows:—1, twenty-four treble, or *soprani;* 2, ten high counters, or *altos;* 3, twelve tenors; and 4, fourteen basses. But the rarity of the high counter voice, which is only a variety of the tenor, has, for twenty-five years, produced remarkable changes in the arrangement of choirs. Instead of the high counter, the second treble voice, formerly called *mezzo soprana* or *contralto*, has been introduced. Rossini and all his imitators have divided the tenor part into two, so that all the choruses are now written in five parts: the result of which is, that it has been found necessary to increase the number of tenors, who would have been too weak in the ancient proportion, being divided into two distinct parts. The contrary has taken place in regard to the treble; for the necessity of forming a *contralto* part, without increasing the number of voices, in order to adapt them to the pecuniary resources of the theatres, has diminished the number of trebles, and has established the following proportion: 1, sixteen trebles or *soprani;* 2, twelve *contralti;* 3, ten first tenors; 4, ten second tenors; and 5, twelve basses. It is not to be supposed that this is invariable, as the quality of voices has much influence upon their proportions. It may happen that the trebles, or the tenors, are too brilliant for the *contralti*, or that the basses drown the sound of the tenors. Generally speaking, the latter, that is, the basses, are the weakest.

A particular singer, whose voice is of feeble quality, may make up for this disadvantage, in an air or duet, by the excellence of his style and his taste; but in a chorus, nothing can supply the place of sonorous voices. With feeble voices, no effect can be hoped for. At the Comic Opera, for example, Ponchard and Madame Rigaut are excellent singers, whose taste, style, and brilliant vocalization, distinguish them in airs, romances, cavatinas, and duets; but their voices are wanting in penetration and force in pieces of harmony. This kind of pieces always produces the greatest effect at the Italian Theatre or the Opera; but upon a majority of the other lyric stages of France, they constitute the weakest part of the performance.

Notwithstanding the progress which music has made among us for some years, the public has still preserved something of its taste for the song; for the French are naturally more of song singers than musicians. The rondeaus, romances, and couplets, are the most applauded parts at the performance in our comic operas; and this taste is, at once, both the cause and the effect of the evil which has just been pointed out. Accustomed to these small proportions, they never think of what is elevated in the arts. The meanness of a composition draws after it an indifferent and mean performance; and the latter prevents the growth of the musical intelligence of the public. There is no doubt that this is the radical defect of the French comic opera. It will never take the rank which it ought to hold in the musical art until there shall be a complete reform of its system, which to a certain point is still that of the ballad opera (*comédie à ariettes*); and until, for an air well sung, a quintet, or a sestet, shall be substituted, like those which produce so much effect in the *Barber of Seville*, *Cinderilla*, or *La Gazza Ladra*, and which our actors shall have learned to sing with the unity, life, and care of the Italians. Such a reform has taken place at the Opera; and we may judge, by the good which has followed from it, of what might be affected at the Comic Opera.

There are excellent orchestras in France, and there

might be still more, with the elements which we possess. In the symphony, the French musicians are unrivalled, especially in life and vigour. The former sometimes seduces them to give too great a degree of rapidity to quick movements, which is injurious to the perfection of the details; but they redeem this fault, which it is easy to correct, by so many good qualities, that they have not the less a right to occupy the first place among the symphonists of Europe, when they are well directed. The reputation acquired by the orchestra, composed of the pupils of the Conservatory, in the exercises of that establishment, is well known. The superiority of this orchestra over all the others is become still more indisputable in the new concerts of the Royal School. This superiority is principally due to the rare talent of M. Habeneck, the best director of concerts that perhaps ever existed.

In regard to the accompaniment of vocal music, it was formerly made a reproach against this orchestra, and, in general, against all the French orchestras, that they played too loud, and neglected the gradations. This reproach is no longer merited; and there has even been, for some years, a remarkable delicacy in the manner of accompanying by the orchestras of the Opera and the Royal School of Music. That of the Italian Theatre has lost, it is true, something of its lightness and unity; but this is the result of peculiar circumstances, which may disappear at any moment, and which it is useless to inquire into here, because they have no relation to the actual state of the art.

In according to the orchestras which have been

mentioned a just eulogium, in regard to the general effect of their performance, it cannot be disguised that there is a great number of gradations which they neglect, and which would add much to the effect of their performances. For example, the *pianos* and *fortes* are but rarely the *maximum* of what those gradations ought to be; the first are not sufficiently soft, and the last not sufficiently loud. When the passage from the one to the other of these effects is not filled up by a *crescendo*, their succession should be much more abrupt than it ordinarily is, which cannot take place, but by carrying the character of each of them to a high degree. The *crescendo* and the *decrescendo* are also gradations which frequently leave much to be desired, because they are not executed in a sufficiently gradual manner. The swelling of the sound is frequently hurried, so that the end becomes weakened, and fails of effect; at other times, it is delayed, so that nothing more than a *demicrescendo* is obtained, the effect of which is vague and unsatisfactory; and, finally, it sometimes happens that the *crescendo* is made unequally, and without concert. All these defects may also be observed in the *decrescendo*. A good leader may avoid them. His gestures and looks are sure guides for the musicians. Every thing depends on the greater or less sensibility of his organs, his intelligence, and his knowledge.

A certain natural indifference (*nonchalance*) is the reason that the performers generally pay little attention to the real value of the notes, and rarely give it as it is written. For example, in movements which are somewhat lively, a crotchet followed by a crotchet rest is performed as a minim by many musicians; and yet the difference is very observable in regard to effect, though it is indifferent in regard to time. Faults of this description are multiplied to infinity, and little account is made of them; but they do much to injure the neatness of the effect upon the audience. In order to feel the necssity of avoiding them, the performers ought to recollect that they are called upon to give the intention of the author, without any modification. Exactness is not only a duty, but it is also a very convenient means of contributing, in so far as concerns each individual, to a perfect execution.

The fine traditions of the French violin school have given birth to a kind of beauty of execution which was formerly unknown: I mean the regularity of the movements of the bow, which we now observe among all those who play the same part. This regularity is such, that, among twenty violinists, who are playing the same passage, there is not the slightest difference in the times in which the bow is drawn and pushed. If we attentively examine these violinists, we shall see all the bows follow a uniform movement, as if the drawing and the pushing were marked by figures. The public does not observe these things, and ought not to see them; but it feels the result, without knowing it; for the bow gives a different tone, according as it is used near the point or near the screw. The choice of the drawn or pushed bow was, at first, an unreflecting instinct; but is now reduced to a regular system, by an observation of what has been found to be good and useful.

There is in all these remarks much that is apparently of small importance; but it is upon the more or less scrupulous attention which is given to these little things, that the success of a piece of music, or even of an opera, frequently depends. The musician who loves his art, does not neglect them, because he finds a charm in them. The secret of a good execution is, to love the music which one plays or sings, to delight in it, to be occupied with it to the exclusion of every other object, and to be interested in it as a matter of conscience. These things make the artist who has the true feeling of his vocation. It may be said that this sense of duty does not always accompany talent. I believe, however, that it is the sign of it. We contract a habit of scrupulous attention as we do that of carelessness. Every thing depends upon the circumstances in which we are placed, and the position which we occupy. One who is but an ordinary scraper in the provinces, becomes a skilful artist at Paris, from the mere fact that more is required of him. The same thing which takes place in individuals happens also in numerous companies. An orchestra is excellent; confide it to an unskilful leader, and in a little time it will become one of the worst that it is possible to hear. There is more than one example of metamorphoses of this kind.

One final observation in regard to execution. It is rare that an author is satisfied with the manner in which his work is performed; his intentions are seldom fully understood; and it follows that we rarely hear music in all its power. When a composer says he is satisfied, he means that he is relatively so, and in the persuasion that he cannot obtain anything more. There are moments of inspiration, however, when the performers go beyond the thought of the composer; and then music attains the height of its power. But such occurrences are very rare.

PART IV.

HOW TO ANALYZE THE SENSATIONS PRODUCED BY MUSIC, IN ORDER TO JUDGE OF IT.

CHAPTER XIX.

OF THE PREJUDICES OF THE IGNORANT, AND OF THOSE OF THE LEARNED, IN MUSIC.

There is more than one degree of ignorance of art. The first, which consists in a repugnance to it, and is the most rare, is incurable. Individuals who are born in obscurity, and remote from cities, are in the second degree; their ignorance is absolute, but their negative relation to the arts may be but temporary, and does not necessarily suppose an aversion for them. The third degree belongs to those inhabitants of cities who cannot make a single step without finding themselves in contact with the results of music, painting, or architecture, but who give them only a slight attention, and observe neither their defects nor their beauties, though they ultimately come to receive from them a certain degree of unreflecting enjoyment. The men of the world, and those who are enabled by a liberal education and an easy position, to see many paintings, and to hear music frequently, do not precisely acquire knowledge; but, at last, attain to the possession of cultivated senses, which, to a certain point, stand them in the place of knowledge.

If we except individuals of the second class, who have no opportunities to escape from their absolute ignorance concerning things which are not connected with their wants, we shall find in the other categories none but those people who are forward to pronounce upon the sensations which they receive from the arts, as if those sensations ought to be the rule for all, and as if they themselves possessed the lights necessary to explain and support their opinion. Observe that people do not say, *This pleases me*, or, *This displeases me;* but they find it more proper and dignified to say directly, *This is good*, or, *This is good for nothing*. Even among beings so unhappily organized as to be insensible to those arts which nature has given us for our enjoyment, there are none who have not also their opinion concerning the objects of their antipathy, and who do not express it with confidence. They do not deny that their own ordinary state presents something incomplete and humiliating; but they avenge themselves by affecting contempt for things which are beyond their comprehension, and even for those persons who are sensible to them. As to the vulgar, they have also their opinion, and express it in their fashion. The delicacy of art never touches them; they understand only its grosser portions. For example, in a picture, all that strikes them is its more or less exact imitation of material objects; what they admire in a statue is, that it is made of marble; what they love in music is made up of the songs, and the airs for the dance. We scarcely discuss with these two classes of individuals; the man of the world laughs at the first, and disdains the other. Disputes do not take place except among sensible and well-bred people, who take their prejudices for their opinions, and their opinions for truth.

He who has lost his health needs not to know the name or the cause of his disease, to be sure that it exists; the pain sufficiently informs him of it. It is the same in music. It is not necessary to know how it is written, nor how it is composed, in order to have a conviction of the pleasure it affords, or of the weariness it causes. But if it be necessary to have studied medicine, to have seen many sick persons, frequented hospitals, and to have perfected, by observation and comparison, an aptness to detect the symptoms of diseases, in order to decide upon their character, and upon the remedies which should be used,—we must agree that it is not less necessary to have learned the elements of the musical art, to have studied all its resources, the varieties of its forms, and to know how to discern defects of harmony, rhythm, and melody, in order to be authorized to decide on the merit of a composition. As, therefore, we simply say, in disease, *I am in pain*, so we ought in music to say, *This pleases me*, or, *It is disagreeable.*

We should be less disposed to give our opinions upon music in a decided tone, if we observed that we changed them more than once in the course of life. Shew me the man who has not given up his first feeling of admiration, to yield to a new one, and who is not at any moment ready to renounce the latter for things to which he was at first averse. How many extravagant partisans of the works of Grétry were there, who, at first, repelled with horror the brilliant Rossinian innovations, and who afterwards forgot their ancient predilections and their new antipathies to such an extent, as to become the most ardent defenders of the new school! How could it be otherwise? The arts belong to human perfectibility, and must follow it in its onward progress; things and events change, and we are forced to change with them. Besides, education more or less advanced, the habit of hearing some things, and our ignorance of others, must modify opinions and feelings. We see, therefore, that it is wrong to decide in a manner so positive as we do habitually, since we are exposed continually to contradict ourselves. In general, we are too hasty in forming opinions.

The artists, and the learned in music or painting, are no more exempt from prepossessions and prejudices than the ignorant; only their prepossessions and prejudices are of another kind. It is but too common to hear musicians maintain seriously that they alone have the right, not only to judge of music, but also to receive pleasure from it. Strange blindness, which makes one believe that he does honour to his art by limiting its power! What, indeed, would painting or music be, if those arts were only a mysterious language, which we could not understand, until we had been initiated into their hieroglyphic signs? They would hardly deserve to be studied. It is because music acts almost universally, and in various ways, though always vaguely, that this art is the worthy occupation of the life of a happily-constituted artist. If it were limited to interesting only a small number of persons, what would be the recompense of its long studies and its longer labours? It is one thing to feel, and another to judge. To feel is common to the whole human race; to judge is the province of the skilful.

But the latter must not persuade themselves that their judgments are always without fault; wounded self-love, opposing interests, enmities, national prejudices, and those of education, are causes which often mislead. Ignorance is at least exempt from these weaknesses, against which the artists and the learned are not sufficiently on their guard. There are so many examples of errors occasioned by them, that we ought always to abstain from forming an opinion, until we have examined our consciences, and separated from our heart and mind every thing that might paralyze the action of the understanding. How many recantations would this wisdom have avoided!

There is an intermediate class between the man who simply abandons himself to sensations purified by education and the philosophic artist. It is that which may be called the class of professional critics (*jugeurs*). It is ordinarily men of the quill who undertake this employment, though they are no more fit for it, than any other persons whose senses have been improved by the habit of hearing or seeing. By the air of assurance with which they every morning throw out their musical theories in the papers, one would take them for experienced artists, if their multiplied blunders did not every moment shew their ignorance of the end, means, and processes of the art. What is somewhat pleasant is, that their opinions have been completely changed within ten years, and their language is as haughty, as if they had held an invariable doctrine. Before Rossini was known in France,—before he had obtained his great success,—they were perpetually crying out against science in music,—that is to say, against harmony, against that brilliancy of instrumentation, which shone at the expense of the melody and of *dramatic truth;* and upon all this they uttered as many errors as words. Now, every thing is changed; the wiseacres of the journals have taken the music of Rossini for learned music, and every one of them has set about affecting a scientific language, of which he does not comprehend a word. They speak of nothing but *forms of the orchestra, modulations, strettes,* etc.; and upon all this they build systems of music as wise as those of other days. The only difference I find is, that, instead of proclaiming the opinions which they form as general principles, they make use of a kind of poetry of circumstances which they apply according to cases and individuals, and by means of which they think to escape self-contradiction. But prepossessions,—favourable or the reverse,—solicitations, hatreds, or compliments, have so much influence over judgments already buried in ignorance, that, if we should compare all that is written upon a new work, in the daily or periodical publications, we should find both sides of all questions. What one approves the other condemns, and *vice versa;* so that the self-love of an author is always gratified and wounded at once, if he is simple enough to attach any importance to such nonsense.

To speak of what one is ignorant of is a mania which affects the whole world, because no one is willing to appear ignorant of anything. This is seen in politics, in literature, in the sciences, and especially in the fine arts. In the ordinary conversation of society, the follies which are uttered upon these subjects do no great harm, because words are fugitive, and leave no traces; but the newspapers have acquired so much influence over ideas of every kind, that the blunders which they contain are not without danger; they give so much the more of a wrong direction to opinion, as the majority of the idle believe them blindly, and as they circulate everywhere. It must be admitted, however, that, for some time, the necessity has been felt of apportioning the preparation of articles for periodical works among those whose peculiar knowledge enables them to speak properly of their subjects; and it is to be observed, therefore, that the world is acquiring more just ideas, and is learning to speak with more propriety.

CHAPTER XX.

OF THE POETIC IN MUSIC.

If there were nothing more in music than a principle of vague sensation, founded only upon a relation of propriety between sounds, and having for its sole result to affect the ear more or less agreeably, this art would be little worthy of the public attention; for, its object being merely to gratify one of the senses, it would not deserve any more consideration than the culinary art. There would, in fact, be but little difference between the merit of a musician and that of a cook. But it is not so. It is not the ear alone which is affected by music. If music unites certain qualities, it produces emotion; in an indeterminate manner, indeed, but more powerfully than painting, sculpture, or any other art.

It must be acknowledged, however, that there was a time when it was believed that the only object of music was to satisfy the ear. That was the period of the revival of the arts. All that remains to us of the music of this period, from the middle of the fourteenth to the end of the sixteenth century, was evidently composed for the ear alone. What do I say. It was not even for the ear that the musicians then wrote, but for the eye. All their genius exhausted itself in the arrangement of sounds in strange forms, which were perceptible only on paper. The madrigals, motets, masses, and, in fact, all the music of these early times of the art, found admirers, nevertheless, because nothing better was known. The rules of an art are never to be inferred from its first attempts.

At a subsequent period, music became more agreeable, and more suited to please the senses. All kinds of it felt the influence of this tendency towards the graceful. It was manifested in instrumental as well as in vocal music, and especially in the opera. Airs, and airs only, occupied an entire drama of several hours. It is of this pretended dramatic music that it was said, that it was *a concert of which the drama was the pretext.* The art was improved by it, but did not reach its true object. Though this music pleased the ear, yet, as it did nothing more, it performed only one of its functions.

In the second half of the eighteenth century, ideas turned towards truth in elocution. It was then required that music should be a language, and singing was neglected for recitative. This was good, as far as it went; but, in seeking to use this language with correctness, they regarded only one of the powers of music; they neglected the others, and, instead of operas, had what they called *lyric tragedies.* In this revolution, the art had evidently changed its object; it could no longer be said to be the art of pleasing the ear; it was settled that it should be that of pleasing the mind; for the fundamental principle of the new system, and the constant answer to every objection, was—*truth.* Now, it is evident that truth does not address itself to the ear. The mind alone enjoys it. Happily, Gluck, who brought this system into vogue, was rather a man of genius than a philosopher; and, in seeking for this truth, which is a pleasure of the mind, he found *expression*, which is a pleasure of the heart. The art thus advanced nearer to its object.

When people had once determined that truth was the principle of music, as of all the other arts, they wished always to be true. Music is capable of imitating certain effects, such as the motion of the waves, a tempest, the singing of birds, etc. It was from thence concluded that it was essentially *imitative;* but it was not observed that this faculty of imitation is merely a specimen of one of its functions; and it was not remarked that it was more satisfactory when it expresses passion, grief, joy, or, in a word, any of our various emotions. Thousands of examples might have demonstrated that it was an art of expression; but, instead of this, every one made it what he wished it to be.

Expression, in its most extended sense, is the presenting of the simple or complex ideas of the mind, or the affections of the heart, in a sensible form. Music is hardly susceptible of anything more than the communication of the latter; but it is not absolutely limited to them, as we shall see hereafter.

When it is said that music expresses the affections of the heart, it is not pretended that it is capable of rendering an account of what such or such an individual experiences: it does more: it excites emotions in the hearer, creates at will impressions of sadness or of joy, and exercises over him a sort of magnetic power, by means of which it places him in relation with external sensible objects. Music, therefore, is not merely an art of expression; it is also the art of producing emotions. It expresses only so far as it touches, and this distinguishes it from language, which is capable of expression only to the mind. This distinction shews the error of those who have thought it a mode of speech analogous to other languages.

Music excites emotion independently of all foreign aid. Words and gestures add nothing to its power; they only enlighten the mind, in regard to the object of its expression. I know that the force which musical expression receives from a neat and well-articulated pronunciation of the words will be urged against me as an objection; but we must make a distinction. If the question be of a word, or of an exclamation which paints a vivid sentiment or a profound sensation, the tone which the singer infuses into it by his pronunciation becomes a very active means of expression, which suffices to move the hearer, and which therefore weakens the effect of the music; for we are not so organised as to receive several sensations at once through the same sense; one effect cannot be produced in us, but at the expense of another. This power of words in music is especially observable in the recitative; in which there is an alternate predominance of the words and of the music. The latter almost always prevails in the repeats.

If the poetry, which serves as a foundation for the music, has not for its object one of those strong and deep feelings, portrayed by a few words,—if it requires a long description,—then the music is restored to its supremacy; then, as I have said, the words are of no use but to convey the ideas. As soon as the mind conceives them, the words become useless, so far as the expression is concerned, and serve only to facilitate the articulation of the voice. The music predominates, and that succession of syllables which strikes the air without affecting the hearer, is no longer heard. This demonstrates that the reproach sometimes brought against composers, that they repeat the words too often, is not well founded, when the purpose of the repetition is to give the music time to pass through all the degrees of passion, which is the important point. It must be remarked that, in speaking of the effect of music upon the hearer, in such cases, I take it for granted that his senses are sufficiently cultivated to comprehend the intentions of the composer, and to convey them to his mind.

From all this, several inferences may be drawn. The first is, that what is commonly called the *expression of the words* is not the essential object of music. To explain: that which the lyric poet puts into the mouth of the personages of his drama is the exhibition of one of two things which they experience; namely, either these personages are under the influence of a passion which is to be shared by the audience, or they are in danger, and the audience is to be interested in their fate. In both cases, it is necessary to produce emotion; and, of all the arts, music is the most powerful for that purpose. The words lend it only a feeble aid; it is enough if they enable the audience to understand the situations. If, on the contrary, the feeling be of a mixed kind, which, without being inert, is still not a strong emotion, the music corresponds with it, by the agreeableness of airs of no decided character, by the richness of the accompaniment, or by the novelty of the harmony, all which produce sensations rather than emotions. In this case, the action of the words is still more feeble. Finally, if it be required that the music should be the interpreter of witticisms, pleasantries, and jokes, it is manifest, at once, that it is completely unsuited for such a purpose. If the musician wishes to bring out any such thoughts of the poet, he must place himself in the background for that purpose, and so immediately becomes feeble and constrained; if he persists in bringing himself forward, he is out of place.

I foresee objections, for all this is not according to received notions. Let us attempt to meet and answer them.

"Grétry," it will be said, "the idol of the French, during nearly sixty years, shone precisely by this very faculty which you refuse to his art,—that of giving expression to the words. He frequently puts more talent into his music than the poet does into his verse; and it is by this very thing that he has obtained such a brilliant reputation." We must distinguish. Grétry, though a feeble harmonist and an ordinary musician, had received from nature a talent for the invention of happy melodies, much musical sensibility, and more mind than his books seem to indicate. Those of his works which have survived him, and which the connoisseurs will still admire, when the progress of the art and fashion shall have for ever banished his operas from the stage, are his melodies, the true inspirations of a creative instinct, and that sensibility which enabled him to discover the tone of every passion. As to the talent, which he piqued himself upon possessing, and which consisted in giving point to a word, in seeking comic inflections, in sacrificing the musical phrase or period to the rapidity of the dialogue,—this perhaps may be something very good in a certain system, but it is not music. It formerly pleased the French audiences, who desired nothing but the vaudeville in their comic operas, and whose senses were not trained to the understanding of anything else; but, even at the epoch when Grétry wrote, the other nations of Europe had begun to see in music an end more noble than to bind oneself to words, and to weaken the one to attain the level of the other. "You talk too much for a man who sings, and you sing too much for a man who talks," said Julius Cæsar to a certain professor of declamation who desired to make music serve as an aid to speech. This criticism is applicable to all those musicians who have had the weakness to suffer themselves to be governed by men of letters, who were jealous of the glory of their couplets, and who thought that their verses were the most important part of an opera.

Not that we ought to banish talent from words designed for music, nor even from the work of the musician. The best Italian, German, and French operas furnish passages in which the musical intonation happily seconds the words. It is enough to recollect that it is not the essential object of the music. Besides, these passages, in which the music divides the effect with the words, are always of short duration. The musician never makes the poet shine, without turning attention from his music.

It will be objected against me also, that there are many comic pieces, in which the hurried articulation of the words produces a good effect; and it may even be objected that there are narratives which have not prevented men of genius from making good music. These objections deserve to be examined.

The Italian comic operas are filled with pieces which are called *note and word*, the effect of which is lively, stirring, and witty; but we must not be deceived. In these pieces, the quality of the musical ideas is less important than the rhythm. The works of Fioravanti are full of these things, which are perfect in effect, though the thoughts of the musician are commonplace. The reason is, that their rhythm is excellent. This rhythm is all that we remark in them. The more or less comic arrangement of the words afterwards draws the attention, and finally, we hardly think of the music, which becomes nothing more than a mere accessory. Observe, besides, that the accent and comic action of the performer are of much effect in these pieces. All this is good in its place; but yet, again, the music only plays a secondary part.

As to narratives, they are of two kinds. In the first, the composer, in order to put no obstacle in the way of the articulation of the words, avoids giving the melodious phrase to the voice, throws the interest into the orchestra upon an appropriate theme, and gives to the voice only an almost monotonous utterance, which permits what the actor says to be distinctly heard. In this case, the effect is complex, in regard to those of the hearers, whose ear is cultivated, and their attention is divided between the play and the music; the others hear only the words, and little or nothing of the music.

The other manner of treating narration consists in taking nothing of a subject but its character, as gay or sad, tranquil or animated, and in making a piece of music in which the words have only a secondary place, whilst the attention is drawn to the work of the musician. Such is the admirable air, *Pria che Spunti*, in the *Matrimonio Segreto.*

In whatever manner we may regard the union of words and music, it is clear that we cannot escape from this alternative: either the music governs the words, or the words govern the music. There can be no possible division between them, unless they are both so feeble that we are as indifferent to the one as to the other. The music which produces emotion expresses situations, and not words; and, when the latter obtrude themselves, the music becomes a mere accessory: in the first case, the soul is moved; in the other, the mind is engaged. Both are good, when properly employed; for it is not given to man to be continually moved; emotions weary, repose is necessary, and especially variety, in our mode of being.

Nothing better proves the power of exciting emotion, which music possesses, independently of the words, than the effects produced by instrumental music. Its effects are felt only by those who have been well educated; but this proves nothing against the proposition, for we have no ideas but by education. Who is there, however little initiated in this art, that has not been moved by the impassioned tones of Mozart's symphony in G minor? Who has not felt an elevation of soul by the grandeur of the march in Beethoven's symphony in C minor? Thousands of similar examples might be cited.

But, it will be said, the nature of these emotions is vague, and has no determinate object. Doubtless; and it is precisely for that reason that they have so much effect upon us. The less evident the object is, the less the mind is occupied, the more the soul is moved; for nothing distracts it from what it experiences. Our perceptions are weakened by their multiplicity. They are the more sensible, as they are simple.

Let us lay aside the habit of comparing those things which have no analogy, and of thinking that all the arts produce their effect in the same manner. Poetry always has an object upon which the mind seizes before the heart is moved. Painting has no effect except so far as it presents to us with truth the scenes or the objects which it seeks to reproduce, and as it addresses itself to our convictions. We require nothing of all this from music: let it excite us, and it is enough. But upon what subject? It is of no consequence. By what means? I know not; and, further, I care not.

Will it be said that this art would be reduced to a mere pleasure of the senses, if it were so? This would be a mistake; for it is like the passion of love, which has a moral as well as a physical effect. It has often been attempted to compare music to something; but nobody has thought of the only passion, the symptoms and effects of which are analogous to those of music. Like the passion of love, music has its voluptuous sweets, its passionate explosions, its joy, its grief, its exaltation, and its vagueness,—that delicious vagueness which presents no determinate idea, but which excludes none. From the fact that it does not address itself to the mind, it does not follow that it is limited to satisfying the ear; for the ear is only its organ, and the soul is its object. Music has not, by itself, the means of expressing the shades of strong passion, such as anger, jealousy, or despair; its tones partake of all this, but they have nothing positive. It is for the words to enlighten the hearer; as soon as he is informed, the music suffices, for it produces emotion. The musician, therefore, ought not to lose his time in seeking the boundaries of shades which it is not in his power to express. All the counsels which Grétry has given in this respect, in his *Essays on Music*, are illusory.

The principles of the poetry and of the philosophy of music are very much bound together, very difficult to apprehend, and more difficult still to present with clearness; but, in whatever manner we consider them, we shall arrive at this conclusion, — that music is neither an art of imitation, nor a language, but the art of expressing, or rather of producing, emotion.

This being established, it becomes evident that the enthusiasts of such or such a manner, of such or such a school, of such or such a style, do not comprehend the object of music. The preferences which certain persons express for melody, for harmony, for simple means, or for recondite and multiplied modulations, are so many errors, by which they undertake to limit the action of the art, which has need of all these things, and of a great many others. Gluck thought that it was necessary to connect the recitative so closely with the airs, that one should scarcely be able to perceive where the latter commenced. The necessary result of his system was a kind of monotony, which has perhaps made his dramatic masterpieces grow old prematurely. For some years past, it has been admitted that the effect of pieces is increased by our perceiving clearly where they begin, because the attention of the audience is greater; and hence composers have sought to separate them as much as possible from the recitative. They have done nothing in this, but to recommence that which was practised before the revolution brought about in dramatic music by the great musician whom I have mentioned. But from the fact that the mode has changed, it is not to be supposed that the system of Gluck was positively bad; for, except in its monotony, there is in this system a vivacity of expression, the application of which may be excellent in many circumstances, and which belongs to the real domain of the art. The simplicity of instrumentation has given place to a richness which sometimes partakes of profusion. Must we condemn either? No: for there are certain situations which demand simplicity, and others which require a greater development of means. Finally, all the composers of the ancient school have considered the luxury of embellishments as destructive of dramatic expression; in the music of our days, on the contrary, they are multiplied to excess. The partisans of the ancient lyric tragedy declare that this last method is ridiculous, because it is frequently in opposition to the sentiments with which the personages are animated; and the amateurs of the new school consider as Gothic that which is not enriched with these brilliant fantasies. Both are in the wrong: the first, because the music ought to have moments of repose, and cannot always be expressive or exciting; the others, because there are situations in which we cannot employ embellishments, trills, groups, and cadences, without destroying every principle of truth. Rossini, who has multiplied things of this kind in his music beyond any former precedent, shews that he knew how to renounce them at a proper time, as particularly in the fine trio of *William Tell*. In a word, to excite emotion or to please the ear being the object, all means of attaining it are good, provided they are properly employed. I do not know any system, or any process, which may not have its effect; the advantage which would result from not rejecting any, would be to obtain a variety which we do not meet with at any epoch of the history of the art, because some particular system always has the preference, to the exclusion of every other.

In regard to instrumental music, the course is still more extended, because the object is more vague. In order to succeed in it, or to judge of it, it is indispensable to divest oneself of all those inclinations or aversions which have their source only in our prejudices. "It must be scientific," say some. "It must, above all, be graceful," say others. "I love brilliancy and rapid passages," says one. "I detest them," says another. "Give me the judicious and pure music of Haydn," says a third. "No," says a fourth, "let me have the penetrating passion of Mozart." "No, indeed," says a fifth; "I prefer the vigorous originality of Beethoven." What does all this mean? Is it saying that each of these great artists, in opening new paths, has had a greater or less degree of merit than the others? And because there is one of them who appeared later than the others, and did things of which the want had not before been perceived, — must it be supposed that he alone knew the true object of the art? Do you wish for only one style? You will very soon be tired of what was at first delightful. Some other novelty will appear, and will displace the object of your affections; and thus the musical art will resemble Saturn, who devoured his own children. In continually going towards an object which we shall never reach, we shall lose, without the power of recovery, the recollection of the paths which we have followed. What extravagance it is to believe only in oneself, and to imagine that our senses are more improved, or our judgment more sound, than those of our predecessors! One feels, or judges, differently from another, and that is all. Circumstances, education, and more than all, prejudices, beset us in every thing that we do, and the results of their action we take for those of a superior reason. Again, let us not reject anything which is to our taste, let us make use of every thing at the proper time, and we shall be the richer.

In order to enjoy the beauties which have passed out of fashion, and to feel their merit, let us place ourselves in the position in which the author was, when he wrote his work; let us recal his predecessors; let us represent to ourselves the mind of his contemporaries, and forget for an instant our habitual ideas: we shall be astonished at becoming sensible to things the merit of which we should have been unable to recognise, if we were to persist obstinately in taking for an object of comparison the productions which are more in relation with the advanced state of the art, and with our inclinations. For example, if we wish to judge of the merit of Haydn, and of what he has done for the progress of music, let us first play a symphony of Van Malder or Stamitz, or a quartet of Davaux or Cambini, and we shall see in him a genius of the first order, creating, as it were, all the resources of which composers make use at the present day. If we, then, come down to Beethoven, in order to compare him with the father of symphony, and examine the qualities which shine in the works of the one and of the other, we shall be convinced that, if Beethoven is superior to Haydn for the boldness of his effects, he is much his inferior in the relations of neatness of conception and of plan. We shall see Haydn developing ideas which are frequently ordinary, with infinite art, and making of them miracles in form, elegance, and majesty; whilst we shall remark in the productions of Beethoven a first gush which is admirable, and ideas which are gigantic, but which, by means of developments drawn out into a vague fantasy, frequently lose in their effect as they advance, and end by making us regret that the author had not finished them sooner.

With this wise direction of his impressions, every one may succeed in stripping himself of his prejudices and his exclusive inclinations; and the art, and the enjoyments which it procures, will gain by the exchange. Enlightened artists have one indisputable advantage over people in general—that of pleasing themselves by hearing the music of men of genius of all epochs and of all systems, whilst others admit only that which is in fashion, and do not comprehend any other. The first seek in the ancient music no other qualities than those which belong to its essence; but the others, not finding in it their accustomed sensations, imagine that it cannot give them sensations of any kind. Men are to be pitied, who thus put narrow limits to their enjoyments, and who do not even attempt to enlarge their domain. It is probable that their number will diminish as soon as composers shall understand that all styles, with all their means, are good to be employed, and when they shall be determined to reproduce in their works the history of the art.

CHAPTER XXI.

OF THE ANALYSIS OF THE SENSATIONS PRODUCED BY MUSIC.

I imagine that, in hearing music, one who has not studied this art, and who is ignorant of its processes, receives nothing more from it than a simple sensation. For him, a choir, composed of a great number of voices, is only one powerful voice; an orchestra, one great instrument. He hears neither chords, harmony, nor melody, neither flutes nor violins: he hears music.

But, as he continues to listen, his sensations become complicated. The education of his ear goes on insensibly; at length he distinguishes the air from the accompaniment, and forms notions of melody and harmony. If his organization, physical and mental, is well adapted to the purpose, he will soon be able to distinguish the differences in tone of the instruments composing the orchestra, and to recognise, in the sensations which he receives from the music, that which belongs to the composition, and that which is the effect of the talent of the performers. The expression of the words, more or less successful, the dramatic proprieties, and the effects of rhythm, are also matters upon which he will learn to form opinions; his ear will not remain insensible either to a want of precision, or to a mistake in the time; but all these things will affect him only by instinct, and the habit of comparing his sensations one with another. Arrived at this point, he will be like those well-educated persons, whom we meet continually at the theatres; for the enlightened public, which makes the reputation of artists, knows no more, and cannot carry its analysis any farther. In harmony, this public does not hear the chords; and a phrase which is represented to it accompanied in different manners, is always the same phrase. The delicate varieties of form, which compose a great part of the merit of a composition, do not exist for this class; so that, if they are less offended than artists with the defects of an incorrect composition, they are also less touched with the beauties of perfection.

Is there not, therefore, any means of going beyond this incomplete perception of the effect of sounds, short of being initiated into musical science? And is it absolutely necessary to make a long and tediously minute study of the principles and processes of this science, in order to enjoy all its results? If I should speak as an artist, I should answer in the affirmative, and say, with pride, that there are certain enjoyments in music for me which will never be shared by people in general; and I would even maintain that they are the most vivid, in order that I might better shew that superiority which my peculiar knowledge gives me. But it is not for this that I have undertaken to write my book; my purpose is, to point out the means of increasing enjoyment, and of directing the judgment, without the necessity of a long noviciate, which one rarely has the time and the inclination to go through. Let us see, therefore, by what means we may, to a certain extent, supply the place of the experience of the artist, and the knowledge of the professor.

Suppose that an audience, capable of appreciating music, is assembled at the representation of a new opera; that the name of the composer is unknown; and that the kind of music is new, and of such an originality, that all the musical habits of the audience are disturbed. This, then, I think, would be the proper way to analyse the new composition.

The first effect of a celebrated name is to inspire confidence, and to give us favourable prepossessions; by a contrary effect, we feel a sort of distrust of an unknown name; and the first impulse is to condemn things with which we are not acquainted. We desire novelty, but we must determine what is new. We fear to compromise ourselves; and as, in general, there are fewer good things than bad, we think it safer to condemn, at first, than to approve. There is much security in reputation; it does not require the annunciation of public opinion, and this is already something; then, it is almost certain that beauties as well as defects will be found in the work; and thus we may express opinions which will not compromise us for the future. Such, one cannot doubt, are the causes of the premature opinions which are every day expressed. These things are the results of human nature and society. The first rule to be established before proceeding to an analysis of the sensations which we experience upon hearing a new work, is, therefore, to distrust our prepossessions, and to be satisfied that we rarely escape being deceived by them at first. The difficulty of escaping deception is increased when the style of music is new; for it is very rare that extreme originality does not offend at first.

Let one recal the unfavourable judgment which was passed upon the music of the *Barber of Seville* at its first representation, and upon the compositions of Beethoven when they were heard for the first time. These examples ought to serve as lessons. We shall have gained much, when we cease to be precipitate in our opinions; for it costs much less to suspend our judgment than to take back what we have said. How often has it happened to us to persist in manifest errors, only because we have avowed them, and because we are interested in them, by an ill-understood self-love!

There are other reasons which ought to put us on our guard against the tendency to preconceived opinions for or against anything. What music is there, however good, which has not lost its charm in consequence of a bad execution? What insipidity has not fascinated the senses, when interpreted by great artists? Music, as it comes from the hand of the composer, is a mere idea: the performance, good or bad, makes something or nothing of it.

It is also a result of human nature to believe that every thing is going on improving in the arts and in literature, as in industry. Hence we think ourselves entitled to call in question ancient reputations, and to pronounce a final opinion upon them. But in these strange decisions, in which we are generally inclined to determine that past generations have done wrong in admiring the productions of their own times, we make no account of the difference of circumstances, of the prevalent forms of fashion, nor of the traditions of execution which are lost. We think ourselves sufficiently informed, after an imperfect hearing, in which we were much more disposed to look for the ridiculous than to listen in a true spirit. How frequent are judgments of this kind! We have seen a striking example of it in our own time, in relation to the famous *Hallelujah Chorus* of Händel. This fine piece, after having been studied with a religious attention in the Royal Institution of Classical Music, directed by Choron, was performed there, with a conviction which drew after it that of the public, and which produced the most lively enthusiasm in the audience. Some time after, the same piece was given by the Concert Society at the Royal School of Music. One might have expected every thing from the choirs and admirable orchestra of those concerts; but the majority of the artists who composed them, being exclusive admirers of Beethoven, and of the modern school, performed this masterpiece of Händel under the influence of unfavourable prepossessions, sneeringly and carelessly. The work produced no effect, and it was settled that this sublime music was as much out of date, as the full-bottomed wig of its author!

When we succeed in divesting ourselves of all the weaknesses which mislead our judgment, and injure our sensations, then will really commence the action of the understanding, in the analysis of our sensations, and in judging of their nature. The first thing to be examined will be the object of the drama, if, as I have said, the matter in question be an opera. If the subject is historical, we may see, at once, whether the overture is analogous to its character; if it is a fancy subject, all we can do will be to judge whether it is agreeable and well made. Whether it is agreeable everybody can decide; whether it is well made is the point of difficulty. The good or bad structure of it depends upon the system which prevails in the ideas. An overture may be rich in invention, and still be badly made; for, if the abundant ideas have no point of union among themselves, they will weary the attention without charming the ear. It is a matter of constant experience, that a phrase, whatever may be its agreeableness, is not understood at the first hearing. It is not until after having been repeated several times, that it engraves itself upon the memory, and that we perceive all its qualities. But if there are many ideas in a piece, and if each of them is repeated several times, the work will be very long and tiresome. Besides, it would be difficult to retain and apprehend equally well a great number of different phrases. There should not be, therefore, more ideas in a piece than its dimensions will admit of, without fatiguing the attention of the audience; whence it follows that a small number of phrases, well arranged and skilfully brought together, compose a piece well made and easy to understand. On the other hand, if the principal ideas of an overture were represented always in the same manner, such uniformity would beget weariness. An overture, then, will be well made, when the ideas shall be successively presented under forms that are rich in harmony or instrumentation, and so that they shall terminate with a brilliant peroration, into which the composer shall introduce unexpected modulations, reserved for that final moment; for if he used them sooner, he would finish more feebly than he began, which, in every thing, is contrary to the progress of emotion.

Once informed of these things, if one has given himself the trouble to follow them into their details, he will at length obtain a habit of distinguishing them readily, and will get rid of that vagueness which brings indecision in its train. It will thenceforward be easy for him to form an opinion of a piece of this sort. Doubtless, one can never become capable, without being a profound musician, of distinguishing, in a rapid performance, one chord from another; of perceiving the advantage which there might have been in making use of one harmony rather than another in a particular passage; or of feeling the beauty of certain movements of harmony, or the defects of certain others. Long study alone can give the readiness of perception necessary to enable us to form opinions of this kind; but we may increase our musical enjoyments, without attaining to this point of positive knowledge.

The pleasure or the indifference experienced in hearing an air, a duet, a concerted piece, or a finale, does not always depend upon the qualities of the music. The dramatic situation has much influence in the effect which these pieces produce. This effect is satisfactory or otherwise, according to the congruity or incongruity of the music with the object of the scene. Thence it happens that certain pieces, which give much pleasure in a parlour, with a simple accompaniment of the piano, are displeasing at the theatre. The bad effect of an air, duet, or any other piece, may arise from the fact that its character is not analogous with the object of the scene, or that it prolongs too much a languishing situation; or lastly, that the principal and prominent idea is not sufficiently developed. The first thing to be done, when one wishes to judge of a scenic piece, is, therefore, to distinguish between the dramatic merit and that of the music, properly so called. It is true that this music, however good it may be, is so only as far as it is suitable to the place which it occupies; but this settles nothing as to the merit of the composer; for there are musicians of genius, who are not born to write scenic music, though they are capable of producing fine things of another kind; whilst there are others, whose ideas are common, though they have the perception of scenic propriety. This distinction is one of the most difficult to make; for, to attain to it, we must resist powerful impressions by which we are governed, and even be persuaded that it is impossible to make it at a first hearing. Professional musicians, even the most experienced, are rarely capable of such an effort. This makes it apparent that we should preserve ourselves from those precipitate judgments which self-love frequently induces us to form.

When we have become able to distinguish that which relates to the scenic merit, from that of the music itself, we must then proceed, in order, to an examination of the latter. Among its qualities, one of the most important is variety; and we must therefore see, in the first place, whether this is provided for. Variety, like monotony, may exist in a great many ways. It is especially observable in the form of pieces. The airs of an opera, for example, as we have already seen, may be presented under the form of rondeau; of cavatina, or air without repetition; of an air in a single movement, or in two or three; alternately lively and slow: or lastly, in the shape of the romance, or simple couplet. If all these forms, or at least, the greater part of them, are presented in the course of an opera, we feel, without noticing the cause, the effect of this variety; but if the same forms are continually reproduced, like the airs in three movements in most of the modern Italian operas, or the couplets and romances in many of the French operas, the inevitable effect will be monotony, and consequently disgust.

It will be still worse if the duets are divided into the form of airs; and, in short, if the nature of the ideas is similar, if the melodies are of a uniform character, if the means of modulation, of harmony, or of instrumentation, are analogous in their character, weariness will doubtless be the result of a composition, each part of which, considered by itself, might, nevertheless, be worthy of praise. This effect is more common than is generally supposed. There are multitudes of pretty airs, which have been successful when performed by themselves, and which lose their whole effect at the theatre, on account of their resemblance to other pieces of the same kind. Next to the examination of the dramatic proprieties, that of the variety or resemblance of the forms is, therefore, one of the most necessary, in order to judge of the merit of a composition.

The melodious qualities of an air or of a duet, like those which relate to dramatic conception, belong to the domain of genius, and are subject to no laws but those of pleasing or exciting; provided that the rhythm and the regular measurement of the phrases be constructed according to rule, the rest is the department of fancy, and cannot be limited by any authority whatsoever. The less the work of the musician has relation to what has been previously done, the nearer it is to the end which he seeks to attain. He cannot please everybody, for there is no artist who has enjoyed this advantage; but no one has a right to discuss the inclination or aversion which is felt for his productions, for we are pleased or displeased involuntarily on hearing a melody. There is, however, a sure sign of the goodness of a melody; it is the approbation of the greater number, which we commonly call the general approbation. I do not mean by this the suffrages of the frequenters of a particular theatre, the inhabitants of a particular city, or of a certain country, but those of all polished nations, sanctioned by time. This kind of approbation has never been given to ordinary things, and it is in this sense that we say, with much justice, that the public opinion is always right.

The mere amateur of music — that is, one who has no relation to this art but by the sensations which it procures him—is deficient in the knowledge necessary to determine whether the invention of certain melodies belongs to the author of an opera in which they occur, or whether they are only a plagiarism; but this is a research with which he scarcely need trouble himself. Plagiarisms are of two kinds: the first consists of those vulgar reminiscences, in which the author reproduces, without shame, what twenty others have done before him, without giving himself the trouble, or perhaps without being able, to disguise his larcenies. Public contempt is commonly the reward of these things, and the utter oblivion into which they speedily fall is the just punishment of those who despise their art sufficiently to treat it with so little conscience. The other kind of plagiarism is one which the greatest geniuses have not disdained. It consists in taking good things, with which the art may be enriched, from forgotten works, and in making them useful, by animating them as genius animates every thing which it touches. The learned, or, if you please, the pedants, never fail to discover the sources from whence they are drawn, and to make a great noise accordingly; but the public care nothing about it, provided they are amused; and the public are right. We have laid aside but too many fine phrases and melodies, to which nothing is wanting, but to be clothed in a little more modern dress, to produce the finest effects; it is saving them from shipwreck to reproduce them in new compositions, by lending them new graces. Whatever the learned may say, an amateur who wishes to analyse his sensations only to give them more activity, will therefore do well not to torture his brain to discover resemblances, which would disturb his enjoyment to no purpose, and would end by making him find imaginary ones.

One of the errors into which most persons commonly fall, when they attend the representation of a new opera, consists in confounding the ornaments, which the singers add to the melodies, with the melodies themselves, and in persuading themselves that the merit of the music consists in these ornaments.

The foundation, upon which these embroideries are placed, frequently remains unperceived, even to such a degree, that it happens to certain frequenters of a theatre not to recognise an air because it is sung in a different manner from that which they were familiar. A slight degree of attention given to the structure of the phrases of the melody will soon produce the habit of separating them from all the flourishes with which they are adorned by the singers; for these embellishments have no musical sense. When we applaud a singer to the utmost for his mechanical skill, it is not because it gives us the slightest pleasure, but because it astonishes. All that is to be done, therefore, is to observe whether the melody presents to the ear those finished proportions which are susceptible of being decomposed into elementary phrases. With this habit, we shall no longer confound that which is the result of the flexibility of the throat, with that which belongs to the genius of the composer. There are some musicians, who affirm that vague melodies, of little character, are the only ones which admit of these embellishments of the singers; and they cite, in proof of the truth of their opinion, the music of Mozart's operas, into which the boldest flourishers cannot introduce anything foreign; but it is always by a false mode of reasoning that we draw conclusions from the particular to the general. The melodies of Mozart, which are ravishing in expression, are almost all stamped with a character of harmony, so that we infer from the succession of their sounds the harmony with which they are to be accompanied; and it results from this, that the singer is restrained within narrow limits by the fear of producing sounds in his embellishments which do not belong to the harmony. Add to this, that these melodies, admirable as they are, have a construction which is not favourable to the free and natural emission of the voice, like the Italian airs. The genius of the composer is always manifest in them; but it is apparent, also, that he was not familiar with the art of singing. In fine, it is not true that a melody is ordinary, merely because it can be ornamented and varied with ease. There is, without doubt, excellent music, which does not admit of embellishment, but for other reasons than are given in this rule. It would be more just to say, that there are some melodies, not composed to admit of embellishments, and others which have been made to favour the singer: both may be excellent, each in its kind; an attentive amateur will never be deceived in them. If the singer confines himself to giving the melody in all its simplicity, it may be concluded that it is not of a nature to be ornamented; for the performers rarely resist their desire to shine by an exhibition of their skill; there are, however, some cases in which they have sufficient taste to feel that the simple melody is better than anything they can add to it; but this is very rare.

From all that has been said, we see that, in order to form an opinion of the qualities of an air, or of a duet, it is necessary, 1, to consider it under the relation of scenic propriety; 2, to compare its form with that of other pieces of the same kind, which occur in the work, in order to be satisfied that it contains a proper variety; 3, to ascertain the regularity of rhythm and the symmetry of construction; 4, to observe whether the melody leaves impressions of novelty or the reverse; 5, and lastly, to separate the work of the composer from that which is only the effect of the skill of the singer. By means of this analysis, we may discuss the goodness or defects of a piece of that kind in such a manner as to give only opinions which are well founded. There are, doubtless, other things which enter into the conception of an air or duet: the harmony, as it is more or less well chosen, the plan of instrumentation, as it is more or less elegant and appropriate, are also qualities which deserve to be examined; but they cannot be made to enter into the education of the ear, until after the subjects of which I have above spoken; for the perceptions of the latter are more simple than those of the others. I do not doubt that, in accustoming the ear and the judgment to make this analysis with readiness, we shall ultimately familiarise them with the combinations of harmony. As to the system of instrumentation, there will doubtless be among my readers some one who is accustomed to the lyric theatres, and is endowed with musical sensibility; and if such an one will examine what has passed within himself since he first heard dramatic music, he will perceive that his ear now distinguishes in the orchestra a multitude of details, which were nothing to him in the beginning, and that he enjoys pleasing passages for the violin, flute, or oboe, which at first struck his ear without effect. There is nothing which we cannot learn to see or to hear, by the mere act of the will to do so.

In proportion as the voices are multiplied with the

personages, and the combinations become complicated, it becomes more difficult to analyse our sensations; and hence the difficulty which we experience in forming an opinion of the quartets, concerted pieces, and finales, at the first representations of an opera. We are commonly struck with only one thing in them, which is the general interest; but most commonly dramatic considerations are those which determine our judgments. These considerations are, in fact, of great importance; for the greater the number of persons employed in a scene, the more necessary it is that the scene should be animated. On this subject, it will be well to make some observations.

Since the invention of concerted pieces and finales, their dramatic object has been changed; but, in general, they have been considered as means of increasing the interest by contrasts of character and passion. Musicians, although agreed upon this point, are not so concerning the means to effect it. Some, considering that the action must become feeble as the number of personages in the scene is increased, provided they do not take an active part in it, require that the quartets, sestets, or finales, should have a rapid progression; and this is the system of the French and German composers. Others, on the contrary, have thought that it is necessary to take advantage of occasions where many singers are united, to produce fine musical effects, at the risk of causing the dramatic action to grow languid; and hence the long harmonised pieces, which we find in the finales or other concerted pieces of the modern Italian school. These two systems have, among amateurs as well as artists, many partisans and opponents: some influenced by their taste for dramatic propriety and their inclination for what is reasonable; others governed by their love of music; for all the difference of opinion is founded in two different systems, both of which have their good qualities and their defects. The dramatic system is more certain of effect upon the first representation of an opera, especially in France, because the subject and action of the piece occupy the attention more than the music; but, in the end, we frequently see that the musical system prevails, and gives more stability to success.

From what has been said, it is evident that the sensations are complex in the hearing of concerted pieces and finales; and it is, consequently, almost impossible to analyse them at once. The most experienced artists do not always succeed in it; and they often pronounce judgments which they afterwards retract. It is not until after having heard pieces of this kind two or three times, that we can form a clear idea of their construction, and appreciate their merit. All that relates to their melody is analysed in the same manner as in airs and duets; but there is one circumstance required for the perfection of these pieces, which must offer more difficulty to any one who has not made a serious study of the art; and this is the arrangement of the voices, and the contrasted movements which result from them. To overcome this difficulty, we must first separate that which belongs to the dramatic expression, and to the melody, from the other constituent parts of the piece, and form an opinion upon them; afterwards, giving our attention successively to the details of the movement of the voices, of the contrasts of character, harmony, and instrumentation, we may gradually form ideas of all these things; and at last become so familiar with them as to experience no difficulty in combining them, and in appreciating them as a whole, instead of receiving from them only a vague pleasure, such as is experienced by the public, which has never learned to reflect upon its sensations.

The music of the church is more simple than dramatic music in certain respects, and more complicated in others. In its origin it was nothing more than an expression of religious sentiment, free from passion, and consequently very simple. But our natural desire of emotion did not allow musicians to remain long within such narrow limits. The Sacred writings, both the devotional and the historical, contain pathetic narratives, bursts of joy, and a figurative language, stamped with all the magnificence of the East. The feeling of piety, clothed in these figures and this language, has not been discerned by many composers, who have only perceived the practicability of expressing the grief and joy of the prophet-king, or the events sketched in the Apostles' creed. From that time it became necessary to have recourse to the ordinary means employed in the dramatic music, and to make use of them with the modifications of a more severe style. These innovations have found both censors and partisans, like all the novelties introduced into the arts. The part of wisdom, in these disputes, is to consider that there are beauties and defects inherent in each kind, and that there is nothing of which a man of genius cannot make a good use. There cannot be any music which does not follow the march of general taste, and which is entirely without relation to the progress of the dramatic species; for the latter is of so general a use, that it is known to everybody, and is necessarily the regulator of the others. After having experienced all the emotions of the theatre, one is hardly prepared to enjoy a calm and simple music during the whole of a service of the church; and the composers, therefore, have been led by necessity to introduce into their sacred music a little of the worldly expression of the opera. It must not be supposed, however, that the calm and majestic music of the church cannot be relished at the present day. Let us take, for example, the masses or the motets of Palestrina, or, in another kind of composition, the psalms of Marcello, and we shall see that, with a good performance, this music will act upon a cultivated audience as a more modern style might do, but with different effects.

In order to be prepared to relish religious music of a grave and antique character, we must, in the first place, divest ourselves of our habits, and be firmly persuaded of this truth — that the art has more than one means of reaching the heart; for the obstacles which our will opposes to certain emotions, against which we are prejudiced, prevent them from arising. When we once have the disposition to attend, and the desire to experience pleasure, we shall not be slow to receive it, if the work which we hear contains real beauties, though they may be of an order foreign to our ordinary ideas. Nothing more is necessary than to analyse our feelings; and, for this, we must proceed in the same way as for music of any other kind.

The melodies of religious music are rarely so easy to be understood as those of the dramatic, because they are more intimately connected with the harmony. Add to this, that we most commonly find in them imitations, fugues, and the other scientific forms, of which we have heretofore given the details, and also that it is scarcely possible to class this kind of melody in the memory, as we do the melodies of operas. On account of this difficulty, it is necessary to receive the impressions of religious music, as a whole; and, to do this, more skill in the analysis of harmony is requisite. Consequently we ought to commence the education of the ear with this kind of music. As the ear can become skilful only by degrees, we must not suffer it to contract the habit of judging of sacred music, until after it shall have become familiar with the dramatic style. Observation on scientific forms will insensibly succeed to the study of harmony in masses; and, if we will only give it a little attention, we shall soon acquire sufficient ideas of those combinations which are characteristic of the religious style.

The last step in the musical education of an amateur, who has not made any elaborate study of music, is the instrumental style. Thus there are few persons, strangers to this art, who like to hear quartets, quintets, or other pieces, not designed to shew the skill of a performer. In this kind of music, the end is not distinct, the object is not palpable. To please the ear is certainly one of the essential parts of instrumental as well as of all other music; but it must also excite; it has its peculiar language of expression, which no other language interprets; and, therefore, we must divine this language instead of comprehending it, and this requires practice. I would say of instrumental music what I have had occasion to repeat several times; we must have patience to hear it without prepossessions, even though it should not please; with perseverance, we shall at length enjoy it, and then we may begin to analyse it; for this kind of music also has its melodies, its rhythm, its symmetrical quantities, its varieties of form, its effects of harmony, and its modes of instrumentation. By the application of the processes of dramatic analysis, we shall acquire notions of it, as well as of every other kind of music.

CHAPTER XXII.

WHETHER IT IS USEFUL TO ANALYSE THE SENSATIONS TO WHICH MUSIC GIVES BIRTH.

I am sure that many readers, in running over the preceding chapter, will have thought—"What does this man mean with his analyses? Does he wish to spoil our pleasure by a continual toil, incompatible with the enjoyment of the arts? These must be felt, not analysed. Away with these observations, and these comparisons, which are at best adapted only to those dry souls who can find nothing else in music, or to the professors of counterpoint. We wish to enjoy, and not to judge, and therefore we have no need of reasonings." This is all very well. Heaven knows that I have no wish to disturb your pleasures; but you will have hardly got the words out of your mouth, before you will exclaim, if you go to the theatre, *What delightful music!* or, perhaps, *What a detestable composition!* This is the way that people pretend to enjoy, and not to judge. The pride of the ignorant is not less real than that of the learned; but it conceals itself under the cloak of idleness.

Does any one persuade himself that I am so destitute of sense, as to desire to substitute an analysis of the products of the arts for the pleasures which they give? No, no; such has not been my intention; but, being certain that we see only that which we have learned to look at, that we hear only that to which we know how to listen,—that our senses, in short, and consequently our sensations, are developed only by exercise,—I have sought to shew how that of hearing should be directed, to render it more capable of appreciating the impressions of music. I have not thought it necessary to add, that the exercises cease of themselves, when the organ is instructed, because that is understood, of course: we no longer need leading-strings, or chairs and tables, when we have learned to walk. The analysis, which I have represented as necessary for judging of music, is made with the rapidity of lightning, when we have acquired the habit of it; it becomes an element in our mode of feeling, to such a degree, that it is itself transformed into a sensation. And what, I ask, is this analysis, compared with that which a skilful composer has to make? He does not limit himself to seizing some of the details of form, to distinguishing the rhythm of the melodies, the more or less dramatic expression, etc. He comprehends all the details of harmony, takes notice of a sound in a chord which is not properly resolved, or of a happy employment of an unexpected dissonance, of an uncommon modulation, and of all the niceties of the simultaneousness or of the succession of sounds; he distinguishes the different qualities of sound of the instruments, applauds or censures innovations upon rules, or the abuse of resources; in short, the immense details of all that composes the grand musical masses are present to his mind as if he were carefully examining them upon paper. Is it supposed that he makes these remarks with difficulty, that this prevents him from relishing the general effect of the composition, and that he derives less pleasure from it, than one who blindly gives himself up to his sensations? Not at all. He never even thinks of all these things; they are present to his thoughts, as if by enchantment, without his knowing it, and even without any attention on his part.

Wonderful effect of an organization improved by study and observatton! All that would seem likely to weaken the sensation, and to increase the share of the understanding, turns to the advantage of this very sensation. No doubt ordinary or bad music gives more pain to a skilful artist, than to one who is incapable of perceiving its defects. In this respect, the latter has the advantage; but, at the same time, how much more vivid are the enjoyments of the former, if all the desirable qualities are united in a composition! These qualities are necessary only as they concur in producing perfection; but perfection results from things so delicate, so fugitive, that we cannot feel it, except so far as these things are within our comprehension, and we are familiar with them. Hence it arises that the merely curious do not perceive the difference between a painting of Raphael and a work of Correggio or of Guido. It cannot be questioned that perfection gives rise to purer pleasure than that which merely approximates towards it; but perfection cannot be perceived until we have learned to see it; and, therefore, we must learn how to see it. Turn the question as you will, you must come to this conclusion at last.

To learn to analyse the principle of musical sensations is doubtless a study which diverts the attention from what may please the senses; this study disturbs the pleasure which one would experience in the hearing of music; but of what consequence is it, if it suspends this pleasure only to render it more vivid? The study will every day become less painful, when we shall have formed the habit of it, and the time will come when the analysis will be made unconsciously, and without disturbing our sensations. If we could be fully sensible of the changes which are produced in the manner of feeling, and of appreciating the beauties and defects of musical works, by habit alone, and independently of all positive knowledge, we should remark that not only is taste modified, but that we at last make the analysis of which I have spoken to a certain point without knowing it, and without knowing the rules by which it is made. Hence it happens that the frequenters of the lyric theatres have a surer judgment than those who attend the representations of operas but seldom. It is evident that what we do without any guide, we should do much better with one. Every thing which is advanced in the world and in books concerning the natural sensibility to art, and the diminution of this sensibility by observation, is neither well founded nor reasonable; but idleness accommodates itself to these follies.

Have I inserted in this book every thing which might be expected in it? I do not know. That I have done so is the less probable, as everybody will not look for the same things. In commencing then reading of it, the greater number of readers will have their opinions, their prejudices, their affections, or their antipathies. How can I expect to remove all at once that which is only worn out by time? But that which will not be the immediate effect of the reading of the book, will be the result of the reflections it will have excited. I believe I have penetrated the causes of the voluntary ignorance which prevails in regard to music: to dispel this ignorance, I have asked only a little attention; the most rebellious will at last give it to me, perhaps even without knowing it.

THE END.

LONDON:
Printed by Manning and Mason, Ivy-lane, St. Paul's.

MANUFACTORY, 108. HATTON GARDEN.

ROWLEY'S

Patent Self-Binding Portfolio,

OR

UTILITY CLASP.

LONDON :—*Wholesale Agents, Joseph Graham, 2, Jewry Street, Aldgate, and Messrs. Whittaker & Co, Ave-Maria Lane.*

IN offering this invention to the public, the proprietor feels confident that he is introducing to notice an article which has long been a desideratum to various important classes of society. His object has been the production of a Portfolio which should combine in the highest perfection those two great requisites—security and facility of reference ; and he is satisfied that his invention will be found to unite the firmness and solidity of the Binder's art, with an ease in referring to any particular document, that has never before been attained. The apparatus is equally fitted for a thick pamphlet or a single sheet ; and while the completion of the file is progressing, as in the case of newspapers, or other periodicals, the SELF-BINDING PORTFOLIO may take its place on the shelf with other books, or will lie open as freely, and every page be referred to as readily, as though the contents formed a portion of any regularly bound book.

The *Nobleman* or *Gentleman* will see, that whilst he holds in this Portfolio a means of freeing the table of papers in the shortest possible time, he also obtains a secresy and inviolability hitherto unapproachable, by tl introduction of lock and key.

The *Solicitor* will find that the SELF-BINDING PORTFOLIO will be applicable to legal business to an extent not to be described in the compass of a few words, and yet immediately perceptible on an examination of the invention.

The *Lover of Literature* will have his newspaper, pamphlet, or periodical, self-bound in the order of the series, and protected from injury, while the file possesses every capacity for library purposes that can possibly be desired.

The *Musical Professor* or *Amateur* will be enabled to convey the Music required for any particular occasion just in the order and quantity necessary, and will lay his portfolio on the stand, using it, in every respect, as though a volume had been specially prepared for each occasion.

The *Man of Business* will find in it the readiest means of filing his correspondence, according to date or subject, that has yet met his eyes. Whether for the desk of the Merchant, the Lawyer, the Wholesale or Retail Trader, nothing has yet been offered combining so much of safety and celerity as the SELF-BINDING PORTFOLIO.

				s.	*d.*
No. 1.	Music size, half bound	15½ by 11	—	6	0
— 2.	Punch & Athenæum..	13 by 10	—	4	0
— 3.	Foolscap folio........	13 by 8½	—	3	6
— 4.	Penny Mag. size, hf bd.	11½ by 7¾	—	3	0
— 5.	Demy octavo	10 by 6½	—	2	6

N. B. Any size made to order.

APPROVED BY

MESSRS. LONGMAN & Co., Paternoster Row.
THE PROPRIETORS of the PICTORIAL TIMES.
Ditto Ditto ILLUSTRATED LONDON NEWS.
D'ALMAINE & Co., Music Sellers, Soho Square.
MESSRS. RUDALL & ROSE, No. 1, Tavistock Street, Covent Garden.
MR. SURMAN, Conductor of the Sacred Harmonic Society, Exeter Hall.
MESSRS. LEAF, COLES, & Co., Old Change.
MESSRS. SOLOMON & Co., Old Change.

[Reduced]

CLASSIC TEXTS IN MUSIC EDUCATION

In recent years the social history of music has begun to receive wider attention. In particular, the role of music in educational thought and practice now forms an accepted field for both graduate and post-graduate studies. But original research is often seriously handicapped by a scarcity of source material.

With *Classic Texts in Music Education*, under the authorship and general editorship of Bernarr Rainbow, some of the most seminal and important titles will now be available in facsimile reprint. The addition of an extended Introduction to each volume enables modern scholarship to place the work of earlier teachers and reformers in historical perspective. Those works not in English will normally have page-by-page translations.

First Series: Popular Education

The books in this first series have been chosen to represent important stages in the development of popular music teaching. Thus, Rhau summarises medieval practice; Agricola and Bourgeois record post-Reformation methods; Bathe rejects medieval pedantry. *English Psalmody Prefaces* traces the development of indigenous sol-fa. Rousseau urges simplification; Pestalozzi's disciples synthesise instruction. Glover introduces child-centred music teaching; Curwen perfects Glover's work. Galin and de Berneval represent innovation in France in the first half of the nineteenth century; Turner, Hickson and Mainzer hold an equivalent place in Britain. Hullah defines the first state-sponsored system temporarily eclipsing the work of other teachers in England. Fétis presents the first widely adopted treatise of the Appreciation movement; Langdale and Macpherson herald the spread of the movement to English schools. Hullah and J. S. Curwen each report on visits to observe music teaching in continental schools. Kretzschmar demands and outlines reform in Germany. Borland describes the achievements and aspirations of the widening field of school music in Britain, early in the present century.

At a time when the range and scope of music teaching in schools has increased to present a bewildering array of traditional and experimental techniques, first hand acquaintance with the work of earlier music educators appears valuable in helping to achieve perspective. That such an investigation is interesting in its own right adds considerably to its attraction. The first series of *Classic Texts in Music Education* has been prepared in that joint belief. A second series dealing with Specialist Education is planned.

The following titles are in preparation.
All have introductions by Bernarr Rainbow
and translations where necessary

Georg Rhau *Complete Manual of Practical Music* (*Enchiridion utrisque Musicae practicae,* 1518)

Martin Agricola *First Steps in Music* (*Rudimentum musicae,* 1539)

H. G. Naegeli *The Pestalozzi Method for Instruction in Song* (*Die Pestalozzische Gesangbildunglehre,* 1809)

H. G. Naegeli *Method for Instruction in Song* (*Gesangbildunglehre,* 1810)

E. Jue de Berneval *Music Simplified* (1832)

H. Kretzschmar *Musical Questions of the Day* (*Musikalische Zeitfragen,* 1903)

OTHER BOETHIUS PRESS PUBLICATIONS

Musical Sources

A Fifteenth-Century Song Book
The Turpyn Book of Lute Songs
The Burwell Lute Tutor
The Sampson Lute Book
John Dowland *Lachrimae* (1604)
The Mynshall Lute Book
The Maske of Flowers (1614)
Tallis & Byrd *Cantiones Sacrae* (1575)
The Board Lute Book
Narcissus Marsh's Lyra Viol Book
The Robarts Lute Book
The Brogyntyn Lute Book
The Willoughby Lute Book
Mozart-C minor Piano Concerto K.491
The Harpsicord Master II and III
Use of Sarum 1-Processionale
Anne Brontë's Song Book
Branwell Brontë's Flute Book
The Trumbull Lute Book
The Marsh Lute Book
The Hirsch Lute Book
Tho. Ravenscroft *A Briefe Discourse*
Jane Pickeringe's Lute Book
Thomas Weelkes: Keyboard Music

Boethius Editions

Richard Charteris *A Catalogue of the Printed Books on Music, Printed Music and Music Manuscripts in Archbishop Marsh's Library, Dublin*

Thomas Lupo: The Complete Vocal Music

John Coprario: The Six-part Consorts and Madrigals

Thomas Lupo: The Four-part Consort Music

Mozart/Wilby: Allegro in F, KV Anh. 90 (580b)

Mahler: Serenade for Voice and Wind Instruments

Ramsey: Two Six-part Latin Motets